W9-AGI-236

The Bassett Women

Grace McClure

THE BASSETT WOMEN

Swallow Press / Ohio University Press
Athens, Ohio · Chicago · London

A Sage Book of Swallow Press

Printed in the United States

Swallow Press books are published by
Ohio University Press Athens Ohio 45701

Library of Congress Cataloging in Publication Data

McClure, Grace.
The Bassett women.

"A Sage book of Swallow Press."—
Bibliography: p.
1. Women pioneers—Colorado—Biography. 2. Bassett family.
3. Cattle trade—Colorado—History—19th century. 4. Frontier and pioneer life—Colorado. 5. Colorado—History—1876–1950. I. Title.
F781.B37M33 1985 978.8 85–7143
ISBN 0–8040–0876–0
ISBN 0–8040–0877–9 (pbk.)

To Amy MacKnight Lube
who opened the doors

CONTENTS

PREFACE

A good share of Western history is oral, based on stories of the old-timers passed from neighbor to neighbor and from one generation to the next. As these stories reached the printed page, they were only as reliable as the people who told them.

The story of the Bassett women has been almost smothered under a blanket of these half-true legends. Seemingly, at times the truth about them and their neighbors in Brown's Park has been deliberately distorted for the sensationalism that sells most readily to the tabloids. They have become almost unrecognizable over the years.

Like other Western writers, I have relied heavily on oral interviews to guide my research in the courthouses, libraries and newspaper files of Colorado, Utah and Wyoming. As I conducted interviews with the family and friends of the Bassett family, I promised no whitewash (nor did they ask for one) but only a balanced and authenticated account, substantiated by printed facts wherever possible.

My first inkling of the distortion of the Bassett story came from Amy MacKnight Lube of Vernal, Utah, when she characterized her notorious grandmother Josie Bassett Morris as a "little brown wren." Our first interview was painful: I was uneasy at bringing up family history which might be embarrassing to her, and she viewed my tape recorder and notebook with suspicion, knowing the damage caused by other would-be reporters. Our later friendship and understanding is a source of great pleasure to me.

Through Amy Lube I met and interviewed her parents, Flossie and Crawford MacKnight of Jensen, Utah, and her brother and sisters: Frank McKnight of Vernal; Betty Eaton of Craig, Colorado; Belle Christenson of Encampment, Wyoming; Dorothy Burnham of Bountiful, Utah; and Jane Redfield of Salt Lake City. The life blood of this book came from the MacKnight family, and my gratitude is profound for their endless courtesy and patience.*

*The seeming discrepancy in spelling the family name which appears in this paragraph will appear throughout the book. Crawford always insisted on the Scottish "MacKnight." All others, even his son Frank, held to the "McKnight" used by Crawford's father.

I interviewed three other members of the Bassett family: Elizabeth Bassett's granddaughter, Edna Bassett Haworth of Grand Junction, Colorado; Arthur "Art" McKnight of Vernal, not a blood relative but the son of Josie's first husband by a later marriage; and Edith McKnight Jensen, widow of Josie's younger son, Chick.

Other people to whom I talked and from whom I received material will be named in other sections of this book or in the notes at its end, but special mention should be made of three contemporaries of the Bassett sisters. First and foremost is Esther Campbell of Vernal. Although younger than Josie and Ann, she was a close friend to both of them in their later years. Her recollections of them, her collection of their personal letters to her, and her voluminous files of written material have been invaluable. Then there is Hugh Colton, a Vernal attorney still in practice. He was not a personal friend of Josie, but his recollections are one of the high points of my story. Mr. Colton referred me to Joe Haslem of Jensen, Utah, who knew both Josie and Ann, and who has earned the right of a good neighbor to speak of the sisters' faults as well as their virtues.

Much important material comes from the sisters themselves. In her old age, Josie taped several interviews with the personnel at Dinosaur National Monument, who kindly opened their files to me. Josie's own descriptions of her childhood, her neighbors, and some of the more lurid episodes in Brown's Park history have given the spark of life and authenticity to what others have said about her and her family.

Ann Bassett Willis has left even more material, for she turned to writing in her later years. The most accessible of her memoirs is the autobiography entitled "Queen Ann of Brown's Park" which appeared serially in 1952 and 1953 in *The Colorado Magazine*, the official publication of the State Historical Society of Colorado. The beginning chapters of another book, *Scars and Two Bars*, were published in *The Moffatt Mirror* of Craig, Colorado, in the 1940s, and many of her letters and fragments of unpublished material are still in existence. Ann's writings are a mixture of truth and fiction. She idealizes and embroiders upon her childhood in the interests of a good story. I have felt more comfortable with Ann's stories when I have been able to find corroboration for them, and have used discretion in quoting her material.

A story based on tradition and hearsay should be presented for just what it is—a story of ordinary people who played extraordinary roles in the settlement of the west. The story does not lend itself to the precise and scholarly footnotes that are possible in biographies of persons who lived extensively in the public eye. Rather than clutter the text with source references, I have described the origins of my information in more generalized chapter notes at the end of the book.

I make no apologies for my speculations as to the motives, inner thoughts, and reactions of my characters. These are based on a certain amount of logic and an equal amount of intuition. This intuition comes almost automatically after many months of research and "Bassett talk" with a variety of people, some of whom loved the Bassett women, some of whom disapproved, and others who withheld judgment. As we talked, a shrug of the shoulder, a slight hesitation, an outpouring of emotion, or a side-stepping of a question gave me valuable clues.

The research for this book was pleasure. In the following months of the drudgery of putting it on paper, I was sustained and assisted by the editing and comments of my son Stephen McClure, my daughter-in-law Judith Flagle McClure, and my friend Marile Creager. Joseph D. Wells of Northridge, California, generously shared his editorial and publishing expertise. My debt to them is surpassed only by my gratitude to William L. Tennent of the Museum of Western Colorado and Dr. Gene M. Gressley of the University of Wyoming, not only for their willingness to check my book for historical accuracy but also for their enthusiasm and encouragement.

During the pre-publication period I have been supported magnificently by the Ohio University Press/Swallow Press editorial staff. However, they threw me into panic when they asked me for a map. My final thanks will go to Fred Tinseth, who rescued me with his imaginatively conceived and painstakingly executed drawing of Brown's Park and the surrounding countryside.

GRACE MCCLURE
Tucson, Arizona
November 1984

INTRODUCTION

In the towns along the tracks of the Union Pacific Railroad in southern Wyoming, and down in the cattle country in Colorado and Utah, the locals still tell stories about the Bassetts. And when they do, they are talking about the Bassett women, those unorthodox and controversial Bassett women, compared to whom the Bassett men are almost shadows.

There were three of these women: the original pioneer, Elizabeth, and her two daughters, Josie and Ann. Elizabeth Bassett is remembered as "head of the Bassett gang." Ann was first called "Queen of the Cattle Rustlers" by a Denver newspaper reporter, and she was known as "Queen Ann" forever after, partly because of her notoriety but also because her imperious ways and her regal bearing made the name a fitting one. The other daughter, Josie, gained her notoriety another way: in a time when divorce was almost unheard of among decent people, she acquired and discarded five husbands, at least one of whom she was suspected of killing. Still, Josie might now be forgotten except that, when almost forty years old, she piled her possessions into a wagon with a spare horse tied to its tailgate and left her childhood home in Brown's Park to establish a homestead of her own. She found that homestead near Jensen, Utah, only forty miles away as the crow flies, but actually in almost another land because of the ruggedness and wildness of the intervening mountains. Josie lived there until her death almost fifty years later. As those years passed, she acquired the respectability of age (despite the stories still told about her) through the sheer strength of her personality, her generosity, her unaffected sense of humor, her companionability, and her stubborn insistence on living the way she wanted to. In her very old age she was as much a legend to the people of her countryside as was her sister Ann.

The Bassetts were early pioneers in a section of northwestern Colorado belonging topographically to the Wyoming Basin, a high arid land of broad plains, undulating hills and occasional outcroppings of rock. This vast, irregular bowl is bordered by high mountain ranges with snowy peaks and thick pine forests; within its boundaries it is divided again and again by lower ranges of bare brown mountains only occasionally relieved by the stunted cedars which grow in country where water is scarce. There is infinite variety in this land of canyons, mesas, ridges, peaks and mountains; there is also infinite monotony in the coloration of its brown grasses, dusty green sagebrush and sober-toned rock. It is magnificently and grimly beautiful. In its bareness and brownness the skeleton of the earth seems revealed.

The Wyoming Basin was the last frontier in "cattle country," which extended as far south as Texas and as far east as Kansas and the Dakotas. In the late 1870s when the Bassetts arrived, the land west of the Rockies in Colorado was still reserved for the Ute Indians, and they lived there comparatively undisturbed by the white invaders. Their displacement was inevitable, of course, once the railroad linking the continent was built. The Utes fought their last battle in 1879.

Even before 1879, and well into the twentieth century, the white invaders were fighting among themselves. They were divided into two groups: the large cattle barons, who dominated those endless square miles of grassland by the sheer size of their herds, and the small ranchers, who sought to establish and maintain smaller herds in the lands immediately surrounding their homesteads. All these cattlemen, large and small, broke the laws of more settled communities because laws had not been written to fit the circumstances under which both groups fought for survival. In and among these "honest" lawbreakers, another group inhabited that vast country—the outlaws, the "professional" lawbreakers, who committed their crimes almost with impunity because the law was represented only in a scattering of barely emerging towns.

By happenstance, the Bassetts settled in the only valley in northwestern Colorado that could assure them a place in the folklore of the region. They filed their homestead claim in Brown's Park, then known as Brown's Hole, a small valley only thirty-five miles long and roughly six miles wide, surrounded by mountains so rugged that only from the east was there easy access. Not far from this eastern entrance was a little area called Powder Springs, a well-frequented stopping place for outlaws on the run. But Powder Springs was overshadowed by Brown's Park, which would become known as one of the way stations on a fabled outlaw trail that stretched from Hole-in-the-Wall in Wyoming to the north to Robbers' Roost in Utah to the south. All three of these spots were in country well removed from the towns being established along the Union Pacific railroad, but of the three, Brown's Park had a particular advantage. It straddled the borders of Utah and Colorado and was only a few miles from the Wyoming line. Thus, if by some unlikely chance a posse from one of the settled areas ventured into the wilderness in pursuit of a badman, in Brown's Park that badman could simply ride across the border into another state and thumb his nose at his pursuers.

In this rustlers' hangout, surrounded by warring cattlemen, the Bassetts lived in a world of rustling and thievery, of lynching and other forms of murder. Their neighbors could comprise the standard cast of a Hollywood western: honest ranchers, rough and tough cowboys, worthless drifters, dastardly villains, sneaking rustlers, gentlemanly bank robbers, desperate outlaws, and ruthless cattle barons. Most Americans assume this world vanished long ago, yet people alive today remember Queen Ann striding along in her custom-made boots and Josie riding to town for supplies with her team and wagon.

Ann died in 1956 when the Korean War was already part of history. When Josie followed her in 1964, the race to put a man on the moon had already begun. Both women were raised in a wilderness but lived to see an atomic, electronic world. Both women brought to that new world a combination of pioneer values and an utter disregard for any conventions that ran counter to their own standards of right and wrong. They were sometimes condemned by their more conservative contemporaries—understandably so, for what they did was not always admirable. They lived their lives as they wished, doing what they wanted to do or what they felt they were compelled to do, with never a serious qualm when they overstepped the bonds of "proper" society.

Since the day when the Pilgrims first stepped on Plymouth Rock, an independent woman has been no rarity in a country which always had a new frontier. Courage, resourcefulness and strength of will were necessities in wilderness communities, and people who possessed these qualities were valued and respected regardless of their sex. It is not surprising that the first crack in the wall of political discrimination against women appeared in frontier Wyoming, where in 1869 the territorial legislature gave women the right to vote in territorial elections. When those Wyoming women went to the polling booths, they were the first women in the United States—even the first in all the world—to cast ballots.

Elizabeth and her daughters were not active feminists; rather, they were pupils of the feminists who had prepared the way for them. And they were apt pupils. They were unusually independent and exceptionally autonomous, for even on the Wyoming frontier the typical woman was a follower of her man, not his leader. If the Bassett women seem forerunners of the feminists of the 1980s, it is because they were indeed in advance of their times in seizing the freedom which the frontier offered. Even so, their story would not be worth the telling if it were not for their personal qualities—audacity and strong will, high temper and obstinacy, good humor and open-handedness, unashamed sexuality—qualities that their contemporaries summed up as "the Bassett charm."

Josie's cabin still stands and can be seen today in Dinosaur National Monument in northeastern Utah. When the old lady died, the National Park Service bought the five acres she still owned and added them to its three hundred square miles of mountains and barely accessible canyons carved out by the Green and Yampa Rivers. The homestead is on the fringe of this wilderness, as is the Monument's museum, a huge, greenhouselike structure covering the remnants of the vast cache of dinosaur bones which gave the Monument its name.

Twice a day the Park Service loads tourists onto a large open-sided bus and takes them out along the Green River, past the red sandstone bluffs with their pictographs left by long-gone Indian tribes, and down across Cub Creek to Josie's homestead.

While the tourists are still on the bus, the Ranger uses his loudspeaker to tell them the legend of Josie Morris. "She was raised in an outlaws' hangout . . . Some people say that Butch Cassidy was one of her sweethearts. . . . She was married five times, and there's a story that she took a shot at one of her husbands but she denied it—she said that if she had been the one to shoot him she wouldn't have missed. . . . Perhaps she got tired of men, for she came here when she was almost forty years old and lived out here—alone—for fifty years, with no running water, no electricity, no telephone. A real pioneer."

The outlines of a carefully laid out working ranch still show despite the years of disuse and the tangle of late-summer weeds. The Park Service has done little to preserve the place except to board up the cabin's windows and put a plywood canopy over the roof to protect it from the heavy winter snows. Even so, it is obvious that this is no hermit's shack, no squatter's cabin.

Peering through the slits in the boarded-up windows, one sees a smallish, square living room with a good brick fireplace and the faded remnants of once-gay blue wallpaper. To one side of this main room is a kitchen, to the other are two small bedrooms. There are porches on two sides of the cabin. On one of these Josie used to sleep, even during the bitter winter months.

Outside, a log fence still bars the mouth of the box canyon where Josie penned her livestock, although the canyon itself is now a thicket of brush and young trees. In what was once her garden area, old fences sag from the weight of her grapevines turned wild. The orchard is a graveyard of gnarled, dying trees. Wild watercress grows in the damp soil near the spring which still fills the pond where Josie kept ducks and geese, before spilling into the meadows below. The chicken house and an old corral still stand, but the springhouse where she stored her butter and the sty where she kept "Miss Pig" can only be imagined.

The Park Service's benign neglect has given a poignant authenticity to what remains of Josie's homestead. The visitors walk and speak softly, as if from respect for the pervading quiet of the place, a quiet broken only by the gurgle of the spring water from an old iron pipe. One can imagine the loneliness of living in such a silent place and the serene strength of the woman who could endure that silence. The silence is provocative, raising questions that the Ranger's rehearsed information does not answer, questions as to what kind of woman Josie really was and where she came from.

If the ghost of Josie Morris could be asked those questions, it is doubtful that she could provide answers, for Josie was always too busy to spend much time on idle introspection.

And if Queen Ann's ghost were at Josie's side, her answer might only raise more questions. "She was a Bassett! A Bassett of Brown's Park!" To Ann, that would explain everything.

The Bassett Women

ARKANSAS TRAVELERS

A highly unlikely partnership began in Hot Springs, Arkansas, on September 21, 1871, when Amos Herbert Bassett took Mary Eliza Chamberlin Miller to be his bride. The incongruity of their marriage is equalled only by the incongruity of their later migration to a Western wilderness where Herbert was to endure manfully his distaste for pioneer life and his wife, joyfully accepting that life, was to become known as "head of the Bassett gang."

Herb was born on July 31, 1834, in Brownsville, Jefferson County, New York, where his forebears had lived for generations. At some time in his younger years the family moved to Sweetwater, Menard County, Illinois. In 1862 he was twenty-nine years old, living on the family farm and teaching school in the winter, when he responded to President Lincoln's call for thirty thousand volunteers from the President's home state. Private Herbert Bassett served in Company K of the 106th Regiment of "Lincoln's Brigade." Since he was a musician, he was assigned to the company band with the official title of Drummer.

While in the Army, Herb was beset by the ill health which later caused him to move to the west. In 1863, barely a year after his enlistment, he suffered from what Army records call a "debility" and was sent home on sick furlough for a month or so. At the end of the war Herb, still a private, was mustered out at Pine Bluff, Arkansas, and chose to stay in that part of the country, very possibly because he had found a Southern branch of his family living there. The name of Bassett is found in Arkansas county records as far back as 1833. This kinship with an old pioneer family evidently smoothed his way despite his being a Yankee, for he eventually became Clerk of the Court, a respected and even powerful position in the communities of the last century.

Herb has been described as a "little old maid of a man." He was only five or six inches over five feet tall, and his legs seemed too short for his torso. Aside from that he was handsome, with thick and curly dark hair, strong features, and well-set blue eyes. Herb's education was better than average and he was a competent musician on both piano and violin. He was deeply religious but not puritanical; although strongly disapproving of tobacco and alcohol, he enjoyed dancing and playing cards, if no money changed hands. He was gentle, kind and good-humored, and despised arguments. Unfortunately, considering the life which lay ahead of him, he appears to have been a passive man with no qualities of leadership.

Mary Eliza (she preferred to be called Elizabeth) had been born in Hot Springs County on August 25, 1855. She was a spirited girl and so voluble a conversationalist that the Utes were later to call her "the Magpie." According to contemporary descriptions, she had the graciousness that marks a Southern gentlewoman, and an inborn magnetism. With this magnetism, an iron will, strong ambition, and indomitable determination to get her way, she controlled the people around her by so intriguing their imaginations that they willingly followed her. She was normally affable and serene, but when she lost her temper she was violent.

Elizabeth and her sister were very young when their parents died, and the girls were raised by their maternal grandfather, Judge Crawford Miller, a breeder of thoroughbred horses. Surprisingly, they were raised with his name. This suggests that something more than an ordinary tragedy may have caused their parents' death. Judge Miller had come from around Newark, Virginia (Elizabeth was always proud of being from one of Virginia's "First Families"), and it is curious that a lineage-conscious Southerner would deprive his granddaughters of their father's name. Elizabeth's daughter Josie was later to tell a grandchild that there was a suicide in each generation of the family. Josie gave no details, but she may have been referring to old and better-forgotten violence. Elizabeth herself possessed qualities which, given bad fortune, could have led her to disaster. But her fortune was good—she married Herb Bassett, who was always to be her balance wheel, even when he could not control her.

If there is a mystery surrounding Elizabeth's parents, there is an equal mystery surrounding her marriage to Herb. Why would the attractive teenage daughter of a well-to-do family marry a graying, middle-aged man?

Perhaps the orphaned girl saw in this kindly and gentle man the father she had never known, although that answer seems rather superficial for someone as complicated as Elizabeth.

Mary Eliza, herself better-educated than many women of the time, would have been contemptuous of a very commonly held opinion that an educated female ran the risk of a withered uterus if uncommon strain were put on her brain. She would have been in complete sympathy with the growing tide of feminism and of women's demands for educational opportunity and equal treatment under the law. At the same time, she was always a lady with strict ideas of propriety, and would have been completely out of sympathy with Victoria Woodhull, who was espousing "free love" on the lecture platforms in the east, and with Amelia Bloomer, who had urged women to replace their petticoats with pants.

A deeper look at Herb shows a man who was progressive and liberal for his time. In later years, for example, he considered his daughters' education as important as his sons'. Herb must have reflected Elizabeth's own ideas—progressive, but conventionally so. She would have felt safe with him, knowing he would treat her as a person of intelligence, despite her womanhood. Moreover, she could trust him to give her the freedom to express herself in her own way and for her own purposes. Her self-awareness must have made it clear to her that she could never tolerate domination. Herb's very passivity and lack of force may have attracted her.

When they married, Herb was thirty-seven years old; Elizabeth had just turned sixteen. Judging by reports of their later years, it was a love match on both sides, which bore up well even under any painful stresses caused by their differences of character.

They settled down in Hot Springs to the life typical of a well-bred couple in comfortable circumstances. In 1874, three and a half years after their marriage, their daughter Josephine (Josie) was born. Less than two years later Elizabeth delivered their first son, to whom they gave the family name of Samuel. Life could have continued in a placid routine except that Herb's health had seriously deteriorated in Arkansas, where the summers are humid and the winters cold but no less humid. Herb described his physical condition when he applied for an Army pension:

> Was treated in Arkansas 20 years ago for liver and heart trouble—had chills and fever frequently for several years after the war was over—was treated by Dr. Henry C. Baker who stated that my liver was in very bad condition—that the chills and fever that I had were very hard to control. While he was treating me I had a very hard chill which threatened congestion and he advised me to leave there at once. I sold out and came here [Brown's Park] in April 1878.

In addition to his "debility," which was probably malarial, Herb was asthmatic. The doctors of those times could offer little help to tuberculous or asthmatic patients except to prescribe a change of climate. It is said that half the people in early Colorado had come there because of "pulmonary afflictions" that might benefit from the dry mountain air.

As if Herb's chills, fever and attacks of asthma were not enough to disturb the couple's tranquillity, in 1874, after six years as Clerk of the Court, he lost his job, possibly because of a change in political climate occurring at the end of postwar Reconstruction in Arkansas. At the time they made their decision to migrate to the west in 1877, Herb may have realized that his future in Arkansas could never hold more than an obscure clerical job or, even worse, working on Judge Miller's horse farm. Elizabeth, with her drive and ambition, may have urged the migration. At the least she would have cooperated enthusiastically in this search for better fortune.

It would seem that they had no firm plan in mind when they boarded the train that would take them west. Family tradition says that their destination was California (another popular haven for asthmatics) but it is very probable that when they left Arkansas they were still not sure where their home was to be. In any event, they broke their journey at Green River City, Wyoming, for a reunion with Herb's younger half-brother, Sam Bassett, who lived about eighty miles to the south over the Utah line in a place called Brown's Hole.

Sam Bassett had been a teenager when he left the family home in Illinois. He had wandered the west from California back to the Dakotas as a miner, prospector, guide for travelers, and scout for General Miles of the Union Army. In 1852 he had done some prospecting in Brown's Hole and had liked it well enough that he returned in 1854 to make it his headquarters between wanderings.

Brown's Hole had been a rendezvous in the 1830s for the fur trappers. For a time there was a small trading post there named Fort Davy Crockett (nicknamed "Fort Misery"), but it vanished when the scarcity of game, as well as the fall from fashion of beaver hats, made trapping unprofitable. When Sam Bassett chose it as his headquarters, he became one of the first white men to live there permanently since the days of that early trading post.

Sam Bassett kept a journal during his early days in the west, and its disappearance is a tragedy, judging by the fragment that survived, quoted by Ann Bassett in her memoirs:

> Browns Hole, November, the month of Thanksgiving, 1852. Louis [Simmons] and I "down in." Packs off. Mules in lush cured meadow. Spanish Joe's trail for travel could not be likened to an up-state high lane for coach-and-four. Mountains to the right of us, mountains to the left of us, not in formation but highly mineralized. To the South, a range in uncontested beauty of contour, its great stone mouth drinking a river. Called on neighbors lest we jeopardize our social standing. Chief Catump, and his tribe of Utes. Male and female he created them. And "Solomon in all his glory was not arrayed so fine." Beads, bones, quills, and feathers of artistic design. Buckskins tanned in exquisite coloring of amazing hues, resembling velvets of finest texture. Bows and Arrows. "Let there be no strife between me and thee!"

Sam had kept in touch with his family over the years. He was a sociable, outgoing man who loved good company almost as much as he loved his solitary prospecting in the mountains; a reunion with his brother must have been a joyful moment for him. It would be equally joyful for Herb to meet again the brother who had written so eloquently of his adventures. The two tenderfeet from Arkansas most certainly did more listening than talking, for Sam was a guide to what they might expect to find when they reached California.

Since Sam had tried California and had not liked it, it is most probable that he discouraged them from going any farther west. Mountain man that he was, he would have told them that California was too crowded, that the good land was all gone, and that, along the coast at least, the air was too foggy for an asthmatic. With the enthusiasm that any man has for a spot he himself has chosen, he would have expounded on the beauty of his own Brown's Hole, its comparative emptiness, its available ground, its mild winters and clean pure air.

Whatever their reasons, Herb and Elizabeth decided not to go on to California but to stay in Wyoming. Herb turned down Sam's offer of hospitality in Brown's Hole, however; he intended to live in town and look for a job compatible with his experience and education. Although he had grown up on a farm in Illinois and had the necessary knowledge to homestead, he lacked the physical stamina required. More importantly, he lacked the desire. Although he had described himself as "farmer" on his enlistment papers, he had actually been a schoolteacher in his youth, and his descendants remember him as a one-time teacher who was a "complete misfit" in Brown's Park.

An undocumented source states that Herb worked a short while in Evanston, Wyoming, as a bookkeeper for a mercantile firm. His grandson, Crawford MacKnight, says he taught school for a term in Green River City. Neither job, however, would have been worthy of his capacities, and he must finally have decided that success in this new land could be found only in homesteading. So word was sent to Sam, and Sam came to guide their wagons on the journey to Brown's Hole.

BROWN'S HOLE

Sam Bassett must have shaken his head in disbelief when he saw the belongings that Herb and Elizabeth were bringing to a wilderness. There were spooled bedsteads and the feather mattresses to go on them; there were walnut bureaus from Elizabeth's girlhood home. These were practical enough; for that matter, so was the huge iron cookstove, even though nothing like it had yet been seen in Brown's Hole, where people still cooked over fireplaces. There were, however, box upon boxes of books, and more boxes of china, silver and dainty glassware. Most wondrous of all, there was an organ! To these had to be added the barrels of flour and sacks of coffee and sugar and beans, the kettles, the skillets, the axes, the hammers, the rifles and shot, the barrel of nails. Any supplies they did not take with them in those two wagons would have to wait until they returned to town in late autumn to buy their winter's supplies.

They made their move at the earliest signs of spring, as soon as the mountain passes were clear of snow. There was an urgent reason for this—in less than two months Elizabeth was due to deliver their third child. Elizabeth's own enthusiasm for this new endeavor can be judged by the fact that she was willing to take the risks of the trip and the hardships of homesteading in her late months of pregnancy.

The wagons swayed and bumped southward over rocks and through sagebrush, following the faint tracks made by those who had gone before. For long stretches they were on comparatively level ground, but for equally long stretches the track took them over formidable hills. Then, like those before them in the trek west, Elizabeth and the children would get down from the wagons, to lighten the load for the straining oxen on the inclines and to save themselves from a turnover on the downgrades if the brakes should fail. One can imagine her walking with a child by each hand, picking the easiest path, mindful of the cumbersome burden she carried within her and matter-of-factly adjusting herself to it.

Josie remembered that first trip:

> I don't know how many days we were coming—I just barely can remember it. I was four years old. And one reason I remember it so well, they had a team of oxen,

> and wasn't I afraid of those oxen! Oh! But I rode with them—I rode with Uncle Sam Bassett and his oxen all the way. But when I was on the ground I wasn't with them, I was someplace else. And that's how I come to remember our trip so well.

There must have been almost a holiday feeling to their journey. Elizabeth was not a woman to be transformed into a semi-invalid by pregnancy. Strong and resilient, she could take discomfort in stride. When they made camp for the night and the men had the fire burning well, she would have helped cook the dinner and put the children to bed with a song. If the two men lingered at the campfire, she would have entered into the conversation as eagerly and as gracefully as if she were sitting safe and secure in her old Arkansas parlor. And it may have been at one of these campfires that Elizabeth started her campaign, often mentioned by old-timers, to change the name of Brown's Hole.

Back in 1869 and 1871, a one-armed Union Army veteran named Major John Wesley Powell had made two voyages of scientific exploration down the hitherto uncharted Green River. In Brown's Hole itself, the Bassetts were to know the Green as a strong but serene ribbon of water pursuing a snakelike course through the valley that the river itself had created. However, to the north and south of Brown's Hole the Green was a treacherous man-eater. It charged through high-walled red-rock canyons so narrow that for miles there would be no place for a boat to land, and poured over rocky beds of boulders that created giant whirlpools. Before Powell's expeditions, the river had been considered nearly unnavigable; it was, in fact, never completely mastered until the construction of Flaming Gorge Dam in the early 1960s.

Major Powell's journals of his voyages had been widely published, and if the Bassetts had not read them back in Arkansas they surely must have read them in the days when they were planning to make their home on the banks of the very river of which Powell wrote. Elizabeth would have read the names that the poetically inclined Powell had given to the landmarks he passed, and would have learned that he had called her future home Brown's Park rather than Brown's Hole.

"Oh Josie, dear," one can almost hear her saying, "did you hear Uncle Sam say *hole?* I thought we were going to live in a *park*! To live in a *park* would be so much nicer, wouldn't it?"

Elizabeth mounted an unremitting campaign, and she won it. At her insistence, neighbors began to use Major Powell's name for their valley, and in doing so they forgot the major completely, giving Elizabeth sole credit for the more euphonious name.

On the fourth or fifth day the wagons entered the eastern end of Brown's Park (as it shall be called from now on) through Irish Canyon. Then they turned west to reach Uncle Sam's cabin, located eighteen or so miles up the valley. As they traveled they surely must have stopped at any cabins along the way, despite Elizabeth's advanced pregnancy. In Arkansas she might have followed the custom that required pregnant women to retire from public view, but in isolated Brown's Park that custom would have seemed rather silly. The shared experiences of the handful of people living there were to create an intimacy in which old customs, old backgrounds, and disparities of education and personality became insignificant. Their lives were to be so intertwined that the Bassetts' neighbors are essential to the Bassett story.

The first homestead on their way belonged to José ("Joe") and Pablo Herrera, two brothers who had fled New Mexico as political refugees.* After a period of time in which they had lived by their wits and their success in the gambling halls in Wyoming, they had come to Brown's Park and established themselves with the help of fellow Mexicans who worked for not much more than their board and room. They carried on a brisk trade with the Utes for their exquisitely tanned buckskin, did a great deal of drinking and gambling, and offered an open house to anyone who happened to drift into the Park. A photograph still in existence shows José Herrera to be a burly, handsome Castilian, well-dressed to the point of foppishness, with an air of strength and breeding. It is difficult to reconcile the sophisticated man of this picture with the one who, J.S. Hoy said, would start sharpening a long knife while talking to someone who disagreed with him.

One of the Herreras' drinking companions and full-time lodgers was A. B. Conway, a practicing lawyer in Iowa before personal problems sent him west. Conway eventually abandoned an aimless and alcohol-dominated existence in Brown's Park and went on to become "Judge Conway," Chief Justice of the Wyoming Supreme Court. When he died, the eulogies of his admiring fellow citizens rang across his grave. This brilliant man's fondness for the Herrera brothers would indicate that, villains though they might be in the eyes of some of their strait-laced Anglo-Saxon neighbors, they were still men of polish. Indeed, in the years before the Herreras returned to New Mexico to engage once more in political agitation on behalf of their fellow Mexicans, the well-bred and well-educated Bassetts counted them as friends.

The wagons then passed the Hoy Meadows on their trip up the valley, although it is possible that Sam would not have bothered to stop here. There were five Hoys—four brothers and an uncle—holding choice meadow lands along the Green River. They claimed to be the first to set up a ranching operation in the Park (the Hoys would not have considered the Mexican Herreras

*The phrase "political refugees" is Ann Bassett's. There was serious unrest in the New Mexico Territory for many decades after the Mexican war in 1846 as its Mexican inhabitants struggled against adverse political and economic conditions.

"ranchers") and had originally hoped to hold the Park as their private domain, attempting to shut out any competition from incoming homesteaders. This had proved to be impossible, but they still stayed more or less to themselves and were not intimate with their neighbors.

There were others in the Park whose names will appear from time to time in the Bassett story. There was the Spicer family, and there were the two Australians, Griff and Jack Edwards, and Jimmie Reed, who was living in a dugout at the lower end of the Park with his Indian wife and their children. There were Scotsman John Jarvie and his wife Nellie, who ran a trading post up at the far west end of the Park. Jarvie was later to build a storage house of stone, reputedly cut by an ex-convict destined to be hanged from the Bassetts' corral gate.

Another neighbor in those early days was James Goodman, a member of Major Powell's expedition down the Green who had come back to settle on this peaceful section of the wild and treacherous river he had helped explore. The Bassetts also soon met "Buffalo Jack" Rife, who was eventually joined by his brothers Ed and Bill. At this time Jack was a bachelor cowboy working up on Diamond Mountain for Jim Warren. He later gained the nickname "Buffalo Jack" by establishing a private sanctuary for the few remaining buffalo, paying the Indians in salt and other supplies to leave them unharmed. His boss, Jim Warren, was an ex-priest (presumably Catholic) and an ex-rustler who had turned rancher when he met and married a good and moral woman.

Soon to come to the Park was another man whose name will appear over and over in the Bassett story: Charley Crouse from Trap Hill, North Carolina. At the time the Bassetts arrived, Charley had a ranch on nearby Diamond Mountain but he moved down into the Park within a year or so. Charley Crouse was an uncouth, rough-talking, hard-drinking semiliterate who had run away from home at the age of nine. His ruling passion was good horseflesh, and he raised fine horses that he took as far away as Nebraska to race for large stakes. When his horses won, Charley was in the money; when they lost, he was not above appropriating a few loose cattle to mend his faded fortunes. Matt Warner, an outlaw who was in and out of Brown's Park, referred to Charley in his memoirs as "that lovable old rustler."

Charley was erratic and more than slightly dishonest, but he was a good businessman. He raised three good children, although the credit for this was given to his wife Mary, daughter of a Mormon convert from England. Mary was well thought of by everyone in the valley, for she was a fine woman who involved herself in all the acts of neighborliness that are so important in a frontier community. Genteel Mary Crouse may have suffered from living with a man whom Joe Haslem describes as "meaner than a bitch wolf in a rainstorm," a man who called his own sons "the red-headed bastard" and "the black-eyed son of a bitch." However, he provided a good living for her, and her own good reputation gained both of them an entree into Brown's Park polite society. Although Charley participated in that polite society, he much preferred a bottle of whiskey and a game of cards with the men who lived in his bunkhouse.

These people considered themselves neighbors, even though their homes were spread out over an area of almost three hundred square miles. Elizabeth's most important neighbors in those early days were the Yampatika Utes who camped on the banks of Willow Creek only a stone's throw from Sam's cabin. In times to come, Elizabeth was sustained by the Ute squaws and educated by them in wilderness ways, and Josie and young Sam played with the Ute children. The bonds of neighborliness were strong between the Bassetts and the Indians as long as the Utes were free to return to Brown's Park.

When Elizabeth first saw Uncle Sam's cabin she must have fallen silent until she remembered her manners. (Josie remembered it as "a funny little old log cabin with two rooms, no floors, no windows.") Uncle Sam may also have been dismayed as he looked at his bachelor's quarters and then at the two wagons full of belongings, the two extra adults, and the two lively little imps who undoubtedly started climbing on his bed, getting into his tobacco jar, and fingering his guns and hunting knives within five minutes of their arrival.

The plan had always been, of course, to erect a cabin for the new arrivals. Although surely it must have been begun, the cabin was not finished a month later, on May 12, 1878, when Elizabeth delivered the first white child to be born in Brown's Park. The infant, Ann, was an active, intense little mite who pulled strongly at Elizabeth's breast and screamed with rage when her hunger was not satisfied. Perhaps because of her spartan life, Elizabeth's breasts did not fill and she had no milk for the baby. Potential disaster was averted, according to Ann's memoirs, when Buffalo Jack Rife stopped by:

> A troop of Ute Indians were camped about two hundred yards from the cabin, among these was an Indian mother, See-a-baka, who had a new-born papoose. Buffalo Jack Rife, good old "Buff", spoke their language like a Ute, so after consultation with Dr. Parsons [this elderly doctor died the next year, to everyone's sadness, since there never again was to be a medical man in residence] he held a pow-wow with Chief Marcisco and Medicine Man Mush-qua-gant, "Star." After making considerable medicine and sign talk, it was decided to permit the squaw to become my wet nurse and me to become a foster twin to her papoose, a boy named Kab-a-weep, meaning Sunrise.
>
> Indians do not coddle newborn infants by covering the head. I've been told it was storming when they carried me to the Indian wickiup, and I can imagine how I must have blinked and grimaced as the snow settled on my little face.

> It was the custom of the Indians to move from the river bottoms where they wintered, to cooler summer camp grounds on the mountain tops. For that reason my Uncle Sam built the "double cabins" for mother at the head of Willow Creek, so she could be near my foster mother. To this cabin See-a-baka came at regular intervals to feed me. I nursed her for six months, until cow's milk could be provided. It was Judge Conway who rounded up a milk cow and presented her to me, so I got into the cow business at a decidedly early age.

Uncle Sam had built the cabin up on Willow Creek by the time the milk cow arrived, but the location of the cabin satisfied neither Herb nor Elizabeth. This was the least of their problems, however; more depressing was the scanty and monotonous diet. Sam had helped select the food supplies they had brought to the Park—beans, flour, coffee, sugar, pork sideback. Sam lived on these staples and may have been satisfied, since they could always be supplemented by game he shot. To Herb and Elizabeth the menu was unappetizing, and for the little children it was a disaster. Judge Conway's milk cow must have been a godsend to them all.

Elizabeth's experience on an established farm in civilized Arkansas could not have prepared her for that first summer, with two small children, a newborn baby, and a sickly middle-aged husband whose muscles had yet to be hardened after years of sedentary life. Sam surely must have helped, but he was neither rancher nor farmer, and preferred prospecting in the mountains. It was late in the growing season by the time Herb cleared enough ground for a vegetable garden of sorts. Because their future was to be in raising cattle, they bought a few head and began the task of learning what to do with them. The cattle were too precious to be used for food, and if Elizabeth did not already know how to use a rifle she must have learned that summer so that she could shoot wild game. The Indians showed her how to make jerky from the deer she shot and told her which fruits and roots were edible among the wild things growing on the mountains.

Somehow they survived the winter, although old-timers have reminisced that the Bassetts were sometimes hungry. The Park women helped as they could; if someone were coming the Bassetts' way, they would send along a few eggs or a loaf or two of bread, whatever they could spare. Such things were offered with tact, as gifts from one neighbor to another. With that same tact Elizabeth brought gifts in later years to other struggling newcomers.

The second summer was better. Herb's health had improved and Elizabeth was acclimated. They had a proper garden, and the problem of food became less pressing. Then in late September of 1879, just as they believed the worst was over, news reached the Park of the Meeker Massacre at the White River Agency station only seventy-five miles away.

This uprising of the Utes resulted in the cancellation of the trust fund set up by treaty and the loss of hunting privileges in their traditional territory in western Colorado. The massacre was used as proof by both the white settlers and the government back in Washington that the Indians could not be trusted to keep the peace. Yet in truth the tragedy was the direct result of what could be described as acts of war by a white man, the Indian agent Nathan Meeker, who had almost life-and-death control over the reservation.

Nathan Meeker was an author and journalist who, under the sponsorship of Horace Greeley (owner of the *New York Tribune* and coiner of the phrase, "Go west, young man, go west!"), had founded Union Colony on the plains of northeastern Colorado, now the prosperous city of Greeley. His colony was to be run on idealistic principles based to a certain extent on the ideas of the French socialist Fourier, who advocated communal endeavor and equal sharing of communal income. A visionary and a romantic, Meeker turned out to be a very poor businessman.

At the end of five years, Union Colony was on the verge of collapse from drought and devastating grasshopper plagues, as well as from Meeker's inexperience and mismanagement. Moreover, his excessive moralism was splitting the Colony apart. According to Marshall Sprague, author of *Massacre*, a definitive book on Meeker, he not only opposed tobacco, liquor, gambling, billiards, dancing and the theatre, but also believed that fishing was cruel to trout and picking wildflowers was childish. His self-righteousness was abrasive as he imperiously insisted upon imposing his extreme ideas.

Meeker personally was ruined financially, and was being sued by Horace Greeley's estate for repayment of loans. (Greeley had died not long after the Colony was founded.) To rescue himself, he applied for the job of Indian agent and was appointed in May 1878. Meeker believed that the only solution to the "Indian problem" was to "civilize" them. He was determined to turn the Utes into farmers as quickly as possible.

The Ute Nation had been getting along quite well with the white men. The principal chieftain, Ouray, realizing the folly of resisting iron cannon, had generally kept the tribal hotheads under control. The Utes continued to wander freely in their old hunting grounds, supplementing the dwindling game supply with the rations distributed by the Agency. Their principal occupation was still hunting, and their hunting was profitable to them, for there was a great demand for their beautifully tanned buckskin, which, according to Dr. Meeker's own statement, sold for $1000 a ton at the railhead. Yet in the report that Meeker sent to Washington (in August 1879, just prior to his murder), he showed no desire to build on the Utes' traditional talents. Instead, he complains of their refusal to plow, to plant, to send their children to school, to forsake their customary hunting expeditions, even as he comments that farm equipment is inadequate and out-of-date, that the schoolroom is rude and ill-equipped, and that the seed furnished by the government had been full of cockleweeds. He suggested a solution to his strongest complaint, that the Utes went hunting:

> If government would take away all the horses in the vicinity, except such as could be useful, the Indians would not go abroad; and if cattle were given instead they would, or could, or should engage in a profitable industry, and one to which they take readily and naturally. To permit any class of human being to do as they please, and, at the same time to be supplied with food, inevitably leads to demoralization. After I get hold of these Indians I can tell a great deal better what can be made of them. I should like to have plenty of land in cultivation, with tools all ready; take away their horses; then give the word that if they would not work they should have no rations. As to how much they would work and produce in such a case, and as to how fast they would adopt a civilized life, is merely to speculate, but my impression is they would not starve.

One of Meeker's early acts had been to plow forty acres and plant it in potatoes although there had been "opposition from the Indians to the occupancy of this valley, since its use to them had been for winter grazing of their horses." Moreover, contemporary accounts say that he ordered their race track plowed up—the track for the displays of horsemanship that were so important to their culture—because they ran races on the Sabbath. Then the well-meaning tyrant ordered that only heads of families could collect the rations on which they depended so heavily, meaning that if the men went hunting, their wives at home would go hungry.

During the summer of 1879 there was increasing petty vandalism against the white settlers throughout the Ute territory. In August the older and wiser heads of the tribe went to Denver to discuss their grievances with the knowledgeable and sympathetic Governor Pitkin. The governor understood the gravity of their complaints and the possible consequences, but he was helpless in the face of the chains of command in the federal bureaucracy. By September the Utes were disillusioned by the lack of response to their peaceful complaints and wild with anger at the man who had so sanctimoniously trampled on their traditions.

The final straw was the news that soldiers were being sent to the reservation to keep order. On hearing this, a radical group of Utes attacked and killed all nine white men stationed at the White River Agency. When outside help arrived, Meeker was found about two hundred yards from his house with a log chain around his neck, one side of his head smashed, and part of a barrel-stave driven through his body. His wife and daughter were nowhere to be found. They had been carried off by the Ute attackers.

The horror of Meeker's death and the resulting fear for their own skins left the whites throughout the area in a state of panic. While the soldiers were out chasing down the captors of the Meeker women, settlers from outlying areas were leaving their homes in droves. Those near the Rocky Mountains headed for Steamboat Springs, a new cattle town at the foot of the Rockies, or its older neighbor, the mining community up at Hahn's Peak. South of Brown's Park in Ashley Valley (later to become Vernal, Utah) the Mormons built a fort for their protection.

Although Brown's Park was in the center of Ute country, its own permanent community of Utes seemed little affected by the happenings at White River. Still, the Brown's Park people felt themselves naked against the threat of an uprising among their heretofore peaceful neighbors. All ranchers of this period lived with the threat, however obscure, of being the victims of some maverick Indian; the present situation was much more dangerous since a whole powerful tribe might unite to drive the white men out of their territory. Most of Brown's Park's population fled, although Indian-wise Uncle Sam Bassett trusted the good will of his Ute friends and stayed where he was. A good number stopped at the ranch of Charley Crouse's brother-in-law, Billy Tittsworth, who lived halfway between the Park and Green River City. They stayed the winter with Billy, living on his supplies and keeping a sharp lookout for the red men with their scalping knives.

According to Josie, her mother was not afraid of the Indians but her father was. When Herb decided that he would take his family to the safety of Green River City, Elizabeth could not argue with the prudence of leaving. Abandoning their cattle and leaving most of their possessions in Sam's keeping, they pushed hastily in a lightly loaded wagon down the valley and through the pass at Irish Canyon toward the security of town.

Homesteading had not been Herb's first choice, and it is very possible that he was happy to leave Brown's Park and had no real intention of ever returning. But Elizabeth had grown to love the valley, with the red bluffs of its foothills giving way to the green expanses of meadows along the river, and the high mountain ranges that seemed to shelter the valley whichever way she looked. She could have almost enjoyed the hardships of their first months, which demanded so much creativity and which challenged her capacities. It may have been the first time in Elizabeth's life she had been given a chance to live up to her full potential, and it is difficult to believe that she was not heartbroken at their defeat.

CATTLE FEVER

In all the unpeopled miles through which the Union Pacific Railroad passed, two separate towns were built only fifteen miles apart—Rock Springs and Green River City, Wyoming.

The first transcontinental railroad had been completed in 1896 when the Western Pacific, building from the west, and the Union Pacific, building from the east, had joined their rails with a golden spike at Promontory Point, Utah. As part of its contract to build the railroad, the Union Pacific had been given alternate sections of land along its right of way. As the construction crews moved across the country, the railroad established towns and sold the land for as little as seventy-five cents an acre, advertising for new settlers who would become customers for its freight and passenger cars.

When the construction crews reached the "dry country," where the typical homesteader could not rely on crops of wheat and corn and barley, the Union Pacific continued to sell land and "choice lots" in its newly established towns; but the land could not sustain enough people to give the towns permanency and, when the construction crews moved on, they became ghost towns. The hopeful investors in "choice lots" moved away, damning the railroad for chicanery and perhaps themselves for gullibility.

Green River City, Wyoming, was spared this fate when the Union Pacific established its yards there permanently. Then the railroad established Rock Springs, where there was coal to be mined for its own use and for shipment to outside markets. Rock Springs was a profitable investment; by giving itself favorable rates on hauling coal, the Union Pacific could undercut its competitors.

Both Green River City and Rock Springs had the unrelieved drabness of any new town established in treeless country, but Rock Springs suffered the additional ugliness of the mine dumps which showered dust on the shoddy clapboard shacks thrown up hastily to house the miners. Green River City, on the other hand, was the county seat, very proud of itself and of its future. It was very nearly a "company town," and its merchants almost "company merchants." Because new businesses were discouraged, being considered dangerous to the financial well-being of the established concerns, ambitious newcomers necessarily turned to Rock Springs to set up their shops.

Keenly aware of the general unfavorable opinion of their town and anxious naturally to get on in the world, these merchants showed all the initiative that Americans are supposed to have, and proceeded to outsell and outsmart Green River City in every way. As time passed, they even used municipal funds to cut a good road through territory belonging to their neighboring state of Utah to entice Brown's Parkers to buy their supplies in Rock Springs, instead of either Green River City or the new town of Craig, east of the Park in Colorado.

Although still ugly, Rock Springs today seems more alive and prosperous than the much more pleasant Green River (as it is now called), which is small, sleepy, and a little down-at-the-heels—the final blow to its importance having come as the Union Pacific's role dwindled. However, at the time the Bassetts fled Brown's Park it was indeed unfortunate that Herb's quest for work landed them in dirty, dingy little Rock Springs. When they arrived in 1879, Rock Springs had a population of around three thousand, a disproportionate share of whom were "foreign labor," brought in by the railroad to work in the mines while being squalidly housed, poorly treated, and abominably underpaid. The good housing for the "whites" was almost as squalid and at a premium, and opportunities for work were limited.

The Bassetts stayed in Rock Springs for over a year and a half before returning to Brown's Park. There seems little question that Herb preferred town life, even in Rock Springs, to chopping brush on a homestead, and perhaps only a lack of funds prevented him from finally taking his family to California. Their eventual return to Brown's Park must have been at Elizabeth's insistence.

Elizabeth may have regretted their flight almost immediately, but it would have been impossible to return in the middle of that first winter, even after the threat from the Utes had subsided. Prudent people do not attempt to pull wagons through the snows of the Wyoming Basin if they can avoid it. Even if she took the winter's delay philosophically, however, she could not have received the news of another pregnancy with joy, for it meant more wasted time. By the time Elbert, always called Eb, was born in June, the short summer season was too far advanced to reestablish themselves. Waiting through another winter must have been nearly unbearable to her, as she sat in a makeshift house in the primitive little mining town, watching cattlemen coming in for supplies.

Elizabeth had contracted a very severe case of "cattle fever," the same fervid enthusiasm that was then infecting investors in Boston, in New York, and even in Scotland and England. In that vast, unsettled western territory belonging only to the United States government there were thousands of square miles of grassland that in previous ages had supported huge herds of buffalo. Since the buffalo had been all but exterminated, all those thousands of square miles were available for the raising of cattle.

Corporations had been formed and the value of their stocks was booming, for small and large investors alike were rushing to participate in what seemed an absolutely sure-fire method of making a fortune. It was so simple! One bought young cattle, turned them loose on the public domain where the food was *free*, then sat back and waited for only two or three years to sell them for ten times what they had cost. And all the while one waited, those same original cows were producing new cows each spring!

A naive investor often ignored the stumbling blocks on this pathway to fortune: the fluctuating prices paid for beef at the markets; "killer winters" when the plains were covered with the frozen bodies of cattle who had starved to death—winters in which whole herds could be wiped out; or, most serious of all, the difficulty of providing water for the cattle to drink in a country where water was scarce. Since cattle can rarely be maintained on land that is more than two and a half miles from water, many of those thousands of miles of grassland were unusable because of a lack of waterholes, and there was savage competition for land which did have water.

The Wyoming Basin had been carved by nature into ranges that followed the streams and the rivers, the springs and the water holes. Early settlers in the years immediately after the Civil War had claimed some of these natural ranges and had built up large herds to fill them. The rest were quickly occupied by the cattle corporations.

These cattle barons, stalemated by their nearly equal strength, lived in peace with surprisingly little dissension as to who "owned" what range, apparently ignoring the fact that the ranges were in the public domain. When their "ownership" was threatened by the later arrivals, the "little men" brought by the advertising of the railroads and the generosity of the Homestead Act, they formed powerful coalitions among themselves to stop the invasion. Each homesteader who filed a claim on a water source was a threat far out of proportion to the one hundred and sixty acres he was claiming, and the cattle barons stood united in fighting him.

The cattlemen fought legally and illegally. Each could legally exercise his own homestead rights to one hundred and sixty acres; moreover, through the inept and often corrupt administration of the Homestead Act, he could use relatives, his own cowboys, or even hired drifters or prostitutes to homestead on adjoining ground. Some cattlemen thereby gained control of twenty or more miles of riverbank.

Any homesteader who "proved up" and gained title to land near a cattleman's domain always knew that his powerful neighbor would gladly buy him out. He also knew that if he stubbornly persisted in holding on to his homestead, his crops could be burned, his cabin wrecked, or his cattle absorbed into the larger herd at roundup time. If the homesteader attempted to fight back, or if his land was in a particularly strategic location, he knew he could even be lynched as a rustler or shot in the back as he rode home from town, and that he could expect no support from the legal authorities. The only real authority in Wyoming, both on the state and local levels, rested in the cattle barons themselves.

During the period Elizabeth Bassett lived in Rock Springs, the war between the large cattlemen and the small ranchers had already begun. That war would continue for twenty-five more years, increasing in violence into the 1900s, when the cattlemen were finally vanquished. Elizabeth was clearheaded enough to realize the difficulties that would face her, but she had a secret advantage over the average incoming homesteader—she knew that Brown's Park was almost pristine territory. Although cattle being driven up from Texas had often wintered there, the land had been for the most part unsettled because it lay in country still reserved for the Utes. She must have been wildly impatient to return to her remote valley to claim her good water and good ground while it was still there for the claiming.

Those who knew them have said that Elizabeth's daughter Josie was just like her mother. In this situation we can imagine Elizabeth using the methods her daughter later used, to convince Herb to return to Brown's Park even against his wishes. She would not have begged or pleaded, nagged or raged. Her tools would have been a contagious optimism, an enthusiastic description of what lay before them, a serene brushing aside of any objections, and an irresistible self-assurance. In a flood of soft Southern words, Elizabeth would have contrasted running their own profitable ranch with Herb's job as a timekeeper at the mine for the gangs of Mexicans and Chinese. Herb hated his job, for it was unpleasant work, poorly paid, and demeaning to a man of his capabilities. If Herb mentioned California as an alternative, she would have reminded him that his brother Sam had been right—that the dry air had already improved Herb's health immeasurably. She could prophesy in good conscience that his asthma would undoubtedly disappear completely once he got away from the blowing coal dust in Rock Springs. She would have painted such attractive pictures of their future as she sat smiling at him, eyes sparkling in anticipation, that Herb would forget momentarily that he was forty-six years old, still suffered from asthma, and hated the idea of being a pioneer again.

Elizabeth's campaign was won, perhaps, through the intervention of A. B. Conway, that previous benefactor who had produced a milk cow for Ann. When Conway had first gone to Brown's Park he had staked out a beautiful piece of ground at the eastern end of the valley near the claims of the Herrera brothers. It lay up against the hills below Cold Spring Mountain across from the Gates of Ladore, those two towering precipices between which the Green River leaves Brown's Park. The property had an excellent spring pouring out just where the hills started their gentle slope down to the valley floor, and its flow was so strong and dependable that it had created a meadow in the land beneath it.

Conway had never done much with his claim and now his law practice and political efforts were so successful that his future was in Green River City. He came to the Park only because he loved the place and enjoyed relaxing there with his old friends the Herreras. He offered to relinquish the site to Herb and Elizabeth, stipulating only that they would help him care for his thoroughbred horses if the Herrera brothers were ever to leave the Park. Here was the perfect opportunity, then, to acquire one of the choice spots in the valley, far better than their first location on Willow Creek. Under the pressure of Elizabeth's enthusiasm, Herb acquiesced.

RANCHERS AND RUSTLERS

The Bassetts returned to their old cabin only to pick up their belongings; then they went back down the valley to their new homesite. On the way, the children broke out in measles. Elizabeth bedded them down under the massive cottonwoods bordering the spring and started to help strip the logs that Sam and Herb were hewing for a cabin. When she was not chopping firewood, cooking meals, washing clothes, feeding the chickens, milking the cow or helping Josie care for the smaller children, she was grubbing out brush for the vegetable garden. After the cabin was far enough along that the family could move in out of the open, there was the chicken house to be built, then the corral for the stock and the sheds for supplies.

After the essential buildings were completed, one can imagine Elizabeth suggesting that an extra supply of logs be cut before winter set in, " for the bunkhouse we will need in the spring."

Bunkhouse! They had no cowboys. For that matter, they had only a handful of cattle. This would not have deterred Elizabeth. She had a clear and constant vision of what must be accomplished and, with gaiety and good humor, she pushed her husband toward the goals she had set for them. (Only occasionally would her violent temper transform the Southern gentlewoman into the brassy-voiced slavedriver.)

If she pushed Herb, she also pushed herself with her need for success. Josie said of her, "My father didn't know how to brand a cow—neither did she, but she tried. . . ." Until her anticipated cowboys arrived, Elizabeth managed the cattle herself. When she was not working at the cabin or in the garden, she was in the saddle—a sidesaddle, of course, as befit a lady—taking salt blocks to her precious cattle, keeping a watch for mavericks, moving her herd to better pasturage, perhaps shooting some game for the dinner table, while Herb and little Josie took care of things at home.

She had her first experience with the casual way in which property rights were treated in cattle country when they first returned from Rock Springs and found that the cattle they had left with Uncle Sam were missing. According to Josie:

> My father bought twenty head of heifers just before the Meeker Massacre and he branded his heifers with "U P." . . . on the ribs. Great big "U" with the "P" connected. But while we were away in Wyoming a man came into the country . . . his name was Metcalf . . . and he branded with "7 U P." He had a "7" in front of our "U P" all over those cows. My father didn't know what to do, he was stranded . . . but my mother did. She said, "I know some of those cows, and I'm taking them." And she took them! She and Mr. Metcalf had some kind of set-with . . . she didn't use "U P" anymore, she had the cattle rebranded.

Once the decision to return had been made, Herb undoubtedly responded with good grace and enthusiasm. While he was neither physically nor psychologically prepared to learn the cattle business, he made contributions of his own to the growth of their homestead. He piped the spring to bring water close to the cabin and to provide irrigation for crops. He established hay fields, becoming the first man in the valley to do more than just mow the natural grasses for winter forage for their horses. He planted an apple orchard. He brought in four-strand barbed wire—another Brown's Park first—and fenced the home fields. When they started summer grazing their cattle in Zenobia Basin up on Douglas Mountain, he built a three-room cabin and a corral with closely placed upright cedar posts to protect the horses from wild predators. (Bears and mountain lions were so thick in the high mountains that horses were belled for protection, and ranchers went on organized lion hunts.) His granddaughter, Edna Bassett Haworth, recalls Herb experimenting with seeds and new plants in a special plot and grafting new varieties of fruit onto existing trees in his orchard.

In addition to cattle, the Bassetts raised horses, and eventually made themselves a local reputation as good breeders; not in vain was Elizabeth the granddaughter of a breeder of thoroughbreds. Esther Campbell's notes describe the day when Ann Bassett first saw Esther's buckskin horse. Ann immediately recognized it as one of a "Nugget" breed that had originated on the Bassett ranch:

> They owned the original mare, the "Tippecanoe" mare, and raised many good colts from her. Her father [Herb] bought the mare from some people traveling through the country from Tennessee. She was high-lifed and they had a wire tied around her tongue to control her. Her tongue was almost cut in two. Mr. Bassett felt sorry for her and bought her. Her colts were always full of life and willing to travel. Ann had a team of buckskins [Tippecanoe's colts] for a buggy team. She

> drove them from Douglas to Craig from sunup to sundown, and they would be pulling at the bits when they trotted up the last hill to Craig.

Breeding good horseflesh to use on the ranch and for an occasional sale was valuable, of course, but their success depended on their cattle. Elizabeth soon learned that even in her remote valley there were intruders.

In earlier days, when the only cattle in Colorado were the Longhorns driven up from Texas, cattle drovers had used Brown's Park as a safe wintering place for their herds. Grass and water were plentiful, and snowfall was normally light because the valley was sheltered by its ring of mountains. Even in a "killer winter" which destroyed herds on the plains, cattle usually survived in Brown's Park. Yet the Park was never large enough to accommodate huge herds. As the land in the Park was homesteaded, continued attempts of outsiders to winter there caused serious overgrazing problems for the full-time inhabitants, who watched their range anxiously for signs of overuse.

As if the damage to "their" range was not enough, cowboys running a large herd often collected local cattle which then were driven out of the area and often lost to the local ranchers. Every rancher expected to lose a few cattle to the weather, a hungry neighbor or an equally hungry mountain lion, but to lose them to an intruder on one's own grass was too much to bear. In retaliation, the ranchers were not too careful of an outsider's ownership rights, and they often carried newborn calves home on their saddlehorns, to be fed in their own home corrals.

Taking home an unweaned calf was, of course, illegal—far removed from the perfectly legal practice of putting one's own brand on a maverick. Originally a maverick had been defined as a yearling which had not been branded, but common practice was to assume that any calf which had left its mother's teats was a maverick, and this was often stretched to include a calf *almost* weaned to grass.

There is no legitimate doubt that small ranchers all over the Basin took as many mavericks as they could lay their hands on, and that the beef on their tables was from cows with an outsider's brand. The common saying was, "Only a tenderfoot eats his own beef." Considering the conditions under which they were struggling to survive, these illegal brandings and butcherings are as understandable as a slum kid's snitching an apple from a grocer's pile of fruit.

The large cattlemen of Wyoming had formed themselves into the Wyoming Stock Growers Association, which almost completely controlled every aspect of the area's cattle business with the cooperation of state and national legislation. On the basis that members owned eighty percent of the cattle in Wyoming, the Association was authorized to conduct the spring and fall roundups and to exclude unacceptable small homesteaders from participation. All mavericks at these roundups were divided among the Association members. Eventually even cattle branded with "unregistered" brands (those not registered by the Association) were confiscated. The ostensible reason was to control rustling, but the real effect was to badly cripple a new settler from the east or a cowboy who had managed to save some money and acquire a few cows of his own.

To these small, persecuted individuals, owners of perhaps one hundred cattle or a few hundred at the most, self-preservation required that they recoup their losses in any way possible. Because the Association itself was composed of rich and greedy men, Wyoming's small ranchers retaliated in the only ways open to them.

The Brown's Park ranchers shared these problems. As the Basin filled up with cattle and the cattle drives from Texas became a rarity rather than a common annual occurrence, the outsiders who had been using the Park for winter graze faded away, only to be replaced by neighbors who presented even more serious problems. The most sinister was an outfit called Middlesex Land and Cattle Company—known from its brand as the Flying VD—which had its headquarters only about twenty-five miles northwest of the Park's boundaries. The owners of Middlesex were big-money men from Boston who had bought up several small ranches, put a ruthless man named Fred Fisher in charge of operations, brought in several thousand head of cattle, and prepared to dominate their own portion of the public domain. Fisher openly announced his intention of driving out all small ranchers in his territory.

Middlesex wanted to establish a base of operations in Brown's Park from which it could spread out and take over the whole valley. Using the techniques of a Chicago blockbuster, Fisher approached several ranchers in the west end of the Park and offered to buy them out at attractive prices. The Park ranchers held a meeting and decided to hold firm; no one sold and the "blockbusting" failed.

Actually, the Brown's Parkers were in a much better position than small ranchers in more open sections of the country. It is easy to visualize this thirty-five mile valley as one huge corral. If Middlesex cattle managed to wander down through the steep mountains that surrounded it on three sides, the ranchers could delightedly appropriate these strays. If Middlesex made a deliberate effort to bring its herds in through the eastern access, the ranchers would be well aware of that fact and could either drive the herd back or cause enough damage that Middlesex would think twice before trying it another year. The ranchers in the Park may have considered themselves a beleaguered group of "little guys," but by banding together and capitalizing on their geographical advantage, they managed to protect their home range with considerable success.

After the Meeker Massacre the Park acquired another large new neighbor not too far from its eastern entrance. Up in Laramie, Wyoming, a highly successful self-made man named Ora Haley was quick to realize that the banishment of the Ute Indians to the Uintah Reservation over in east central Utah had opened up an important new range not yet appropriated by anyone.

In 1881 Haley bought a spread on Lay Creek, about thirty miles as the crow flies from the site on which the Bassetts were then establishing their new homestead. Bringing down cattle from his extensive holdings in Wyoming and buying others in Utah, Haley put twelve to fifteen thousand cattle on his new range. According to John Rolfe Burroughs, this was by far the largest herd ever assembled in northwestern Colorado under one ownership up to that time. Haley's brand of two slanting bars gave the outfit its common name, the Two-Bar.

In the early years, Two-Bar caused Brown's Park ranchers little trouble and made no real effort to appropriate their range. Still, cattle wander. They drift in small groups, paying no attention to whose range is being invaded or whose water is being used. There was little, if any, supervision of these herds except at the semiannual roundups when the Middlesex and Two-Bar cowboys moved the herds—in the spring to the mountain plateaus for summer grazing and in the fall to the more temperate lowlands. Two-Bar's cowboys would come into the Park and search for their cattle at these times.

During these roundups the new calves were branded and cattle ready for market were cut out of the herd. Usually a large operator expected a ten percent "leakage" each year from death, rustling, and casual butchering on the range by persons unknown. This leakage factor also took into account the utter impossibility of finding all the thousands of cows in hundreds of square miles of gullies, washes and canyons. However, because of the magnitude of his operation, the large cattleman still made a profit—if not too many cattle had winter-killed and if the bottom did not drop out of the price of beef.

Both Middlesex and Two-Bar knew that their leakage factor would be doubled if their cattle strayed into Brown's Park, and if they classed all Park inhabitants as no better than the rustlers who were reputed to hang out there, those inhabitants only smiled grimly and hoped their bad reputation would protect their range from deliberate invasions. They were fighting for their own protection, and thought themselves no less honest for gathering mavericks or even unweaned calves, and eating Two-Bar's beef.

There were actually not very many badmen and professional rustlers in the

Park once the homesteaders arrived. Back in the 1860s and early '70s, the truly vicious Tip Gault gang had often used Brown's Park as a hideout between its raids on the wagon trains of west-bound pioneers, but that gang had been broken up before the Bassetts and other homesteaders had arrived. For the most part, the badmen who came through the Park in the Bassett days were small-fry criminals running from the charge of stealing a horse or shooting a man in a saloon brawl. Their principal rendezvous was at Powder Springs, twenty-five miles northeast of the Park, and any lawbreaker who came into the Park proper usually behaved himself. If the ranchers themselves had been asked to describe the lawlessness in their valley, they most probably would have talked about their own respectable neighbors, Jesse S. and Valentine Hoy, who were perpetrating legal thefts far more serious, in Brown's Park eyes, than the occasional theft of a horse.

Everyone in the Park started as a squatter because the land had never been surveyed, and it was even unclear exactly where the state of Colorado ended and Utah began. Not until the summer of 1884 was a survey completed, allowing the homesteaders to establish clear title to their acreage. As the survey party brought its chains and transits into the valley, some of the local people were hired to help them, including Valentine Hoy as the party's cook. Herb Bassett may also have been hired; it is certain that the party camped temporarily near his ranch.

When the survey was completed, Major Oates, the leader of the party, gave Herb the metes and bounds of the Bassett property, and the legally knowledgeable Herb went immediately to the county seat at Hahn's Peak and recorded his claim, as shown by the county records of September 22, 1884.

Not all the ranchers were as prompt. Valentine Hoy, having gained early knowledge of the legal descriptions of the ground, was able to claim certain parcels whose occupants did not move quickly to record their land. With his brother Jesse, he hired outsiders to file claim on desirable parcels; when these hired homesteaders had acquired clear title, the Hoys bought them out and enlarged their own holdings of valuable pasture land along the river bottoms.

All this was completely legal, exactly what other well-to-do ranchers were doing all over Wyoming, but the neighbors resented the Hoys bitterly. Ann called Valentine Hoy a "land grabber." Josie described his scheme in her taped memoirs, using a quaint colloquialism, "swift," the exact meaning of which seems to have been lost:

> The Hoys came first . . . and tried to make a monopoly of everything. . . . V. S. Hoy wasn't a good man. . . . You see, when the survey was made, V. S. Hoy was a smart man [as] all the Hoys were. . . . V. S. Hoy was cook with the

> survey party. He had a nice business, he was there for a purpose. . . . Now he knew the numbers of places and put swift on them, bought the land, and what he didn't buy with swift he had people coming here from Fremont, Nebraska and Leavenworth, Kansas . . . to take up homesteads. Then he met them at Glenwood Springs, where they'd take up proof, paid them each a thousand dollars and they were gone. He had their homes and that's how the Hoys got all of the Hoy bottoms. . . .
>
> He tried to swift my father's place, but my father's filing on the homestead had gone in just before his swift got there, so that didn't work. My father never liked the Hoys, that made a bad spot. My dad was a very forgiving man but he never forgave that, no sir! He said, "I've been a friend to V. S. Hoy and thought he was a friend to me, and to have him do that—I'll have nothing to do with him." And he never did.

Valentine was more active in acquiring land than his brother Jesse, but Jesse was still deeply enough involved to earn his neighbors' anger. Furthermore, they resented Jesse's readiness, over the years, to write letters to the newspapers denouncing lawless conditions in Brown's Park, and his equal readiness to file suit upon even a suspicion that someone was tampering with Hoy property. Most of the ranchers were too busy or too unlettered to take court action, and they preferred to handle their own problems, either firing a dishonest cowhand and running him out of the Park or quietly retaliating later. Glade Ross's files contain a comment by an early rancher: "Horses weren't worth anything. So when someone branded a horse belonging to another, no fuss was made because it wasn't worth anything then. If they came up in price, then we'd brand one of his."

Jesse S. Hoy is one of the more interesting and controversial of the many controversial personalities of Brown's Park. He had had certain successes in Wyoming before he settled in the Park permanently and persuaded his brothers Adea, Henry and Valentine, and his uncle Frank to join him. While still in Wyoming he had served one term in an early legislature, and after moving to Brown's Park he represented Wyoming as justice of the peace.

Hoy was an educated man, passionately fond of all animal life. In his old age, when his judgment was slipping, he managed to burn his barn to the ground by lighting smudge pots in it to protect his horses from flies. Almost without question he was a eunuch. There is one romantic tale that he was castrated by a jealous medical student during a stay in Paris; a more mundane but plausible version is that he had suffered a severe and permanently damaging case of mumps in his childhood. Whatever the cause, the fact remains that some of his more disrespectful and unsympathetic neighbors called him "the old steer."

Perhaps because of his physical handicap, he was an embittered and unsociable man who quarreled violently with his own family; he was never on speaking terms with all his brothers at any one time. As he grew older, he became suspicious of his neighbors almost to the point of paranoia; if a man had business to transact with Hoy he turned it over to his womenfolk to handle. Hoy took self-righteous pride in the fact that he had never in his life butchered so much as one cow belonging to someone else. The Brown's Parkers, however, never quite forgot the way he had acquired some of his lands.

In his old age, Jesse retired to Denver and wrote his memoirs describing his early life on the plains and his years in Brown's Park. These memoirs, known as "The J. S. Hoy Manuscript," were unearthed from the files of a publisher in Denver. They had been mercilessly edited, probably by a Hoy relative who either feared libel suits from the people in Brown's Park or who believed that the old man had unjustly blackened his neighbors' names. The manuscript contains only the barest information on his Brown's Park days, and no particularly specific accusations have survived the censor's scissors. Even in its expurgated form, however, it clearly shows that J. S. Hoy felt that most of his neighbors were thieves and rustlers and that the worst ones were the Herrera brothers and Elizabeth Bassett.

While the manuscript contains mentions of "the Bassett gang," Elizabeth herself is mentioned only once. After a censorship of several pages, one sentence remains which condemns as it excuses: "In fairness to Elizabeth Bassett it must be said that . . ." There follows a moving paragraph on the hardships women endured in pioneer life.

Whatever the Hoys' opinions of Elizabeth, tradition says that her fellow ranchers admired her spunk, her ability, and her leadership. Among the ranchers, Elizabeth's voice was respected. As for Herb, they thought enough of him to elect him their representative on the county commission of Routt County in 1882. County records show his $5000 bond was made by Pablo Herrera, Anton Prestopitz, and Griff Edwards. He evidently served only one term, for in those days it was impractical for Brown's Park to be represented at regular county meetings held three days' journey away at Hahn's Peak. However, from 1884 until his resignation in 1892, Herb still represented authority in the Colorado part of the Park, for he was appointed justice of the peace, with Griff Edwards and Solomon Rouff as his bondsmen.

Indeed, Herb was a leader in many community affairs. His education was broad enough that he could give good advice on subjects affecting the ranchers' welfare. While they might think him a poor sort with cattle, they never questioned the integrity of this man who, on many a Sunday morning after an all-night Brown's Park party, would lead the hymns and conduct a simple religious service for this churchless community.

Even after the early days of building, Herb Bassett took no active part in running the cattle and bossing the cowboys; that was Elizabeth's bailiwick. Even though Herb's health returned and he lived to be very old, it is hard to picture this quiet little man, who had always been a clerical worker, directing six-foot cowboys at roundup time.

Equally incongruous might be the picture of a woman in a sidesaddle bossing six-foot cowboys. Elizabeth was a successful manager, however, using that famous "Bassett charm" the old-timers speak of. She did not issue orders; she made requests, and she accompanied them with a warm, very feminine smile. Skeptical cowboys soon found that they had an efficient boss who would work right along with them. She had put in her apprenticeship before they had arrived and had learned her lessons well. One woman who knew her said, "She was as good a cowhand as any man."

In *Where the Old West Stayed Young,* John Rolfe Burroughs writes:

> It is impossible to overemphasize the loyalty that Mrs. Bassett inspired in the breasts of the homeless and oftentimes outlawed young men, any one of whom it is said "willingly would have died and gone to hell for her." If high strung, she was a strong-willed, self-controlled woman not at all motivated by romantic considerations. But such was her vitality, her personal magnetism, and her sympathetic understanding of the essential loneliness of her footloose constituency that men willingly flocked to her standard.

Elizabeth was too practical to rely on only that "personal magnetism," which was, after all, instinctive and not contrived. More important, she gave her men the privilege of building their own herds so that a man could work for himself as well as for the Bassetts. This attracted the ambitious, for many outfits had halted the practice, believing that it tempted the poorly paid cowhands to change a few brands for their own benefit.

Equally important from a human standpoint, she welcomed her ranch hands almost as guests within her family circle. Her bunkhouse was comfortable and her food was good. If a man liked to read, Herb's library was available. If he enjoyed children, the Bassetts could supply him with five, of assorted ages. Ann Bassett has described bucking contests where each small child had for a bronco a cowboy who would do his best to throw his rider into the clean hay strewn in a makeshift arena.

Aside from the fact that Elizabeth was a good cowhand and a good range boss and Herb was not, Herb's complete separation from the cattle side of the ranch was possibly because he disapproved of the way Elizabeth was running things. Herb was a deeply religious man with a strong moral sense; moreover, in Arkansas he had been an officer of the court, sworn to uphold the law. It could be that he refused to have anything to do with any activities smacking of illegality, no matter how Elizabeth and the neighboring ranchers might justify them.

An example of the opposing attitudes of husband and wife is the story Ann tells of the day on which one of their cowhands, Jack Rollas, was shot:

> He was a pleasant-mannered young fellow from Texas who came to the Bassett Ranch in 1882. A good hand with horses, he was hired to break broncs on the ranch. It was in the late fall of that year that three strange men arrived about noon, and were asked to eat dinner with the family. While Mrs. Jaynes, who cooked for us at the time, was preparing the meal, one of the strangers asked her if Jack worked there. Mrs. Jaynes replied, "Yes, that is Jack saddling a horse at the corral." The three men walked from the kitchen and went on down to the corral. One of them pulled a gun and shot Rollas as he was reaching for a bridle. He ran behind a barn, where he fell, mortally wounded.

The ranch hands, Herb, and Elizabeth managed to get the men at gunpoint while Mrs. Jaynes rushed out and gathered the children into the shelter of an outbuilding. Rollas had been carried into the bunkhouse, and the furious Elizabeth marched the marauders in to confront him.

> The one who had done the shooting said his name was Hambleton and that Rollas had shot and killed his brother in Abilene, Kansas. Hambleton had trailed Jack Rollas for two years to kill him. Rollas confirmed Hambleton's statement in part, explaining that a man of that name had married his sister. He abused the sister and Rollas had killed for it.
>
> Mother spiritedly informed Hambleton that it was not the custom of the northwest to shoot an unarmed man in the back. By the determined threat of her leveled Winchester, she lined the trio up against the bunkhouse wall, and directed the wounded Rollas to kill his assassin, or all three men, if he wanted to.
>
> Rollas was too weak to hold a gun, and he died a few hours later. While mother and Mrs. Jaynes were administering to the dying cowboy, father and Perry were guarding the prisoners. Harry Hindle went to notify the settlers of the park, and to get Charles Allen, Justice of the Peace, to the scene of the crime. [This was before Herb's own appointment as justice of the peace.] Night came and father began to think with deepening apprehension. A lynching could be in the making. He advised the captives to go to the barn and feed their horses, and he warned them to ride directly to the county seat, over a hundred miles away, and surrender themselves to the law. When neighbors arrived at the Bassett ranch, the murderer and

> his companions had escaped. Naturally, they failed to do as father had instructed, and were never heard of again. . . . The method subscribed to by father in the matter of advice to the shooters *would have been in direct conflict with the opinion of mother and Mrs. Jaynes. Therefore, he did not commit himself and tell the true story for some time afterwards. . . .* [italics added].

Although Ann's accounts of Brown's Park life are sometimes slightly colored, Elizabeth's domination and Herb's subservience in this instance have a ring of unvarnished truth.

While Elizabeth was undoubtedly the head of the Bassett family, J. S. Hoy exaggerates when he calls her head of a "gang." (As far as is known, the term "Bassett gang" was used *only* by Hoy, not by other contemporaries.) She was primarily a rancher managing a herd of legitimately acquired cattle which was increased by calves from legitimately owned cows. It is unbelievable that this woman, this gentlewoman, was a "night rider" engaged in actual rustling on a large scale. Moreover, since large-scale rustling was unacceptable to all ranchers, large or small, her neighbors would have stopped her, distasteful as it might have been to them to prosecute a member of the "weaker sex."

But while Elizabeth may not have been a night rider there is a tradition that she did brand more lost calves and butcher more stray beef than less energetic ranchers might have done. There is also an undocumented story that she added to her herd by buying cattle at cut-rate prices from professional rustlers, who normally took their stolen cattle either to Rock Springs to be butchered and sold to the mining camp, or down to the Mormon farmers in Ashley Valley, always ready customers. Given Elizabeth's character, it would not be surprising if she had done so, especially in those earliest days when the family was living hand to mouth. She absolutely had to build a herd, or "turn tail and run" for an uncertain future in California. In that sort of dilemma, Elizabeth would have put her own survival before a rich man's property rights.

An interesting story is repeated by Burroughs, in *Where the Old West Stayed Young,* involving five hundred head of Middlesex cattle purportedly made off with in a single raid. "Cornered in Zenobia Basin on Douglas Mountain, it is said that Elizabeth Bassett and her helpers 'rim-rocked' the herd, i.e., drove them over the cliff into Lodore Canyon, thus destroying the evidence that might have been used against them."

Elizabeth's grandson, Crawford MacKnight, made a notation in the margin of his copy of Burroughs' book: "I think this 'rim rock' business is all B. S. What in hell would they do with that many cows, even if they had gotten away with them?"

Crawford's objection is practical, for rustling is a stealthy business, and hiding five hundred cows would be as difficult as hiding a Greyhound bus. Still, old-timers remember the pile of whitened bones that could be seen in Ladore Canyon for decades.*

There is a possibility that Middlesex had decided to summer some of its own cattle in Zenobia Basin and that Elizabeth, enraged at this intrusion on "her" range, told her cowboys to rim-rock the cattle. Possibly the story grew in countless tellings into a case of rustling. If, for whatever reason, Elizabeth actually did push those cattle into Ladore Canyon, she must have sincerely mourned the destruction of good beef.

A more credible story is told by Edna Bassett Haworth, who remembers Herb telling her mother Ruby about the early days at the ranch. Herb heard a terrible bawling out in the corral and went out to find that it was full of calves. The calves were not yet weaned, so the corral was besieged on all sides by cows bearing various brands, bellowing loudly for their young ones to be returned to them. In the middle of the uproar was Elizabeth, calmly using her branding iron.

Herb had a habit of clicking his heels, a silent way of showing disapproval or frustration. When Ruby asked Herb what he had done about it, Herb told her that he had "clicked his heels and walked away."

Poor Herb! He was a strictly moral man in a world where morality was sometimes considered an unaffordable luxury. Left alone, he might have been defeated by the special needs of survival in this harsh situation. Everyone respected him—his grandson Crawford says that he was the finest man he ever knew—but his wife, his children, and his neighbors all knew that in Brown's Park he was entirely out of his element.

---

*The most spectacular elements in Brown's Park are two cliffs between which the Green River leaves the Park. John Wesley Powell, the explorer of the Green, named them "The Gates of Ladore." In establishing a Brown's Park post office, the Post Office Department spelled it "Lodore." The two spellings have existed simultaneously ever since.

THE BASSETT GANG

In the pioneer west, where survival was serious business, no decent rancher would turn away a hungry man. A traveler in strange country felt no hesitancy about stopping at any ranch house along his way if he had a tired horse and an empty stomach.

The Bassett ranch was the first one in clear view on the trail leading into Brown's Park, and because of its location it became the nearest thing to a country inn. There was usually at least one guest at the dinner table. He might be a neighbor returning from town, a cowboy searching for work, or a suspicious-looking character of dubious reputation. It made no difference. All were welcomed and treated as honored guests, in accordance with the universal custom of the west and Elizabeth's own Southern open-handedness. Cash might be scarce in a bad year, but food was always there for the asking.

An unemployed cowboy rode into the Bassett ranchyard in about 1883 looking for a meal and a bunkhouse with an empty bed. He was a tall, broad-shouldered, slim-waisted, dark-skinned black man named Isom Dart. When Elizabeth asked him to stay on, she could not have realized that this new cowhand was to become a mainstay in her life and in the lives of her children and grandchildren.

Isom had come up from Texas on a trail drive of around six thousand head of cattle destined for the Middlesex ranch. His trail boss was his boyhood friend, Madison M. "Matt" Rash, who had been born near Acton in Hood County, Texas, on January 4, 1865. Matt was about eighteen years old at the time he left Texas, more than old enough to be a trail boss in those times when the Texas cattlemen depended consistently on teenagers to drive their cattle north. Crawford MacKnight describes Isom and Matt as "boyhood friends"; since Isom was ten years older than Matt (he was born in 1855) possibly Isom worked near Matt's boyhood home or even for his family.

Isom's powerful physique and superior coordination made him an all-around cowhand of exceptional competence. It was his personal qualities, however, that endeared him to three generations of Bassetts. He had natural dignity and integrity, and although the Bassetts would not completely erase the line between the races, they accorded him concern, respect, and a friendship that was close to love. Crawford remembered him as almost a member of the family, someone who shared their life more intimately than an ordinary cowhand would have done, and who "put a good meal on the table when it was his turn," although he was not hired as a cook and was too valuable on the range to be kept in the kitchen.

Isom was a loner who went infrequently into Rock Springs and mingled very little there, even with members of his own race. He seemed to prefer life back at Brown's Park, where he could play with the children and entertain them with his fiddle or the mouthharp on which he was a master. He loved to work with rawhide—Crawford called him a "rawhide artist"—and fashioned quirts and lariats of carefully cut strips of cowhide which he blended into articles of heirloom quality.

His real love was horseflesh, dating perhaps from the time in his early youth when he was stableboy for a governor of Texas. All the time he was with the Bassetts he had his own herd of cattle, which he augmented by catching the wild broncs so plentiful in those days, breaking them to saddle and then trading them to the surrounding ranchers for cows. A measure of the man can be taken by the fact that when he was breaking a bronc he took off his spurs and hung them on the corral fence. To Isom, it was cruel to use spurs on a wild creature, and he had the strength and stamina to break a bronc without them.

Isom lived on with the Bassetts, semiautonomous, with his own herd and his own ways of bringing in money. He ate his meals in the main house along with the other cowboys, played with the children, and pursued his own interests in his quiet, dignified, independent way, gaining admiration and respect from the ranchers in the valley.

In the meantime, his trail boss, Matt Rash, had stayed on at Middlesex after delivering the Texas cattle. Soon Matt transferred to Tom Kinney's Circle K ranch just west of the Middlesex ranches and worked for Tom as a foreman. But Middlesex, which had been thwarted by the Brown's Park ranchers' concerted opposition when it tried to expand to the east, turned to the west, where Tom Kinney ranged his cows. Here the expansion was more successful. Tom was forced to sell out his cattle and turn to sheep-raising. Matt, a self-respecting cattleman, parted company with Tom at that point, but Tom did not hold this against Matt, and even helped him financially until he could get his own credit at the bank. Matt came on over to the Park driving a herd of his own, mostly young heifers he had got from Tom Kinney in their final settling up.

Although Matt stayed in the Bassett bunkhouse when he first entered the Park, he soon built himself a cabin a couple of miles west of the Bassett home and became independent. Friendship grew between the Bassetts and him, and the relationship deepened into another "family" association as time went on. Matt was from a good Texas family—his mother was a sister of Davy Crockett, it is said—and he spoke the same language as the Bassetts. Although Elizabeth was cordial to her neighbors, she had little in common with many of them and had developed no intimate friends. It was a pleasure to both Herb and her to have the company of this bright, aggressive young man.

Not too long after the arrival of Matt and Isom, a teenager joined them at the Bassett ranch: Jim McKnight, a rangy, six-foot Scotsman with chiseled features and blue eyes that turned green when he was angry. Jim was the namesake of a father whose own family had disowned him when he left the Catholic faith to become a Mormon. Eventually the elder McKnight became involved in so severe a doctrinal argument with the church elders that he was forced to leave Utah. He went on to the state of Washington, where he edited a newspaper, and never returned to Utah. His devoutly Mormon wife Mary stayed on at the family farm in the Salt Lake area, continuing to raise her children in the ways of righteousness.

Young Jim became disillusioned with Mormonism as his father had, and in 1881, when he was only twelve years old, he ran away to Rock Springs. Luckily for Jim, he captured the interest of a wealthy rancher, an immigrant from Pennsylvania named Butterworth. Jim worked on Butterworth's ranch during his early teens, and his employer saw to it that he got an education and stayed out of trouble. When Jim felt himself grown he headed for Brown's Park to begin ranching for himself, and ended up at the Bassett ranch as another cowboy ambitious to start his own personal herd of cattle.

Jim joined Matt Rash, Isom Dart and Elizabeth in an informal but closely cooperative working relationship in which they handled their various herds almost as one. When J. S. Hoy spoke of "the Bassett gang," he was referring to these three men, and he regarded Matt Rash as the senior member. It is interesting to note, however, that for all of Hoy's disapproval of Rash, and for all his eagerness to file complaints against his neighbors, no charge was ever brought against Rash, nor against Elizabeth or Jim McKnight for that matter. Isom was not as lucky, and was accused at least twice.

John Rolfe Burroughs tells of a time when Deputy Sheriff Philbrick came out from Rock Springs to arrest Isom on J. S. Hoy's complaint of "larceny of livestock." On the way back to Rock Springs there was an accident; the horses, the buckboard, the deputy and his prisoner all tumbled into a deep draw, leaving Philbrick with smashed ribs and several bad cuts. Isom, unhurt, got the team back on the road, took Philbrick to the hospital at Rock Springs, delivered the horses to the livery stable, then walked over to the jail and turned himself in. The grateful Philbrick testified at Isom's trial, pointing out that such merciful treatment and willingness to accept arrest were not the actions of a guilty man. The jury found Isom innocent of the charges.

Burroughs tells of a more serious incident in 1890, when three of the Bassett cowhands—Angus McDougal, Jack Fitch and Isom Dart—were accused of burning down Harry Hoy's barn. Angus and Isom were further accused of altering the brands on three horses belonging to another brother, A. A. Hoy. Angus McDougal was sentenced to five years in the Colorado state penitentiary, although Tom Davenport, Elizabeth and young Sam Bassett were subpoenaed to testify for the defense. Charges against Fitch were dropped. Burroughs states that Isom jumped jail (perhaps with the approval of his jailers?) and was never brought to trial. If so, it is possible that the authorities had no more of a case against him than they had against Fitch, since they did not bother making another trip to the Park to bring him in. Considering his reputation and his behavior with Deputy Sheriff Philbrick, it seems that they could have dropped him a postcard and he would have come to trial of his own accord.

If Elizabeth's helpers can be considered a "gang," then there was one other member, an important one. Even before Elizabeth acquired her first cowhand, little Josie had been a working member of the family. As each baby arrived and as the workload on Elizabeth grew heavier, Josie took over an increasing share of the care of the smaller children and the household tasks. She graduated from the work/play of "helping" Elizabeth pat out the biscuit dough with fingers still chubby with baby fat to making those biscuits herself. The first child, Josie accepted her responsibilities as a matter of course, and her lifelong generosity and solicitude for others (along with her habit of command) became as natural as breathing.

Josie has been called "another Elizabeth." She must have been a charming little girl. Her curly hair was the color of a copper penny; her fair skin was liberally sprinkled with freckles. She learned from her mother the art of tactful persuasion and acquired her mother's well-mannered poise and serenity. She had Elizabeth's quickness and drive, her ability and need to control, her indomitability, her strong will, and her well-controlled but volcanic temper. But where Elizabeth was admired and respected, Josie was to be loved, for her strengths were tempered by the warmth and affability she gained from her father.

Young Sam was more like Herb, an easy child to care for when Josie became his surrogate mother. Since Sam was over four years old when the Bassetts returned to Brown's Park, he too would have soon become a working member of the family. Like all the Bassett children, he learned to ride as soon as he could straddle a horse, but even before he was trusted on horseback he must have gathered eggs, hauled water from the spring and brought wood for the cookstove.

Ann was altogether different. If Josie was the picture of her mother, Ann was Elizabeth's caricature. Like Josie, she had fair, freckled skin, and although her hair lacked the brightness of Josie's, it still had auburn highlights. Ann could be as winsome as her mother and behave as sweetly and politely as her older sister Josie when she wanted to, but she lacked the self-control and self-assurance that her mother and Josie both possessed. Whereas Josie's temper was slow to rouse and responded only to strong provocation, Ann's temper was her primary weapon in her determination to have her own way. She had been a demanding child from the first time she found no milk in her mother's breasts, and as she grew older her temper tantrums became part of her standard repertoire.

In those beginning years a relationship between Josie and Ann was formed that was to continue throughout their lives. It was a close and loving one, for family ties were important in the Bassett family, but it was never peaceful. Josie chided and scolded her younger sister when she was naughty, and exercised her delegated authority with complete assurance. Josie had an honest conviction that what she was saying should be listened to by any well-brought-up girl, especially a Bassett girl. She infuriated Ann, who usually refused to obey. Ann was impudent, and she soon learned to bait Josie into losing her temper. Elizabeth and Herb would, of course, scold Ann for being naughty, but the brunt of their displeasure must have fallen on Josie, who, after all, was older and supposed to know better. Ann, looking angelic with tears in innocent eyes, would thoroughly enjoy the uproar she had caused.

Their next brother, Eb, was another Ann, although he lacked Ann's steel-willed violence. When George came along in 1884 he was "Herbert's child," and this must have been a decided relief to Josie. As the years passed, each boy in turn was introduced to the outside work and was gradually absorbed into tasks in the fields and on the range. Ann, however, was expected to follow in her sister's footsteps, become a little lady, and turn into what the neighbors were later to call Josie—a "homebody."

Ann had other ideas. She looked at Josie, who actually liked to work around the house, and at her mother, who spent much time in the saddle, and decided that her mother and her brothers were having all the fun. From the time she could climb on a horse she was out following her brother Sam. If Sam sent her home, she went outside with Eb, playing rough and getting grimy—something allowed little boys but not nice little girls. Although her parents attempted to keep her in the house with Josie, Ann either ran away or did her housework so ineptly that Josie would do the work herself.

In *The Colorado Magazine* Ann tells of her pride in an Indian costume she was given and of bursting into a roomful of visitors from the east "all done up in war paint and eagle feathers." She contrasted this to her sister Josie, "all perked up in starched gingham and ruffles to announce dinner." It was tiresome to Ann to be constantly compared to Josie, but it would have been more tiresome to have copied her. She continued to be a wild, unbroken colt of a girl, slipping away to the bunkhouse to listen to the cowboys' talk and picking up incidentally a vocabulary that she sometimes used even when she had turned into an elegant young woman. When she was just a little thing, it is said, she would use those words as she threw stones when one of the unpopular Hoy brothers happened to ride past the schoolhouse yard.

There was a cruel streak in Ann. She herself told how she could not keep from laughing when a "slow" little boy named Felix Myer would try to recite. Although the teacher remonstrated and her mother whipped her, Ann still laughed. The teacher could only send her out to sit on the steps whenever poor Felix had to recite.

Dick Dunham tells a story in *Flaming Gorge Country* involving a bride of one of the Rife brothers, who bragged excessively at a community supper about a cut-glass bowl she had brought from the east. At this time Ann was old enough to be helping the women wash the dishes. No one could ever be sure that it was intentional, but Ann picked up the bowl to polish it, juggled it for a moment, then watched it go crashing to the floor.

Yet there was kindness and loyalty and a demand for justice in her that balanced the cruelties of her nature. She was never hesitant to speak up in defense of the weak or the oppressed. In her childhood the Utes were still slipping back into Brown's Park to hunt and to dry their jerky. They camped at the mouth of Vermillion Creek, not too far from the Bassett ranch, and Ann would go down to play with the Indian children, just as Sam and Josie had. Because the Indians were her friends, she was always to defend them and espouse their cause, even in the face of the distrust and contempt that many whites felt for an "Indian-lover." Actually, throwing stones and cursing the Hoys was a child's way of thirsting for justice.

The children had a wonderful life. They worked hard, but they accepted this as natural. They also fell naturally into the fellowship of adults which their work earned them. Children were not segregated and given children's activities in Brown's Park. Instead, they were incorporated into the full life of the community and were genuine participants at the house parties, on the roundups, and at the horse races down on the old Indian track below Harry Hoy's place.

The Bassett children had a particular possession of their own, a private retreat up in the great outcroppings of polished maroon rock behind their home. They could climb up the rocks to what they called "the cave," although it was actually a geologic oddity more delightful than a cave. In past eons an ancient spring had poured its water on one of those huge slabs of rock until a perfect circle, almost six feet across, had been melted out of it. The water had hollowed out a large room beneath the opening and had carved a huge opening on one side. Sunlight streamed down through the roof and made patterns in the loose sand in which the children buried their treasures, and from their "picture window" they could see their whole world laid out below them. They played their games in a setting that seemed created just for the delight of children.

Even though strangers rode through the Park, and though peculiar characters sometimes camped in a secluded wash, there was no thought that the children should be sheltered from every possible harm. Once their chores were done, they could ride the hills as free as the jackrabbits that bounded away at their approach. The one incident that has come down to us in which this freedom might have been dangerous is found in Glade Ross's files:

> Sam and Josie went up Bull Canyon to get horses, Sam on a scrawny iron grey and Josie on a sorrel mare which looked good but was not as good a horse as she looked. As they were coming back down, a tall man—ugly, dirty, red stubble about an inch long, riding an old grey horse just about played out [stopped them]. He had corduoroy [*sic*] pants on, stuffed in his boot tops, no sign of a gun and no pack or supplies. The horse was shod. Said, "Sis, let's trade horses." Josie refused but he insisted, took her off her horse and changed saddles. Sam said, "Better let him do it, Jose," but Josie was mad and really cussed him out. He said, "O.K. kids, I"ll see you around," and left on her horse. No one knew who he was, and Mr. Bassett tried to find out but never did. Knew the country or he couldn't have gone through the country so light and avoided everyone. The grey horse was much better than the sorrel and Josie had him several years until he died. Everyone kidded Josie about being quite a horse trader, but she didn't like it.

The children's most meaningful education was carried on informally in their own cabin as they listened to their father read aloud. There were readings from the Bible, of course, but also from Shakespeare, Emerson, Sir Walter Scott and all the other writers whose books filled Herb's shelves. However, formal schooling was also provided for Brown's Park children from the first possible moment after Herb's arrival. He organized a public school in 1881, just after the first survey party came into the Park to establish the Colorado-

Utah line. Herb had eked out the number of pupils required under Colorado law by enrolling his own Josie, even though she was still a bit under age, and rounding up Jimmie Reed's half-Indian children.

The first school building was concocted from an abandoned barn belonging to the deceased Dr. Parsons, the doctor who had attended Ann's birth. Herb partitioned off a section with a tarpaulin, covered the windows with oiled paper, and built a fireplace. A dugout down by the river was used during another school term. Eventually a real school building was erected, and the people had a community meeting place at last.

Elizabeth celebrated Christmas as lavishly as possible, baking pies and cookies, making candy and popcorn, and stringing berries from the wildrose bushes for the Christmas tree. Christmas once past, the children started their stint of formal education, which ended before the time for spring chores. The ranchers in the far reaches of the valley eventually built tiny cabins around the school where their children could stay for the three-month term under the care of a grandmother or an older sister. Josie recalled that during her first school year in the Park she was sent to stay nearer the school in the teacher's crowded dugout, going home only for Saturday and Sunday.

As the family grew and the ranch prospered, the Bassetts' original two-room cabin was expanded to a cross-shaped building of five spacious, many-windowed rooms, each with its own fireplace. It acquired a finished look, surrounded by hay meadows, vegetable gardens and well-constructed out-buildings. The apple orchard matured so that Elizabeth no longer had to ration out the store bought apples at one per child per day.

The cabin itself was charming. Herb had replaced the original hard dirt floor with puncheons, splitting green cottonwood logs and smoothing the thick slabs on each side with his broad-ax, then fitting them close together throughout the house. With the picturesque bear and buffalo skins scattered on the good puncheon floors, the beautiful old furniture from their Arkansas home, the truly impressive collection of books, and the marvelous organ that added so much to the lives of their neighbors, it became something of a local showplace. In addition to what the Bassetts had brought with them, Herb added to its beauty, as Ann relates:

> Birch grew in profusion along all the streams. Rawhide was plentiful. He [Herb] solved our problems by making small tables and chairs of all sizes, using birch for the frames and rawhide strips for seats and backs. There were high chairs and easy ones, of the various types devised by his ingenuity. Cushions were of buckskin stuffed with milkweed floss. . . . The curtain problem was mother's to solve, which she did with most satisfactory results. She traded Indian Mary ten pounds of sugar for a bale of fringed buckskins, smoked to a soft tan. Father fashioned

rods of birch and sawed rings from the leg bones of deer carcasses. When hung, these draperies were the cause of much complimentary comment.

The pleasant cabin saw many parties. It was the custom in the Park for the word to be sent out to everyone that so-and-so was entertaining, and people came from all over the valley for a dance that would go on until dawn. As the evening progressed, the children would be laid crosswise on the beds like so many sardines in a can as they fell asleep, one by one, listening to John Jarvie play his concertina or Herb Bassett his organ. Herb also loved to play the violin; when he later lost two fingers to blood poisoning he would have his grandsons tape the bow to his mutilated hand and then play until the tight bindings stopped his circulation. Guns were checked at the door at Brown's Park parties, and any drinking was done in the barn. If a man took a few nips too many and became objectionable, he was relegated to the barn for the rest of the evening. There was no saloon atmosphere at these community parties, especially at the Bassetts'.

When it was another neighbor's turn to have a party, the Bassetts piled their organ into their wagon and took it along. It is said that the organ traveled the rutted roads of the Park so often that it finally succumbed from overexertion. Its passing was mourned by everyone, for its music had given beauty to people who would travel thirty miles by wagon for one of these lively parties.

THE HARVEST

As the country opened up and more people came in, Brown's Park was still at the end of the world. It was not until 1890 that a permanent post office was established there, replacing an unreliable mail delivery (which had ended completely two years before) to John Jarvie's store at the far west end of the Park. Herb was appointed postmaster of "Lodore," Colorado in January of 1890. The government's mistake in spelling the name made the post office no less welcome.

Herb built a separate cabin to serve as post office and store stocked with a modest selection of supplies. The mail was brought in each week from Maybell, Colorado, a miniscule hamlet sixty miles away, delivered to Herb by a carrier who spent the night at the Bassett ranch before making his return trip. The carrier usually forded Vermillion Creek or rode across the ice during the winter. Since fording was dangerous during the spring runoffs, Herb devised a pulley system to be used at such times. The mail was transported across the creek to him by use of this pulley, and he in turn sent blankets and food to the carrier, who was forced to spend the night in the open.

Herb loved his post office. Gradually he moved in his books and newspapers, turning it into his own private retreat. It gave him a personal responsibility of his own, unconnected with Elizabeth's ranching operation.

In that same year of 1890, Herb also applied for an Army pension based on his old "debility." The records of the National Archives are not clear as to exactly when this pension began to be paid, but most probably the first checks were spent on school tuition for Josie. She had been sent to board in Craig to acquire the high school education not available in Brown's Park. Then, in 1890, she was enrolled in St. Mary's of the Wasatch in Salt Lake City.

Josie loved St. Mary's and loved the nuns. Reared on the classics and good poetry and always a receptive student, she responded well to the educational standards and insistence on "social polish" in this excellent Catholic convent school. Both parents must have taken pride in her good record at the school, and Herb may have hoped that perhaps, given an understanding of potentials in life outside the Park, Josie might escape completely. He had never been happy there, and he wanted better things for his children. Unfortunately, Herb's hopes were never to be fulfilled. His children were all given educations far beyond the norm of the times, but they were to love ranch life as much as their supremely contented mother.

In the autumn of 1892, as she looked at what she had achieved in their twelve years of homesteading, Elizabeth had good reason for her contentment. She and her friends had weathered the terrible blizzards of 1886 and '87 that had wiped out Middlesex; the threat of Two-Bar was well contained, and Brown's Park had been more or less converted into a cattle "empire" belonging to the ranchers who lived there. Herb had his post office and his pension, which relieved the constant search for hard cash that was the affliction of most small ranchers. And Elizabeth and her good friends Isom, Matt and young Jim McKnight had reached a level where they were all prospering. She must have looked at their comfortable home, their well-fenced fields, and their strong herd of cattle on the range, and reflected with pride that her labors had been fruitful and the future was secure. Being Elizabeth, she must also have had many more plans for the future.

But sometimes the unthinkable happens.

In December 1892, just as Elizabeth would normally have been starting her Christmas preparations, she took to her bed with an illness, the cause of which is still obscure. At the end of two weeks, Elizabeth—so full of vigor and boundless energy, at the height of her capacities, only thirty-seven years old—was dead.

Josie was to say later that appendicitis killed her mother, but Ann's story to Esther Campbell, which seems to fit more closely with the available facts, was that Elizabeth had a miscarriage.

While still in bed, her favorite milk cow was caught up in a herd of cattle being rounded in the Park. In a fury, Elizabeth rose from her bed, saddled her horse, and gave chase. She retrieved her cow and cut it out of the intruder's herd, but at the cost of her life. As Josie described it:

> She went to bed at night all right, and woke up about four o'clock in the morning just deathly sick. Just terribly sick. Father was there and Jim McKnight was there, and—I don't know—some of the cowboys. And they couldn't get a doctor, of course. All they could do—all they thought of was hot applications . . . and that relieved her, of course, but she died.

So died a southern gentlewoman who had bested many strong men in a rough, competitive world. That competition had brought out the best in her, and perhaps some of the worst.

There is no way of knowing what scars were left on the Bassett children by the premature death of their mother, and whether or not these scars contributed significantly to their later development. Probably they did not, for their personalities and attitudes had already been formed when Elizabeth died.

The children had lived with a reversal of roles between their mother and father that was to form their adult attitudes toward the relationships between men and women. Elizabeth was, in effect, the breadwinner of the family, and their physical welfare had depended upon her. Herb had given his children laughter, tenderness, gentleness and the unhurried attention for which Elizabeth had never had time. As a result, Josie was to say, "We girls respected our mother, but we adored our father."

Loving their gentle father as they did, they absorbed the lessons that he taught them by his own example: the necessity for honesty, charity and love of God and neighbor. These values were reinforced by everyday life in the community, where a man's word was his bond, neighbor was loyal to neighbor, a hungry person was always fed, newcomers were assisted, and the sick were nursed and cared for. The Bassett children learned these lessons well and followed them in their adult lives.

Their mother had followed these same precepts, but from her and others in the Park the children had also learned to deal with the real world of survival. They learned that laws were to be disregarded if those laws favored lawless men; that Brown's Park belonged to them and was to be defended against marauders; that one gave without question whatever was asked by a friend, but that the property of outsiders was fair game. These principles were of course never taught formally but they were universally understood. So arose the dichotomy that would be seen later in the standards of some of the Bassett children.

The *Empire Courier* in Craig, Colorado, published an obituary of Elizabeth Bassett that hints at the controversy surrounding this extraordinary woman even during her lifetime:

A Sad Event

A messenger from Brown's Park arrived Monday bringing the sad intelligence of the death of Mrs. E. Bassett. Her children, Sam, Josie [*sic*]* and Anna who have been attending our school immediately started for home, accompanied by Mrs. William Morgan.

Mrs. Bassett's death occurred on Sunday after an illness of two weeks.

The deceased is one of the best known women in the country, where she has lived since the earliest settlement. She was a natural pioneer, possessing the most remarkable courage and energy.

She was highly esteemed by those who best knew her and commanded the re-

*Josie was actually in Salt Lake at St. Mary's of the Wasatch school.

> spect of those who, from conflicting business interests, were her enemies. The most conspicuous and admirable trait in Mrs. Bassett's character was her unwavering loyalty and devotion to her friends. She was only 35 [*sic*] years of age and apparently in the meridian of health and vigor. The sympathy of the community is extended to the motherless children.

Who were these "enemies" whose business interests conflicted with hers? Surely not her fellow ranchers, for to them she was a leader, loyal friend and a helpful neighbor in time of trouble. Surely not the men who worked with her. Her only possible enemies were the strong, important men who controlled the range in Colorado, who dominated the free grasslands—even fenced those grasslands in defiance of federal law—and who were quick to give the name "rustler" to anyone who opposed them. The only neighbor who ever damned Elizabeth Bassett was the bitter, greedy, sanctimonious J. S. Hoy, who had been thwarted, partially by Elizabeth, in his attempt to make Brown's Park his own private cattle kingdom.

They buried Elizabeth on a hillside overlooking the home place, thus establishing a family cemetery that now holds most of the Bassett dead. For over thirty years, however, she lay alone, as her family contended with the difficult times and the changing fortunes that would eventually almost destroy what she had built.

Elizabeth's daughters were to display in varying degree all her restlessness, ambition, unruliness and determination. They would be blessed by her dynamism and cursed by her strong will. They would always have her pride; it sustained them in bad times, and set the standards by which they lived. They would always think of themselves primarily as "Bassetts of Brown's Park," meaning that they were the daughters of Elizabeth Bassett, head of "the Bassett gang."

THE SURVIVORS

As Herb and his children faced the first difficult days of surviving without the driving force of Elizabeth, any fears that they would suffer materially were quickly allayed. Jim McKnight and Isom Dart were still in the bunkhouse and Matt Rash still lived down the road. Elizabeth's coterie of friends automatically continued to handle the Bassett cattle and acted as unofficial guardians of her heritage until her own boys were old enough to stand alone. The children could readily accept this, for Isom and Matt had always been central to their lives. The ranch's business went on as before.

The relationship between Herb and his children also continued unchanged. They loved him and respected him for his intrinsic goodness, but they still did not turn to him for practical advice in their own lives. Herb was sunk in a morass of grief, for he had loved Elizabeth as only a generous man can love. His grief was probably complicated by a feeling of helplessness when he looked at the children for whom he was responsible. Any advice he might give them, any authority he might attempt to exercise, were weakened by the fact that he had never been the master in his own house during Elizabeth's lifetime and therefore could not become its master when Elizabeth was gone.

After Elizabeth's funeral, young Sam and Ann went back to high school in Craig and Herb hired a housekeeper, "Auntie" Thompson, an Army nurse during the Civil War and now the wife of "Longhorn" Thompson, who had a homestead just east of Brown's Park. Ann has given Auntie a certain immortality in the story she tells of Auntie's confiscating the *Police Gazettes* the cowboys had stashed in the bunkhouse and using them to paper the bunkhouse walls—but hanging all the pages upside down to make them more difficult to read. This may have broken a few hearts in the bunkhouse, but it no doubt confirmed Herb's belief that Auntie would make a good guardian for his younger boys.

When Herb spoke to Josie about returning to St. Mary's she refused to go, saying she was needed at home. During that first sad time, Josie's state of mind was perhaps the most pitiable of all the family. She could not indulge in simple, uncomplicated grief for her mother, but had to suffer the added grief of knowing that she was about to give a further wound to her father. Josie now knew for certain what she had not suspected when she had left for Salt Lake City in the fall—that she was pregnant by Jim McKnight, and that unless nature graciously intervened and she miscarried, her school days were over.

She procrastinated as long as she could, but the time came when there could be no more stalling. On March 21, 1893—two months after her nineteenth birthday, three months after Elizabeth's death, and only four months before the baby was due—Josie and Jim were married in Green River City. The names of the witnesses on the marriage license, Charles H. Miller and Sarah C. Boorum, are not familiar in Brown's Park annals. It is possible that Josie and Jim went alone to Green River City and waited until after the ceremony to confront Herb with the news. Their son Crawford was born on the twelfth day of July.

If Herb was sad, disappointed or shamed, the other folks in the Park were neither surprised nor too dismayed. Like wise people everywhere, they may have quoted the old saying that "a baby usually takes nine months to grow, but a first baby can come any time."

Josie was universally liked by the Brown's Park people. She was never "above herself," as Ann later became. She talked easily to the women about women's affairs and at the dances made the older men feel like gay young blades again. She was completely genuine and completely at home with her neighbors. Although she had a background and education that most of her neighbors lacked, she slipped easily into the colloquialisms of the country with no touch of condescension. She loved life in the Park and was part of it.

She could have had any man in the Park with a flick of her finger. Like all the Bassetts, she was handsome. She was small-waisted and full-breasted, and had a glorious mop of curly chestnut hair. Although she genuinely enjoyed the customary womanly tasks, she had also ridden the range with the cowboys, and she spoke their language. She was always more interested in men's talk than in exchanging dress patterns with the women, and she had enough of the famous Bassett charm and enough confidence in her own desirability to be a flirt and a coquette. The combination made her irresistible.

There must have been gossip, of course, and much discussion, but even the most condemnatory of the gossips probably excused Josie by saying that it was the Bassetts' own fault, keeping a grown girl in school when she should have been married and settled down, and that Herb Bassett had better not make the same mistake with Ann, or she would "get in trouble" even faster than her sister Josie.

As the gossips were to learn in the years ahead, not even marriage could permanently tame a Bassett woman. For Josie as for Ann, the intensity of her emotions and the strength of her will made it unthinkable that she could have denied herself sexual satisfaction when she was ready for it. No moral consideration, no fear of gossiping tongues, not even the larger fear of pregnancy could have prevented it. She was always to be this way. She would never count the cost.

Uncle Sam gave Josie a magnificent wedding gift. In earlier years he had filed a claim on Beaver Creek, eight or ten miles up the valley from Herb's ranch, and had built a cabin to use as a base of operations between prospecting trips into the mountains. Now he promised to leave it to Josie, on the condition that she was to take care of him until his death. Sam's prospecting days had ended, for he had suffered a stroke which left him with an unsteady gait and unclear speech.

The young couple moved up to Beaver Creek and built a cabin for themselves near Sam's. They put in a garden and erected some outbuildings, but it was obvious that they would have to do something about the water supply if they wanted a hayfield or crops. While it was true that Beaver Creek ran through their property, its banks were so high that the water level was below the level of their land.

Josie came up with the solution and Jim put it into effect. Using a horse and plow, or digging by hand where necessary, Jim cut an irrigation ditch extending four or five miles across the brush to a point where the creek came out of the hills, grading the ditch in a gentle slope to his home fields. The neighbors were unbelieving, said the bizarre idea would never work, and called it "McKnight's Folly." Josie herself was serenely confident throughout the digging, and her confidence was justified when the irrigation floodgate was opened and the water came flowing smoothly down the ditch. "It stands to reason," she is quoted as saying, "that water would have to flow downhill." The ditch was used to irrigate that ground until the paving of Highway 40 in modern times.

Matt Rash was the real manager at the Bassett ranch after Elizabeth's death, and although Isom Dart had maintained a friendly relationship with him through the years, Isom had been Elizabeth's man. He turned now to Elizabeth's daughter Josie. If Josie herself were not enough reason for this, there was the baby Crawford, and Isom loved children. By the time Josie's second child Herbert—always to be called Chick—arrived in early 1896, Isom was working full time with Jim McKnight. Isom, who had his own herd and land, developed the same working relationship with Jim as they had both once had with Elizabeth. Again, Isom became almost a family member. When Josie had her hands full at home or wanted to ride down to the Bassett ranch to visit her father, Isom would do some of the cooking and would babysit for the boys and for helpless old Uncle Sam.

Herb's greatest difficulty in those days was trying to decide what on earth to do with Ann; as time passed, it became a question of what to do with Ann *next*. At the time of Elizabeth's death, Ann was a tomboy and a hoyden, still trying to keep up with her brothers, still spending time out in the bunkhouse with the cowboys, and still refusing to be ladylike.

Herb believed in ruling children by love alone, and Ann was the only one of the children to whom he had ever administered corporal punishment. One day when he was making puncheons out of cottonwood logs he found Ann trying to make her own puncheons with his sharp ax. When he admonished the child, she screamed at him, "You son of a bitch, I'll do what I want to do!"

"Now that's enough, girlie—you've stirred up enough for a time," he said, and gave her a sound thrashing.

Herb's reliance on love as a discipline might have been effective had he been a stronger and more impressive figure. As it was, the family seems to have been rudderless after Elizabeth's death, with little effective control over a recalcitrant child.

As soon as Ann reached the proper age, Herb sent her to St. Mary's of the Wasatch, where Josie had been so happy. In later years Ann was to write a tender and poetic account of what the convent school had meant to a young girl from the back country, but this must have been her opinion only in retrospect. At the end of the year the nuns asked Herb not to send Ann back; they considered her incorrigible.

Ann was also an indifferent student, one who seemed to learn by osmosis rather than through mental effort. After St. Mary's closed its doors to her, Herb was still determined that his daughter was to be educated. She was sent east to school, probably to Cleveland where Herb had a half-brother; possibly other schools were involved. In 1899 the Craig newspaper reported that "Miss Anna Bassett of Omaha and Miss Blanche Tilton have arrived in town from Brown's Park. . . ." What Ann was doing in Omaha is lost in the mists of time.

In her memoirs, Ann claims to have attended Miss Porter's School for Girls in an exclusive Boston suburb, but Josie told her family that this was just another of Ann's exaggerations. The exaggeration did serve to enhance Ann's reputation, and in later years the people in Colorado and Utah considered her a highly educated woman; one old-timer in Vernal now insists that she was a Vassar graduate. Ann told a story of a happening at Miss Porter's that smacks of truth and surely must have occurred at some school or other. This is what she wrote in *The Colorado Magazine*:

> . . . A wild barbarian who knew nothing about "correct style" must be taught horsemanship by a competent instructor. The school employed a riding "mawstah" to teach the girls correct positions in the saddle and how to post. One morning about a dozen of us were lined up for inspection before taking off for a decorous canter over chosen bridle paths. Everything appeared ship-shape. But there was rebellion in my soul, revolt that demanded action.
>
> The "Mawstah" walked back a few yards for some words with one of the stable boys. That was my Heaven-given chance to air "ronickie" dun out a little. I was perched like a monkey on a stick, atop of a locoed old sabine gelding with one glass eye. I threw my right leg up over the side saddle and raked his flanks. Then uttering a wild yell that must have scared him half to death, I put him through several range stunts while the girls screamed with glee.
>
> The outraged "Mawstah" came on the run, giving off a stream of sarcasm meant for me. He grabbed for my bridle reins at the same time ordering me sharply to "Dismount."
>
> He got nowhere reaching for *my* bridle. I was completely "r'iled up" by that time. I swung the horse about, with a prancing and rearing he had probably never before even attempted. Leaning from my saddle, I exclaimed vehemently, "Go to hell, you repulsive, little, monkeyfaced skunk!"
>
> His eyes almost popping from his head with shock, he turned and ran for the school office to report the scandalous event. Our riding lesson was promptly cancelled for that day. And I was brought before the stony-faced faculty, on the carpet, with all the girls of my riding class also there to testify to my use of profane language. Not one of them could remember a word I had said! Indeed, they had not heard anything out of the ordinary.

Whatever the truth of exactly where she was educated, exposure to the outside world created a metamorphosis in Ann. As she grew into her later teens she became aware of her own sexuality and of how pleasant it was to be attractive to men. She learned to dress herself in the height of fashion; she carried herself so straight and held her head so high that people recognized Ann Bassett's back even from a block away; she adopted eastern speech patterns and an eastern accent, and used them until they became her customary way of speaking. She even flaunted convention by using forbidden rouge on her cheeks. Her first loves were still the range and the outdoor life—these she was never to outgrow—but now her riding was done in tailored riding habits, and she protected her freckle-prone skin by wearing a broad-brimmed hat and fringed gauntlet gloves. Sometimes she used a full black mask—a stocking in which she had cut eye holes. One cowboy tells of seeing her from a distance and thinking he was about to be accosted by a masked desperado.

Ann combined city ways with Bassett charisma to gain a glamorous position among the people of her home country, and played her new role magnificently. Ann was always an actress, with a passionate desire to be the star. Possibly her strong compulsion to be in the limelight stemmed partly from her childhood struggles to keep up with her brothers, but it undoubtedly had a great deal to do with being the younger sister of the highly competent and universally admired Josie.

It infuriated Ann that she was not able to best Josie as a rider, in shooting accuracy, or at rounding up cattle. Finally, in becoming a lady of fashion, Ann found an area in which she could excel and in which Josie would not compete.

Ann wanted to be like her mother in her domination of the range and the people around her. But she never learned Elizabeth's tact. Ann made her suggestions in an abrasive and opinionated style that usually kept her family silent for fear of one of her tantrums, but nevertheless failed to convince them.

As in their childhood years, Josie was Ann's primary target. The ordinarily self-controlled Josie could take only a certain amount of Ann's bragging, baiting, and goading. Then her own volcanic temper would erupt, and truly monumental battles would be waged. Even in their later years, a quarrel between Josie and Ann could end in fist fights and hair pulling. Ann seemed compelled to attack Josie's composure, and Josie was too strong-willed to resist Ann's challenges.

Between their periodic clashes, these daughters of Elizabeth—each having many of Elizabeth's qualities but so different from each other—were good friends who confided and depended on each other. Each had a strong sense of family, and this bond existed for the rest of their lives, knitting them together in a never comfortable but always close relationship.

Ann was disruptive in all family relationships, and Eb was almost as much so. Herb could only stand by helplessly as the quarrels of childhood turned into the more bitter disagreements of almost-mature adults. Eb was subject to swings between high good humor, in which he was as charming as only a Bassett could be, and deep, ill-tempered despondency. (The family called his black moods "Eb's higolly-go-flips.") Sam and young George were as peaceable and quiet as their father, trying, along with Josie, to be patient with the mercurial Ann and Eb, who seemed to have inherited Elizabeth's aggressiveness untempered by her self-control.

If Herb suffered in the turbulences of his own home, he could find no compensation in how things were going for Josie down on Beaver Creek, for Josie and Jim were obviously unsuited to each other. Had they had time to consider carefully, without the pressure of Josie's pregnancy, they might have realized that fact and saved themselves a lot of grief. But Josie was certainly desirable, and her capacity for hard work and knowledge of ranch life made her an ideal wife for a man living on what was still a frontier. From Josie's standpoint, Jim McKnight represented many things that were important to her: he was hard-working, ambitious, and more polished than many of the men in Brown's Park; he had the physical virility that was always to attract her; and he was tall and broad-shouldered, with a good seat in the saddle.

However, each was entirely too dominant to live with the other peaceably. Generous though Josie was, she gave only on her own terms. Jim needed a pliant, more conventionally docile woman, who would unquestioningly follow whatever path he chose to take.

Ranch life fulfilled Josie. She moved from one task to another, washing her clothes in a kettle over a fire in the open yard and making lye soap in that same kettle, putting bread out to rise, making clothes for herself and the children, tending her vegetables and her beloved flowers, and pruning the apple trees that she had set out as soon as she moved to Beaver Creek. Motherhood was equally fulfilling, although when she became pregnant with Chick almost before Crof was out of diapers she decided there would be no more children. She learned the crude contraceptive methods of that era from older women knowledgeable about folk medicines and Indian herbs, just as she learned from them the art of midwifery. She profited from what they told her; she had no more children, and she became a skillful midwife.

For recreation, Josie was content with Brown's Park parties and the visits of neighbors who would drop in for a meal as they passed the McKnight cabin. And once a week she would hitch up her two-wheeled buggy and drive the eight or ten miles to the Bassett ranch to visit her father. Since Auntie Thompson no longer kept house for Herb, Josie washed his clothes and saw that he had baked bread to eat. Even the onerous tasks involved in caring for stricken Uncle Sam were not unbearable to Josie, for he was part of her family.

Jim was not equally at ease in his married life. He had started out on his own at the age of twelve and had lived the life of a bachelor cowboy ever since. He had eaten his meals first with the Butterworth family and later with the Bassetts, but he had always been able to retreat to the bunkhouse for cards, a drink or two, and some untrammeled male conversation. Now he unsaddled his horse and went in to a cabin where he was greeted by two demanding babies and a pitiful old man, unsteady on his feet and drooling a little as he tried to form words with his paralyzed mouth. As Sam's condition worsened and affected his control of his bowels, it became even more unpleasant. The fact that at bedtime Jim was greeted by a voluptuous woman did not completely compensate him for the loss of his old freedom.

Jim started fording the Green River to visit what had become the unofficial

Brown's Park Men's Club—the saloon Charley Crouse ran in his bunkhouse. There he could meet with an assortment of like-minded neighbors, generously larded with Charley's sometimes disreputable cronies and strangers of dubious background. Their presence did not disturb Jim—the talk was free and easy, the card games were usually honest, and the liquor never ran out. Jim felt at home at Charley's.

While ranch life kept Josie content, the marriage itself was disappointing to her. Whether she realized it or not, her father's subordination to Elizabeth's control had shaped Josie's ideas of what a satisfactory marriage should be. She was always attracted to strong men, but she seemed to expect them to act like Herb in their relations with her. She found it difficult to understand why Jim could not be as satisfied with the absorbing routine of work as she was, and why he would not spend his evenings as her father had done, reading aloud to the family while she caught up with her mending. Reared in a more cultivated, intellectual, and nonalcoholic environment than Jim, Josie could not, or would not, admit his attraction to Crouse's "saloon."

Ann's unruliness and Josie's unhappiness distressed Herb, but his greatest disappointment was that his chidren did not accept his own standard evangelical Christianity. As he grew older, he gave more and more sermons and tried harder and harder to convert them, but he failed. His children were not irreligious, but they did not want to be "saved." (Josie was to tell one of her grandchildren that "religion is like a dose of salts, fine in small doses but a disaster in large ones.")

Herb was even more distressed when he looked at his brother Sam, so obviously close to death. Sam proclaimed himself either an atheist or an agnostic, and had no use for traditional evangelical doctrine. Herb talked to Sam and prayed with him and begged him to read the Bible. Sam tried. He read the Bible, but then turned it back to Herb.

"It's no use, Herb," said Sam. "It still seems like a fiddle to me, ready to play any tune you want it to."

Herb's world was alien and disappointing. He spent more and more of his time in his post office, hiding in his books and dreaming of the time he would be able to escape.

THE OUTLAWS

In February 1898, while Brown's Park was still in the grip of winter cold, a bloody manhunt brought in lawmen of three states. Headlines in newspapers as far away as Denver confirmed the country's opinion of Brown's Park as a place overrun by vicious men, and there was general public outcry that something be done to clear out the rascals. Because of the manhunt, badmen who had used Powder Springs as a hideout realized that the west was changing and that the Brown's Park area was no longer a safe haven. They quickly disappeared, leaving Brown's Park to its legitimate owners for the first time since the valley was settled.

There had always been a murder now and again within the Park's boundaries, and some of them had involved honest men who had the misfortune of getting in the way of one of the seamy characters who drifted around in the Park. It was the general opinion of the Park's residents, moreover, that a couple of strange deaths up on Crouse Creek at Charley Crouse's cabin might have been the doings of Charley himself, for he was not a man to tangle with.

None of these deaths was condoned, but the ranchers were few in number and the lawmen in the three surrounding states too far away to apprehend a killer before he skipped the country. Even if the suspected man was caught, evidence was difficult to obtain, and in those wild days a man who put in a plea of self defense could usually get away with it.

In the dreadful happenings in February 1898, however, the evidence was so clear and the lawmen so providentially close at hand that, for once, the murderers were apprehended.

Two small-time wrongdoers started the bloody chain of events. P. L. "Pat" Johnson was a surly, hard-drinking man in his late twenties who had killed a man in a barroom brawl before coming to the Park back in 1892, the year of Elizabeth's death. He had never amounted to much. He worked in the valley for one rancher and then another, not getting into any conspicuous trouble but not earning much respect for himself either. John Bennett was much the same. In earlier years, John had peddled illegal liquor to the Indians, and had once served a stretch in the Colorado state prison. While in prison he had learned the art of stone-cutting, and it was he who had reputedly dressed the stone for John Jarvie's new storehouse up at the west end of the Park. Like Pat, he was a more or less permanent Park resident, picking up work here and there, and rustling cattle from time to time.

The preceding summer in Baggs, Wyoming, Bennett had acquired the nickname "Judge" after presiding over a kangaroo court held by Butch Cassidy's "Wild Bunch." It seems that this notorious gang of outlaws had been celebrating between jobs at an establishment known as the Bull Dog Saloon. During the course of their party, their old friend Dick Bender had died because of the indifference, or perhaps the unsuccessful administrations, of the local doctor. Despite the fact that "old Bender" was not a bona fide member of the Wild Bunch, Butch and his friends felt his death should not go unpunished, and they organized a drunken kangaroo court, badly frightening the poor medic before they finally let him go.

"Judge" Bennett, a mere petty thief himself, was delighted to have been given such a distinction by the aristocratic Wild Bunch. These men planned their crimes with great precision, executed them efficiently, and confined themselves to operations that would bring in large sums of cash. Men of their caliber, who robbed trains and banks and left the local ranchers alone, were given a certain respect by many of the people in that part of the country. To them the word "outlaw" had a special meaning. Josie once said of Matt Warner, one of the Brown's Park badmen, "He was no outlaw! His game was robbing sheep camps and stealing cattle."

Butch Cassidy was especially forgiven, even admired, by many of the country people in this three-state area because it was well known that his gun had never killed anyone. Butch had been born Robert Leroy Parker to good Mormon parents in a solid, God-fearing Mormon community. Despite the fact that the Mormons wisely provide recreation for their young people and sponsor dances in their communities, the atmosphere in a religiously oriented Mormon town was oppressively workaday for a farm youngster who dreamed of the glamorous life of a cowboy. Young Bob Parker got his start in his life of crime in a not uncommon fashion. He became involved in a minor scrape concerning a stolen saddle, perhaps actually stolen by one of his friends, and took that opportunity to light out for the ranch country of Wyoming and Colorado.

Bob, eighteen years old in 1884 when he left his Mormon home, spent the next few years gravitating between lawful cowpunching and unlawful horse and cattle thievery all over Wyoming and Colorado, doing honest ranch work so conscientiously that his employers were always sorry to see him leave. He seems to have drifted in a zigzag course, rather than purposefully blazing a straight path into big-time bank robbery.

His first bank robbery was in 1889 when he helped two older men, Tom McCarty and Matt Warner, rob a bank at Telluride, Colorado. The robbery was successful and they escaped a pursuing posse, but the experience seems to have sobered young Bob Parker, for he headed for Brown's Park and went to work eventually for Charley Crouse. First, however, he worked for Elizabeth Bassett and spent the winter in the Bassett bunkhouse.

Josie remembered Bob Parker (she would never call him Butch) as "a big dumb kid who liked to joke," who would ride through the gate, wring the necks of two or three chickens, and then invite himself to dinner. When he lived at the Bassetts' he spent his time reading the newspapers and magazines in Herb's post office, only occasionally going to the local dances.

It is in this period that he is supposed to have courted Josie Bassett. Josie herself would neither confirm nor deny the story in her old age. Smiling cryptically, probably enjoying herself, she would tell the curious only that she and Butch had been "good friends." If there really was a courtship it could not have been a serious one, for in 1889 Josie was fifteen years old, interested in all the boys but serious about none.

Bob's friend Matt Warner (his partner in the Telluride bank robbery) had established a ranch of his own up on Diamond Mountain above Charley Crouse's ranch. Bob Parker used Matt's cabin as his headquarters during his later stays in the Park, as did his good friend Elza Lay. Elza had been a personable young teenager when he first came to the Park with a haying crew. Like Bob Parker before him, Elza had wintered in the Bassett bunkhouse and had gone to school with Josie and the other children to acquire a little more education. Much time had passed since then, however, and now both Bob and Elza were part of a rollicking, cattle-stealing bunch of scalawags who bore little resemblance to the "big dumb kids" they had once been. Neither were they yet the hard-bitten professionals of the kind whom Bob later organized into the Wild Bunch when he became known as Butch Cassidy.

Bob was sent to the Wyoming state penitentiary in 1894 on a horse-stealing conviction, and when he was released two years later he headed for Matt's ranch on Diamond Mountain. He was there with Elza Lay, the two of them helping Charley Crouse with his horse-breaking and his rustling, when serious news came from their old friend Matt.

Matt had been arrested in Vernal, Utah for a triple shooting so enraging to the townspeople that he was transferred to the jail in Ogden to protect him from a lynching. He managed to get a note to Butch ("Bob Parker" was now gone forever) saying, "Butch we're gonners if we don't get money quick to hire Lawyers." Butch and Elza could not ignore their friend's appeal, and shortly thereafter they robbed a bank in Montpelier, Idaho, netting $16,000 to pay for Matt Warner's defense. There was no turning back after that robbery. They rustled no more cattle. From then on, they preyed on banks, payrolls and railroads with the Wild Bunch, whom Butch recruited and managed with all the finesse of the manager of a big eastern corporation.

As the fame of the Wild Bunch grew and newspapers became full of their exploits, Herb Bassett told Josie, "That's a mistake. That young fellow would never do that." Many other people shared the same fondness for Butch. Several poor ranchers in western Colorado thought of him as a Robin Hood for his generosity to them and his strict refusal to cause any loss, even of a horse, to a common man. Butch paid for his meals and for horses like the honorable man he considered himself to be, and he usually paid in gold.

These were the "outlaws" who were not only tolerated but made welcome in the Park—polite gentlemen who never stole a horse, insulted a decent woman, or committed the social blunder of wearing a gun into a private home. If they stole money that did not belong to them, Brown's Parkers looked the other way.

In that little group of socially acceptable lawbreakers were, for instance, the Bender Gang. These men "worked" in the summer and spent their winters in Brown's Park. Ann Bassett wrote in detail about a Thanksgiving dinner the outlaws gave for the families in the Park around 1895, recreating it for Esther Campbell so that Esther might use it for a community program. Ann is quoted here, with the faulty spelling and casual punctuation she used in letters to her personal friends:

> . . . Brown's Hole was a rest retreat for the men we called the "Bender gang." Billie Bender and Les Megs were men of education and refinement. They had several younger men who came with them regularly. It became known in our country that Bender and Megs were agents for smugglers working from the Mexican border to Canada. Several years after they no longer came to Brown's Hole, Bender died in Wyoming and Megs became a real estate broker in Los Angeles. None of them ever gave the people of Brown's Hole any trouble. They were quiet peaceful citizens while there. Their profession or business was rather a mystery to the settlers but it was not our business to question that since they were well behaved and kept their boys in line.
>
> Butch and Lay were on friendly terms with Bender and Megs and their boys, so they gave the Thanksgiving party for the Brown's Hole families together and did not spare expenses in putting over a grand spread of the best delicasies Rock Springs could supply.
>
> Tom Davenport raised the turkeys and the "gang" bought them. The dishes, linens, and silver was furnished by the women of the Hole.

The Menue

Blue point cocktails, roast turkeys with chestnut dressing, giblet gravey, cranberrys, mashed potatoes, candid sweet potatoes, creamed peas, celery, olives, pickled walnuts, sweet pickles, fresh tomatoes on crisp lettuce, hot rolls and sweet butter, coffee, whipped cream, Roquefort cheese, pumpkin pie, plum pudding, brandy sauce, mints, salted nuts.

How the people dressed

Men wore dark suits (vests were always worn) white shirts stiff starched collars, patent low cuts. No man would be seen minus a coat and a bow tie at the party—if it killed them and it almost did I am sure. If a mustach existed that must be waxed and curled.

The women wore tight fitted long dress with leg-o-mutton sleeves and boned collars—hair done on top of the head either in a french twist or a bun and bangs curled into a friz. Girls in their teens wore dresses about 3 inches below the knees—spring heeled slippers and their hair in curls or braids tucked up with a big bow of ribbons at nap of neck.

Esther Davenport had the pretty dress for the party. A yellow silk mull over yellow taffeta she looked very pretty. Now I will tell you what Ann wore at the party—silk mull powder blue accordion pleated from top to bottom, camesole and petticoat of taffeta, peter pan collar, buttoned in the back puff sleeves to the elbows, belted by a wide sash with a big bow in back. The mull pleated well and how it swished over the taffeta undies. A narrow black velvet ribbon around the neck a gold locket fastened in the front. . . .

Now for the stockings—hold your hat on and smile—lace made of silk and lisle thread black to match shoes. They were precious and worn only for parties. We had to be careful with them they cost *3.00* per pair and lasted a long time.

I wore my hair in three curles fastened at nap of neck held in place by large barrett beau catcher curl on forehead. Spring heeled shoes like the babydoll shoes shown in catalogues now.

The older women wore black taffetta with tucking at the neck and sleeves. High button shoes often with white tops and high curved French heels (always too tight as were their corsets.) Josies dress for the party was a sage green wool [bunting]. Many-gored skirt, tight to the knees then flared to the floor to sweep up the dirt.

Josie was married, I was not and girls were not permitted to wear long dresses, put up their hair or wear high heels.

The party lasted about six hours. That evening we danced at the Davenport home, I say evening, I mean until sun up the next day. . . . Program at the dinner was put on by the guests. The hosts waited table, Megs-Bender, Butch, Lay and Harry Roudenbaugh. [*Author's note*: Does she mean Harry Longabaugh, the Sundance Kid?] The other boys helped in the kitchen. All but the cook wore butcher aprons over their white shirts and suit trousers. Megs, Bender and Lay received their guests then slipped on aprons to help serve the crowd of 35 or more, lots of work for the dinner was served in courses.

This was a joke, that is it was to some of us young rough necks, just itching for an excuse to kick each other under the table and highly grin. Butch was pouring coffee, poor Butch he could perform such minor jobs as robbing banks and holding up pay trains with out the flicker of an eye lash but serving coffee at a grand

> party that was something else. The blood curdeling job almost floored him, he became panicky and showed that his nerve was completely shot to bits. He became frustrated and embarrassed over the blunder he had made when some of the other hoasts better informed told him it was not good form to pour coffee from a big black coffee pot and reach from left to right across a guests plate, to grab a cup right under their noses. The boys went into a hudle in the kitchen and instructed Butch in the more formal art of filling coffee cups at the table. This just shows how etiquette can put fear into a brave mans heart.
>
> By the way, Josie played a "Zither" and rather well. . . . She was accompanied by Sam Bassett on the fiddle and Joe Davenport with a guitar. . . . I gave a short reading on the meaning of Thanksgiving after being coached by Mr. Jarvie for a couple of weeks. . . .

If a posse had come for any of these men, nobody would have hindered them in the performance of their sworn duty. However, since all these lawbreakers went into the towns openly and transacted their business with impunity while the sheriffs apparently looked the other way, it was unlikely that those same sheriffs would come all the way to Brown's Park to make their arrests. And certainly none of the Brown's Park people considered it their business to handcuff the culprits and take them in, especially since they were such agreeable neighbors.

But Butch Cassidy, Elza Lay and the Bender Gang were not killers. When it came to murder, Brown's Park's attitude was different, as is evidenced in the affair of Pat Johnson and "Judge" Bennett.

At this time Pat Johnson had leased some land from Valentine Hoy on a share basis, and was living in the bottom story of Hoy's house on Red Creek, while Valentine himself lived on the upper floors with his wife and her aged parents, the Blairs. Hoy had been missing cattle and had petitioned for a warrant for Johnson's arrest, as all the legalistic Hoys usually did, rather than just kicking the culprit out. Johnson found out about this, and was so angry that Valentine and his wife moved to other quarters for safety. He left the Blairs in the house, however, because he trusted that Johnson would not vent his anger on aged and helpless people.

Johnson had two people living with him in his own part of the house, his friend John Bennett and a fifteen-year-old youngster named Willie Strang. What happened to poor Willie was undeserved and unintentional, but it was the catalyst for other tragic events in the following days. Willie was a teenage tease, and in jest he tipped Johnson's elbow while Johnson was drinking a dipperful of water. Johnson, still half-drunk from the night before, was enraged by the boy's practical joke. Willie ran for the barn, and Johnson took a shot at him, meaning only to teach him a lesson. But the bullet hit Willie's spine and he died a few hours later, leaving Johnson remorseful, Bennett dismayed, and the Blairs horrified. The guilty man lit out for the rustler hideout at Powder Springs and Bennett, to his great misfortune, went with him.

While all this was happening, Sheriff Charles Willis Neimann of Routt County, his deputy Ethan Allen Farnham, and a rancher named Boyd Vaughan, who lived outside the Park, were sleighing into Brown's Park from Steamboat Springs, Colorado, to arrest this same Pat Johnson on the comparatively minor charge of tampering with Valentine Hoy's cattle. Neimann's party stopped at the Bassett ranch overnight, and there they found Willie Strang's older brother, who had just arrived with the bad news about Willie. Octogenarian Mr. Blair had already waded through the snow to a sheep camp to summon the law, and a Wyoming posse was already in Brown's Park searching for Johnson. (Hoy's Red Creek ranch was in Wyoming's jurisdiction.)

Neimann remembered a strongly suspicious trio he had met as his sleigh had come into the Park, and he sent young Strang to give this news to the Wyoming posse. He also told Strang to notify the local men along his way, so that they could come help with the search that Neimann himself intended to launch as soon as morning came.

Strang stopped at Jim McKnight's cabin and gave him the news. Jim left for the Bassett ranch, where he was joined by William Pigeon (a partner of John Bennett's until bad blood rose between them) and by Valentine Hoy himself. Auntie Thompson's husband Longhorn and young Eb Bassett were also there, armed and ready to help. On hearing the news that her father's ranch was going to be overrun with visitors, Josie bundled up her children and went to the ranch also, and Auntie Thompson came over to help prepare the meals.

The three men who had aroused Neimann's suspicions had been headed toward a trail over Douglas Mountain that would lead them to safety in Utah. Neimann's posse started searching that area and in early afternoon almost caught the mysterious trio, coming so close without being detected that the men were forced to run away in such a hurry they took only their rifles with them.

It was already midafternoon; darkness would fall shortly, making it impossible to follow the trio's tracks. Sheriff Neimann very wisely started his posse back to the Bassett ranch to wait for morning. Since he took the fugitives' gear and horses with him, Neimann had little worry that the men, hungry and on foot, could escape him.

The posse returned to the Bassett ranch, still unsure of just exactly whom they were chasing but assuming it was Johnson and Bennett and some unknown third person. They did not know that Johnson had run across two escaped convicts from Utah when he reached Powder Springs: David Lant, who had been serving a term for embezzlement and who was as comparatively innocuous as Johnson and Bennett, and a truly hardened and vicious killer named Harry Tracy.

On the second day of the hunt, the posse tracked their men to a spot that could be reached only through two closely positioned rocks. Cautious Sheriff Neimann wanted to lay seige to the position rather than take the risk of storming it. The posse, however, on their second day out in the cold, were getting impatient. None of them was really afraid of Johnson and Bennett, who, after all, were not known for either bravery or viciousness.

Valentine Hoy declared that he, for one, was going in after them. As he reached the two rocks, so close together that only one man at a time could squeeze through, the ruthless Harry Tracy shot him in the chest with a blast from a shotgun, and Valentine was a dead man as he hit the ground. Somehow or other, the rest of the posse snaked their way back to safety and headed for the Bassett ranch.

Eb Bassett had not been up on the mountainside when Valentine Hoy was killed. He had been sent down to round up some more horses, which he was to take back to the ranch. Here is Josie's story of what happened, slightly abridged:

> Well, my brother Eb went to Lodore to get some extra horses they needed and there he met John Bennett. Ed Bassett was just a big boy then, about seventeen, and he was scared to death of Bennett. Bennett was kind and pleasant to Eb and Eb was to him, and they took the horses and went home to Bassetts'. My father had the post office and he sold tobacco and little things like that. So Bennett said, "We're all out of tobacco," and that made Eb more scared than ever. He thought, "We! Who are 'we'! Wonder who the other people are."
>
> I was baking cookies in the kitchen, and he [Bennett] came in; and I took some cookies and I said, "Won't you have a cookie, John?"
>
> "I will," he said, "because I haven't had any dinner today."
>
> The sheriff, two sheriffs from Routt County, Charlie Neimann and Farnham, were in the bunkhouse resting and Bennett didn't know it, of course, and that made me more frightened than ever. I thought, "He won't be arrested until he has killed someone." So he sat down at the table eating his cookies and Farnham came in. Bennett finished his cookies. Farnham went around to where he was and said, "Is your name John Bennett?" He said, "Yes, that's my name."
>
> I had quit baking cookies to listen to what was going on. I was so scared—I could hardly speak, I was so scared. Farnham said, "Hold up your hands, put them up high." And I thought, If he's got a six-shooter he'll kill Farnham. But he had set his gun down at the back door when he came in. So he held his hands up high and Farnham put the handcuffs on him.

Judge Bennett did not act like a hunted man. He had shown no alarm upon meeting Eb, had calmly accompanied Eb to the ranch, had checked his gun at the door, the custom when entering a private home, and had sat quietly eating cookies. It is extremely probable that the "we" who were out of tobacco were men over in Powder Springs waiting for Bennett to return. Bennett had evidently decided that he had no reason to head for Utah with Tracy, Lant, and his friend Pat Johnson. He was therefore infuriated by his arrest, swearing and making threats against the lawmen and every man in Brown's Park. Josie says, "He carried on like a gray wolf," and shouted that "old Bassett is the only white man in Brown's Park."

Sheriff Neimann was not inclined to let Bennett go until he had sorted out just exactly where he fit into the picture. He had Bennett taken over to the post office, which was well suited for a temporary jail since it had a fireplace, a water bucket and a kerosene lantern. Bennett was kept handcuffed, under Farnham's guard, all night and into the next day. After jailing Bennett, Neimann sent a messenger to Vernal, Utah, through the snow and the dark to notify the sheriff there that possibly Utah should send a posse to help.

Members of the original posse had fanned out to neighboring ranches and gathered other men, Isom Dart among them, to track down the murderers. The news that Valentine Hoy had been killed added fuel to indignation already at white-hot point over the killing of young Willie Strang, and by morning half the ranchers in Brown's Park were on hand to help with the manhunt.

About ten o'clock that morning, four-year-old Crof asked Josie, "Mother, who are those men with the funny hats?"

Josie looked out the window to see eight men on horseback ride through the gate. Each wore a mask of some sort; one had draped a piece of pink lady's underwear over his face and another had cut eyeholes in the sleeve of a black rubber slicker. Josie, who later commented that she had kept that piece of black rubber for a long time, continued the story:

> They took him [Bennett] out. They didn't make any noise at all going in there, but somehow I heard a door shut or something. I was right on my tiptoes anyhow. I said, "Oh, Dad, they are going to turn him loose. They are going to take him out and turn him loose."
>
> My father said, "Now you stay in the house, that's not for you to see." He knew from the masked men that something was going to happen. They hung him, they took him up and buried him, and then we all had dinner and it was very peaceful.

Although Josie knew all of the lynching party—they all came in to wash up and sit down at the dinner table—she never officially revealed their names.

That night the enlarged posse split up into smaller groups and spent the night in the open, determined that the killers should not escape. It was the next day when they finally caught Tracy, Lant and Johnson, half-starved and with feet bleeding from the ordeal of climbing around on Douglas Mountain in high-heeled leather cowboy boots. They were taken back to the Bassett ranch for the night, and J. S. Hoy, justice of the peace for Wyoming, was brought there to conduct the inquest into the slaying of his brother.

The inquest was held in the Bassett living room, and a vivid description of it, probably written by J. S. Hoy himself, was given to John Rolfe Burroughs, who quoted it in *Where the Old West Stayed Young:*

> People, including Josie McKnight and Mrs. Thompson, were wedged in the room until there was not a square foot of floor space unoccupied, and the crowd overflowed into the adjoining bedrooms and the kitchen. The red-faced, bewhiskered men, many of whom were gaunt and hollow-eyed after sleepless days and nights in the open; the prisoners, scarcely resembling human beings they were so ragged and unkempt; the continuous restless undercurrent of murmurings and recriminations circulating through the assemblage, practically every man-jack of which was in favor of according these prisoners the same speedy "justice" that had been meted out to Judge Bennett—all combined to make the preliminary hearings of Pat Johnson, Harry Tracy and David Lant a fascinatingly colorful event. . . .
>
> That night there were more than sixty members of the Colorado, Utah, and Wyoming posses and local residents at the Bassett ranch. It was the largest congregation of law officers and law-abiding citizens ever seen in those parts, and except for the Sheriffs and their deputies, to a man this group was in favor of lynching the three prisoners. . . . The men lounged around a big bonfire in the yard. Sheriff Neimann maintained a night long vigil, passing from one group to the next, reasoning with the men, and discouraging any lynching talk that he heard. Even so, the only thing that saved the lives of the prisoners was the lack of a forceful leader to channel the lynch sentiment into action.

There would indeed have been a lynching that night, had the Brown's Park men known the destiny of the three prisoners. Tracy and Lant were taken first to Hahn's Peak, then all the way to a stronger jail at Aspen, Colorado. Nevertheless, they broke out and nearly beat their jailer to death in the process. Lant, never more than a small-time criminal, went back to Utah and went straight. Harry Tracy, however, killed five or six more men before, four years later, he killed himself with his own gun when his capture was inevitable. As for Pat Johnson, who killed Willie Strang, he was put on trial in Wyoming and the jury freed him. The lynched John Bennett was the only one who paid the ultimate price for the murders of Hoy and Willie Strang, and all he had really done was help his friend Pat Johnson lift a few of Valentine Hoy's cattle.

By the time of the Bennett lynching, Butch Cassidy had probably abandoned both Matt Warner's cabin on Diamond Mountain and the cabin he had built for himself at Powder Springs. He had moved his base of operations down to Robbers' Roost, Utah, which could be more easily defended against lawmen and where he found the other big-time outlaws with whom he was to work. At their zenith, Butch and Elza were seen no more in Brown's Park. Within four years the whole country became so hot for Butch Cassidy and his lieutenant Harry Longabaugh, the Sundance Kid, that they fled to Argentina in 1904. Unfortunately, Elza Lay could not accompany them; he had been captured and was serving time in a New Mexico prison.

Elza was released in 1906 and settled on some land not far from Brown's Park, where he lived the upright life of a legitimate rancher before emigrating to southern California in his later years. Contrary to widely accepted reports, Butch was not killed in Argentina, but returned to Utah to see his surviving family, after which he wandered anonymously throughout the west, occasionally visiting with one old friend or another whom he happened to come across. He was in Rock Springs, Wyoming, one year and heard that Josie was in town. Butch said he would enjoy seeing her again, a mutual friend arranged a visit, and they had a nice chat about old times. Ann was also to run across him many years later in a mining camp in Nevada, according to a story Crawford MacKnight told to author Dora Flack:

> This Doc Masson showed up. . . . He got acquainted with the crew and kept looking Ann over. She didn't know why. He got her alone one night where he could talk private with her. He came right out: "Ann, you are the dumbest person I know." She dried her hands on the dishtowel and looked at him hard.
>
> "Ann, the last time I saw you was over on the Douglas Mountain. You were riding a big palomino horse called Old Gus. Do you remember Old Gus?"
>
> "Yes, I remember Old Gus."
>
> "You were riding him. Do you remember Old Pete?"
>
> "Yes, I remember Old Pete. Just who in hell are you? You know me but I don't know you."
>
> "You know me but I am not going to talk."
>
> "I'll figure you out. But anyone could tell me I was riding old Gus. Anybody could say that."
>
> "When we were young I knew you well. I had many a meal at the Bassett cabin. Do you remember Old Pete had a running sore on the side of his nose?"
>
> Then she knew it was the straight goods. It couldn't be anyone but Butch Cassidy. They took pictures of him with a whole bunch and he didn't know it. He had a little goatee nearly black. Then they compared them with pictures Florence Kelly and Maude Davis had and by holding your hand over the lower part of his face, it was the same person. Anybody that ever knew him would know it was Butch.

The departure of Butch and Elza, the manhunt for Johnson, Tracy and Lant, even the knowledge that there were not as many desperados over at Powder Springs after Bennett's lynching—all that had no material effect on the lives of the Park people. The outlaws had seldom bothered them with their presence and were barely noticed in their leaving. In the ensuing years, however, Brown's Park was to be invaded by a new group of badmen—men whose evil was almost officially sanctioned and who inflicted real pain on its inhabitants. It is little wonder that the people of Brown's Park saved their fear and hatred for the newcomers and remembered their outlaw neighbors with something like fondness.

THE SHOOTING OF JIM McKNIGHT

The *Empire Courier* of Craig, Colorado, was issued weekly in 1900, usually in an eight-page edition of which six were "boiler plates" furnished to small newspapers by a forerunner of the Associated Press. These boiler plates had little real news, except perhaps in a presidential election. They specialized instead in serialized thrillers and romantic fiction, articles on elephants in Africa, the mating customs of South Sea Islanders or high-born Englishmen, and bizarre murders currently scandalizing people in New York City, Detroit, or Hutchinson, Kansas. The advertisements were mostly for patent medicines and usually contained testimonials such as one for Peruna from a Catholic nun of an unknown order, or from a housewife in Dayton or Schenectady or Missoula who had cured herself of anemia, hemorrhoids or "female disorders," or who had stopped her husband's drinking habit by dropping miracle tablets into his coffee.

The newspaper's remaining pages were filled with legal notices and items about local people who had either gone to Denver or returned from Denver, or who had married, had a baby, or died. Because all these local events had to be crammed into two pages, any event with a headline and more than two inches of copy was of great importance.

The inches of copy and the headlines given over to Josie Bassett McKnight's troubles with her lawful husband Jim McKnight suggest how unusual a divorce was in those days and what a furor it must have caused among the good people of Routt County.

The first article appeared in March 1900. It was comparatively short and restrained. It stated that A. H. Bassett and Mrs. Josie McKnight had been to Steamboat Springs and had then stopped in Craig to arrange for a restraining order against Jim McKnight. Behind that brief news item was a long story of arguments and fights, probably physical as well as verbal, that had been shaking the rafters of the McKnight cabin during the winter months.

The crisis between Josie and Jim had come in the sixth year of their marriage when old Uncle Sam had another stroke and mercifully passed away.

Jim, ambitious and not as devoted to ranch life as Josie, proposed that they sell the ranch, move to Vernal and start a saloon.

The highly moral town of Vernal, in bone-dry Utah, was situated immediately adjacent to the Uintah Indian reservation, whose headquarters was just down the road at Fort Duchesne. At the request of the owners of a nearby gilsonite mine, the United States government had given autonomy to a small piece of the land reserved for the Indians. This piece, known as "the Strip," was outside the jurisdiction of both the officials at the Indian reservation and the sheriff in Vernal. The result was that the Strip became one of the wildest pieces of real estate in the west, almost equaling the bawdiness of San Francisco's Barbary Coast. Since it was the only place in hundreds of miles where a man could walk into a bar and order a drink, it attracted everyone from solid Vernal citizens with legitimate but illegal thirsts to Butch Cassidy's Wild Bunch, to the lowest piece of human scum in the area. All these citizens, good and bad alike, gathered in the Strip's saloons, and many of them patronized either the tawdry cribs or the more genteel whorehouses of its hundreds of prostitutes.

Even a wild neighborhood such as the Strip had its more respectable areas, however, and a strong man who ran a decent saloon and kept a gun handy under the bar could keep out of trouble and make a very good living at the same time. This was what Jim proposed to do. To Josie, leaving the country and moving to town, especially under such circumstances, was out of the question. She refused to move, and Jim refused to stay. The conflict ended their already unsatisfying marriage.

It was not a friendly divorce, and it undoubtedly was preceded by shouting matches when both of them let loose their violent tempers. Jim McKnight was a strong-willed man and he must have been infuriated at being kicked out of Josie's life. The fact that Uncle Sam had left his property solely to Josie, that she could veto his plans, and that she could manage very will without him must have enraged him further. He had no way of forcing her to submit. Eventually Jim made off with their cattle and—for revenge against Josie, for love of his children, or perhaps for both reasons—spirited his children away from her. In *Butch Cassidy, My Brother*, a taped conversation with Crawford MacKnight, one of those children, is reproduced:

> My dad kinda kidnapped me and my brother, took us to Salt Lake and then up to Smithfield and turned us over to old Aunt Jodie Heath. I don't know if she was Dad's aunt really but she was a fine old woman. I liked her a lot. Well, mother wanted us kids brought home naturally, and she had papers made out and they deputized a little guy in Rock Springs to come out to serve papers and a warrant for his arrest and a subpoena to appear in court.

It was to regain possession of her children and her share of the cattle that Josie and Herb had gone to Steamboat Springs.

Then, in the April 14 issue of the *Empire Courier* came an explosion of large headlines and an almost unheard-of amount of copy as the newspaper gave its eager public the news of more bloodshed in Brown's Park:

SHOOTING AT BROWN'S PARK
James McKnight Probably Fatally Wounded
by Deputy Sheriff W. H. Harris

James McKnight, of Brown's Park, was shot and probably fatally wounded by Deputy Sheriff W. H. Harris, also of Brown's Park, on Wednesday evening, April 4, about 9 o'clock at the Edwards ranch on Beaver Creek. [*Note*: In *Colorado.*]

Mr. and Mrs. McKnight have had some domestic troubles during the past year and Mrs. McKnight and her father, A. H. Bassett, an old resident of Brown's Park, were at Craig and Steamboat Springs and commenced divorce proceedings. . . . and [obtained] a summons and an order from the county court restraining McKnight from disposing of his property, and a bond for $2500 for his appearance, were placed in the hands of Sheriff Farnham to serve on McKnight at Brown's Park.

The Sheriff arrived at Bassetts' on the 31st of March, a day in advance of Bassett and Mrs. McKnight. The Sheriff found that McKnight had already disposed of his property and left for Utah. [Farnham was not] aware that he was just across the line and only a few miles away. Not knowing whether or not McKnight would ever return, Sheriff Farnham appointed W. H. Harris, formerly of Rock Springs, to serve the papers should McKnight return, and left for Craig.

On April the 4th Mrs. McKnight sent word to her husband that she was very sick and wished to see him and "fix up matters." About dark he made his appearance. Those present at the ranch were: Miss Blanche Tilton, Miss Ann Bassett, Carl Blair, Larry Curtin, Geo. Bassett, Eva Hoy, [Mrs.] Valentine Hoy, and Mrs. James McKnight. Mrs. McKnight was in bed and the women were giving her medicine and applying numerous mustard plasters.

A little later Harris happened along and went into the house. McKnight said, "How do you do, Harris?" and the latter replied, "How do you do, Jim?" Miss Tilton then invited both men to stay the night. Harris turned his horse in the corral and McKnight said he guessed he would go home, which is just across the line in Utah, and started for the door. Harris said, "Jim, I have a letter here for you to read" and handed him the summons which Jim read and threw them on the table and remarked "that is only a matter of form." He then started for the door and Harris asked him if he could give bonds for those papers. He said "yes!" and started for the door again and Harris said he would put him under arrest until morning. McKnight did not answer, but opened the door and went out. Harris followed and called to him three times to stop but [McKnight] paid no attention to the command and Harris shot twice, one ball taking effect in the left side near the spine and glanced upward. Jim fell and called on Harris to shoot him in the head and finish the job. All rushed out of the house and the excitement was at a high pitch, Miss Annie Bassett, sister of Mrs. McKnight, being very demonstrative

> about the catastrophe which had befell her brother-in-law. Mrs. McKnight was quite ill and could not realize the gravity of the excitement.

It is easy to understand why Josie was so ill in a neighbor's house—the house happened to be on the Colorado side of the state line. Obviously her letter to Jim had tricked him into coming into Colorado so the papers could be served. Jim's rage at having fallen for her trick must have blinded him to the possible consequences of his refusal to heed Harris's order to halt.

The newspaper article continues, describing Jim's being carried into the house, other neighbors being sent for, and a doctor being summoned from Rock Springs. It ends with mention of a ride to Vernal by a stranger at this moment of this story, a stranger who was to gain prominence in the Park in the following months:

> Tom Hicks rode to Vernal, a distance of forty-five miles, in four hours and a half, and wired McKnight's relatives at Salt Lake and his brother, Frank McKnight, arrived Friday night and is looking after him. McKnight signed the papers on the 7th and Harris came to Craig, arriving last Monday, and delivered them to Sheriff Farnham and returned to Brown's Park on Tuesday.

Two months passed before the *Empire Courier* resumed its coverage in its issue of June 2:

> There was quite a delegation of Brown's Park citizens here this week. They left Thursday for Hahn's Peak to attend the county court next Monday when the divorce case of Mrs. James McKnight against her husband will be tried before Judge Voice. Those who will appear in the case are A. H. Bassett, father of Mrs. McKnight, Miss Anna Bassett, George Bassett, Carl Blair, Joe Davenport and Mrs. E. B. Thompson.

And in another item in the same weekly issue:

> Low Ranney arrived here last Sunday from Brown's Park. He accompanied James McKnight who was on his way to Hahn's Peak to attend county court. Mr. McKnight has about fully recovered from the wound he received in April at the hands of Deputy Sheriff Harris. His injuries were not as serious as at first anticipated and, although three efforts were made with Xrays the bullet was not located and he still carries it as a reminder of his unpleasant experience.

And then on June 16:

> Mrs. Josie McKnight secured a divorce from James McKnight in the county court at Hahn's Peak last week on the grounds of cruelty. . . .

> Elaborate preparations had been made for a bitter legal fight on both sides, but Mr. and Mrs. McKnight, after meeting at Hahn's Peak, decided between themselves to settle the question of allimony [*sic*] costs and custody of their two children out of court so as to avoid airing their troubles before the public. . . .
> Mrs. McKnight left for Salt Lake last Tuesday for the children, armed with a letter from Jim to his sister, with whom they have been living, to turn them over to her.
> Mrs. McKnight will make her home in Craig with Mr. and Mrs. McLacklan for a short time. Mr. McKnight will embark in the sheep business in Utah.
> When they bade each other goodby at Craig no animosity existed between them and they parted with best wishes for each other.

So the matter was settled. Jim was eventually to open his saloon and a livery stable as well, and raise Arabian thoroughbreds on ranch property he acquired. Hugh Colton of Vernal remembers him as a well-regarded businessman until Prohibition sent him north to find a new occupation.

Jim and Josie were never really friendly after their divorce, but they spoke politely if they happened to meet. In Josie's tapes she said, "He was undoubtedly Scotch. It was hardly in his favor. He wasn't a bad man—he was just a Scotchman, that's all." And she warned her granddaughter against ever marrying one.

The shooting of Jim McKnight was the first building block in what was to become the Josie Morris legend. Country people like nothing better than to hunker down on someone's porch and swap stories, and a divorce in the Bassett family was eagerly accepted as a sequel to their tales of the daring and unwomanly Elizabeth Bassett, who worked side by side with her cowboys while Herb Bassett sat at home. As they went over and over the McKnight divorce and Jim's shooting, someone's guess one day was quoted as truth the next.

Jim McKnight must have received his own share of attention from the legend-makers. The *Empire Courier* had said that no bullet was located after three x-rays. Perhaps, some said, there was no bullet. One old story is that people laughed, saying Jim only thought he was wounded, that actually he was struck by a spent bullet and became frightened.

If Jim was thus accused of being craven and a hypochondriac, Josie acquired the image of a woman who tried to kill her husband. Shots fired by a deputy sheriff were not dramatic enough for the storytellers. Soon everyone knew that without question it was Josie who shot Jim McKnight, and it is in connection with this story that Josie said, "No, I did not shoot him. If I had, I wouldn't have missed!"

There seems no reasonable doubt of the true story. Jim McKnight married again and produced a son Arthur, who was to write that his father carried the bullet until his death and had told him that he had been shot by a "damned political hanger-on" named Bill Harris. When both sides in a war agree on the facts of a story, surely history can accept it!

Since Josie never allowed gossip to upset her seriously, the stories did her no real harm. However, great harm was to come from acceptance of her father's advice as to what she should do with her future. Herb himself, now that his youngest child George had finally reached sixteen and could be considered a man by frontier standards, was finally ready to make a break for freedom. In one of the isues in which the *Empire Courier* reported Josie's divorce proceedings, there was also a nice little article about Herb:

> A. H. Bassett, the pioneer of Brown's Park, was a pleasant caller at this office last Tuesday. Mr. Bassett has resided in the Park twenty-two years and many is the traveler who has partaken of the hospitality at his ranch at Ladore during all those years. He is a genial, whole-souled man, with a fund of good stories of pioneer days and ever ready to extend a welcome hand to the stranger who is "just looking over the country" or to the weary cow puncher who finds his way to Ladore. Mr. Bassett contemplates leaving Brown's Park and returning to his former home in Arkansas where he was a prominent figure during the war and for a number of years after the "unpleasantness." He has been postmaster at Ladore ever since the office was established ten years ago. Mr. Bassett recently resigned his position of postmaster and Mrs. W. H. Blair has been appointed his successor. The post office will be moved to the Blair ranch on Green River, about five miles from its present location.

If Herb had quietly returned to Arkansas, no damage would have been done. Instead, he used his influence to "rescue" Josie from the wilderness; and she, confused and distraught at the temporary loss of her children and anxious to do what was right for them now that they had been returned to her, made the mistake of listening. She would not sell her ranch for Jim McKnight; now she foolishly sold it for her children. In her tapes her regret comes through plainly:

> My father thought that the . . . he said—that was wrong of my father—he said, "Now, a woman with two little children to send to school has no business living alone on the ranch." I had six hundred and eighty cattle, and I could have managed that outfit just as well, far better than I could living in town, because I wasn't used to that town business, and don't like it and I never did. George Bassett could have helped me and would, and that's why I should have stayed. . . . But I sold out on father's advice and went to Craig and went into the hotel business, something I didn't know a thing about. But I made out all right, I made a living and lived very decent.

Herb had struck a mortal blow to those of his children who would remain in Brown's Park. Bad days were coming to them, and they would face those days without the presence of Josie. As forceful as her mother Elizabeth, Josie might have provided a steadying influence on Eb and Ann, might have been a help to young George, who was sometimes to bear the brunt of their indiscretions.

Moving to town was unmistakably disastrous to Josie herself. She lost her inner contentment when she left the country that was so important to her. She had committed herself to a life that was foreign to her, one that could have broken her permanently had it not been for her ability to seize what she could under any circumstances and extract some good from it.

Thus Josie left, reluctantly. Herb, the eager one, was not to leave the Park that year, for within a month after Josie's divorce such tragedy struck the Bassetts that even Herb, distasteful as the Park was to him and disappointing as were his children, surely must have postponed his leaving until the worst of the crisis had passed.

SCARS AND TWO BARS

The events that were to occur in Brown's Park in the summer of 1900 started with a pot of trouble that had been simmering for a decade or so in northwestern Colorado, and they can be understood only in the context of what had been happening in Wyoming throughout the 1890s.

In the struggle between the cattlemen and the homesteaders, actual armed warfare had taken place as early as 1892 in Johnson County, Wyoming, when the cattle barons had openly hired twenty-five Texas gunmen, to be known as "the Invaders," to come in and "clear out the rustlers." Ordinarily the homesteaders might have welcomed this, since rustlers were a threat to them as well as to the barons. However, so many honest men had been molested that now they believed they would be on the "hit list" along with those men who stole cattle as a matter of habit. Consequently, they united against the Invaders, and were actively besieging the hired gunmen and ready to fight a pitched battle when they were stopped by federal troops.

All during this period the Wyoming cattlemen had been hiring private stock detectives to accumulate evidence of rustling. Any court action on charges they brought was ineffective, however, because the juries were made up of townspeople, farmers, and small ranchers. The attitude of these people was that a big cattleman could always find, or if necessary manufacture, evidence against any man who was in the way. Like Elizabeth Bassett, they considered that they were engaged in warfare, and that the ordinary man was more sinned against than sinning. It was next to impossible to persuade these juries to return a guilty verdict when the complainant was a cattle baron.

Thwarted in the courts, the cattlemen secretly authorized their stock detectives to enforce the law by violence. Though no longer openly employed by the Cattlemen's Association, the detectives were put under the direction of a "cattlemen's committee," with activities hidden from the public's eye. The detective's standard fee for a "kill" was said to be five hundred dollars.

It was at that time accepted throughout the country that a duly elected sheriff who killed a man for whom a reward was offered was within his legal and ethical rights in accepting the money. However, the thought of a gunman being hired to kill by private interests was abhorrent to everyone—except the big cattlemen attempting to control the free lands which they thought of as their own.

In 1894 the cattlemen around Cheyenne, Wyoming, hired a former Pinkerton detective named Tom Horn, a name that was to become used by mothers to frighten rebellious children. Down in New Mexico and Arizona, Horn had been a stage driver, a teamster, and a scout during the period when the Apaches were being subdued. In Wyoming, Horn's method of operation was to go into an area seeking evidence of rustling and, when evidence was found, to send a warning note to the suspect giving him thirty days to get out of the country. If the warning was not heeded, a shot would ring out in the night. Just the rumor that Tom Horn had entered an area was often enough to make a bona fide rustler saddle his horse and leave.

Western Colorado had been settled a bit later than Wyoming. However, Routt County (which at that time took in all of western Colorado from the base of the Rockies at Steamboat Springs to the Utah border) was bound to have Wyoming's problems, once the Utes were pushed out and the big cattlemen moved in. Although the eastern part of Routt was too cold to support cattle in the winter without heavy reliance on hay and was too split up by canyons and the foothills of the Rockies to accommodate large cattle herds, the county's western portion had the open grazing lands and more temperate climate of southern Wyoming. Inevitably, the big ranchers in Colorado would feel as crowded by the homesteaders as had their Wyoming counterparts.

The cattlemen of Routt County had their own organization, the Snake River Stock Growers Association. It was never as powerful or as dominant in the state legislature as the Cattlemen's Association in Wyoming, but it did effectively control the management of the Routt County range, and there were the same tensions over grazing lands and water as there were in Wyoming. However, in the mid-1890s when the Wyoming association was negotiating with Tom Horn, Routt County's ranchers, both big and small, found themselves agreeing on one issue: The sheepmen across the border in Wyoming were not to be allowed to bring their nasty, evil-smelling, close-grazing, sharp-hooved animals into the state of Colorado. They agreed to take concerted action. Perhaps some small ranchers would have liked to turn to sheep-raising themselves, now that the huge herds of cattle had damaged the range, but pressure from the cattlemen of the Snake River Stock Growers Association prevented them from doing so.

There had been some sheep in the Brown's Park area since 1880 when, according to John Rolfe Burroughs, the two Welshmen from Australia, Jack and Griff Edwards, had thrown their sheep just outside the Brown's Park eastern entrance to help prevent the encroachment of Middlesex cattle upon the Park. Middlesex was long gone, ruined by mismanagement and the terrible winters of 1886 and 1887, but the Edwards sheep remained, and by 1895 their combined flocks had grown to a very respectable sixty thousand. The brothers normally used a summer range in Wyoming, but in the winter they returned their flocks to Routt County, grazing some of them in Brown's Park itself, but for the most part using the land they had traditionally occupied outside the Park's borders.

The cattlemen were determined that even an old-timer like Jack Edwards must go, lest others follow his example. Edwards had set up shearing pens in the spring of 1896 on Four Mile Creek in Colorado, and was herding thirty thousand sheep in that area. On June 1 a group of Routt County cattlemen attacked his flocks, clubbing some of the sheep to death and scattering the others. In the fracas, two of Jack Edwards's sheepherders were murdered.

Jack Edwards was a fearless man, and when he heard the news he rode out alone to assess the damage. A group of cattlemen seized him and stood him under a tree with a rope around his neck while they discussed with him the inadvisability of continuing to graze sheep in Routt County. When Jack refused to take his sheep back to Wyoming, they hoisted him up and let him choke for a while; then they let him down to reconsider. Jack still refused. The second time they hoisted him almost finished him, and when they gave the choking man a final chance he agreed, realizing that the cattlemen meant business. Eventually, within a year or so, Edwards kept his promise and took his sheep back across the Wyoming border.

Routt County's worries about sheep were not too important to the Brown's Park ranchers. They had their own neighboring cattle baron to worry about. Ora Haley had just expanded his Two-Bar ranch down on Lay Creek by purchasing a ranch immediately outside the eastern entrance to the Park. Grimly the ranchers speculated that Brown's Park was likely to be used increasingly by the Two-Bar cattle, and that they were going to have difficulty holding out against the onslaught.

Ora Haley, who himself knew little about raising cows, had succeeded in the cattle business by hiring the best available managers for his various holdings and then giving them almost total authority. He had jumped at the chance to buy a new headquarters west of Lay Creek; his operation could not be expanded toward the crowded range around the Yampa River, whereas the land to the west was, in his opinion, underutilized. The manager handling this enlarged operation was Hiram H. "Hi" Bernard, one of the most knowledgeable cattlemen in all the Wyoming Basin.

At the time Hi Bernard took over the management of the Two-Bar he was thirty-nine years old, a big, powerful, slow-talking Texan with blue eyes sunk deep in a square face pockmarked from smallpox and mottled from years on the range. He had been working with cattle since his poverty-stricken youth in Texas where, at the age of twelve, he had started helping Charles Chisholm "moonlight" Longhorns. It was hard work, scouting for the wild cattle's feeding grounds in the daylight hours and then going out at night to rope them as they came out of the impenetrable brush, but for Hi it was the beginning of his escape from the miserable conditions under which he had been raised. He followed the Chisholm Trail on a couple of cattle drives and then settled down in Wyoming to become a manager of cattle ranches. He was highly respected, not only for his knowledge of how to handle cattle profitably but also for his skill in getting the best out of his cowboys without driving them harshly. In addition, he was more than just a good range boss: Ora Haley, who made as much money in short-term speculations on the cattle market as he did in raising his own cows, relied heavily on Hi's judgment of when to buy and sell on the market.

Hi had never owned a cow, being content to take a salary more than ample to provide well-tailored clothes, custom-made boots, and rich living when he went to the city. He preferred to leave the headaches of ownership to his employer; however, he was proud of the fact that no outfit under his management had ever gone broke. He was a well-paid, dedicated "company man" with a willingness to trade his independence for financial security because of his memories of his childhood days back in Texas. Frank Willis quoted him later in his unpublished "Confidentially Told."

> When small ranch seekers came to squat on our ranges, I was not in sympathy with them and used every means in my power to move them on, using force if need be. Every poor family moving in a covered wagon to settle on a lonesome claim, to chuck into a little rough dugout or a dirt-covered log shack brought back memories of bed bugs, my childhood, and my little sad mother in poverty, drudging wearily along and bravely enduring such an existence. The thought of struggling individuals going the hard way and bucking against odds they could not conquer was hateful, and turned me sour.

When he took on responsibility for the Two-Bar, Hi immediately went over to Brown's Park to meet with the ranchers. His main concern, he told them, was to promote the anti-sheep campaign and be sure that the sheepmen were not allowed to move into the underutilized range in Brown's Park. The Park's ranchers listened skeptically. They did not feel their range was underutilized; rather, it was just not being overgrazed. If Bernard wanted to talk about sheep, they themselves wanted to talk about Two-Bar's huge herds of cattle.

The opposing sides reached a compromise. The ranchers formed their own organization, the Brown's Park Cattle Association, and elected Matt Rash its president. They would cooperate in keeping sheep out, but only on the condition that their long-time neighbors were allowed to continue in the sheep business just as they had been doing. The Park's sheep belonged to good friends: Jimmy Goodman raised them, the Davenports had a flock, and Jack Edwards's brother Griff had sheep in Brown's Park handled by his foreman Willis Rouff. It was agreed that these flocks would not be molested.

The more important part of the compromise as far as Brown's Park was concerned was that Two-Bar agreed to a line of demarcation between its range and the range in Brown's Park. The line was established at a point halfway between the Snake River and the Park's Vermillion Creek, running north–south along a clearly defined limestone ridge. This line was called the Divide.

The agreement worked well, considering the difficulty of sequestering herds on the open range. The Park men threw up a cabin on the ridge and took turns patroling, driving back any Two-Bar cows that wandered over the line. Bernard assigned a man named Billy Sawtelle to guard Two-Bar's interest, and he was more than equal to the task. He was the typical cowboy of a Hollywood Western, a tough man when riding the range and even tougher when he went to town, where he acted the part of a hard-drinking gambler of professional caliber who held his cards to his chest and left his man lying dead on the floor of the saloon if necessary.

The outside cattle interests were not satisfied with this compromise, but Hi Bernard had probably realized that he should take what he could get in the negotiations. He knew that the Brown's Parkers were not really interested in the sheep question and that, if hard-pressed by an influx of cattle, they might even turn *en masse* to sheep-raising, leaving him in a worse situation. The arrangement, however, did not please the Snake River Stock Grower's Association.

Six months after the near-lynching of Jack Edwards, in Christmas week of 1896, a group of cattlemen, so large that it took seven wagons to bring in its supplies, moved into Brown's Park and started visiting those involved in raising sheep. There was no violence—the sheer numbers of the invaders were too intimidating, especially since the whole country knew what had happened to Jack Edwards and his luckless herders. Willis Rouff, Griff Edwards' foreman, got Griff's permission to move his sheep; Jimmy Goodman agreed also. The cattlemen left, and Jimmy, getting old by this time anyway, sold his ranch to Matt Rash and left the area.

The ranchers realized that the threats against their sheep-raising neighbors had apparently come from all the cattlemen in Routt County, but even so they still blamed it on the "Big Four"—The Sevens, Two-Circle-Bar, Charley Ayer, and their own neighbor the Two-Bar. After all, sheep that graze in a group and can be controlled had not been particularly disadvantageous to Brown's Park ranchers. There had been room in the Park for both sheep flocks of reasonable size and the ranchers' own small herds of around six hundred cattle. It was the big operators, who controlled over seventy-five percent of the Routt County range, who were now objecting to competition. The men of Brown's Park waited to see if the agreement on the Divide would be broken as easily as the agreement about the flocks of their neighbors.

With the sheepmen well under control, certain members of the Snake River Association turned their attention to cattle rustling. With the myopia of the cattle barons of Wyoming, they saw as a rustler anyone who contested their control of the range or who tried to recoup losses. To combat this menace they formed a Wyoming-style *sub rosa* "cattlemen's committee" with the understanding and approval of the official membership.

The original committee consisted of three large ranchers whose ranges were on the Snake River—Charlie Ayer, W. W. "Wiff" Wilson, and Two-Bar's manager, Hi Bernard. Just when it was formed and what, if anything, it accomplished are not known; all that is clear is that it was indeed formed. This is attested to by J. H. Ratliff, a man of unquestioned integrity, of whose courage and determination more will be heard.

This first cattlemen's committee was evidently enlarged before it took any action. This inference can be drawn from a letter from J. Wilson Carey of the Two-Circle-Bar ranch to John Rolfe Burroughs, dated April 9, 1859. Carey told Burroughs that at a meeting of men from five big cattle ranches (Pierce-Reef, Clayton-Murnan, Yampa Livestock, Two Bar and Charlie Ayer) he had been delegated to collect one hundred dollars each month from the members and turn the money over to Charlie Ayer, who was to hire a man to move into Brown's Park and secure evidence of rustling. Carey said that he did not know whom Ayers hired, but felt that it was Tom Horn.

The sinister implications revealed in that letter almost sixty years later could only be guessed at as Routt County watched the tragedies taking place in Brown's Park in the summer months of 1900.

In early spring of that year a man named James Hicks entered Brown's Park looking for land on which to start a horse ranch. He traveled up and down the valley, visiting one rancher and another, including the Bassetts. (He was most surely the "Tom Hicks" who rode to Vernal when Jim McKnight was shot.) Eventually he moved in with Matt Rash and worked with him as a cook during the spring roundup. It is told that during this period he came across Isom Dart skinning the hide from a young bull belonging to a rancher named Sam

Spicer. It is also said that Isom, having had trouble with this particular bull and believing it to be dangerous, had shot it, and that he had told Spicer about it and settled up with him.

Ann Bassett met James Hicks while he was helping on Matt's roundup crew and took an immediate dislike to him. Her story in *The Colorado Magazine* tells us:

> I did not take kindly to the new cook. His bragging that he had been a great Indian fighter, his boastful, descriptive accounts of the human slaughter he had accomplished single-handed, were exceedingly obnoxious to me. I emphasized this point with vehemence in several heated arguments.
>
> Matt Rash attempted to iron out the discord and remarked "most all the big Indian battles were fought around the campfire as men smoked and talked."

Hicks was an unprepossessing man. He was swarthy as a Mexican and had the high cheekbones of the Indians he bragged of having killed. It is said that he never looked anyone square in the face, but kept his lids lowered over his black eyes and looked at the ground. A. G. Wallihan, who lived over near the original Two-Bar ranch at Lay, said, "I didn't like him. My wife had lived all her life on the frontier, and she was not afraid of God, man, or devil, but she said: 'That man Hicks is a bad man. . . .' "

Hicks left the area rather abruptly. Soon after his departure several ranchers found notes on their front gates warning them to leave Brown's Park within thirty days or suffer the consequences. Tom Davenport and Longhorn Thompson were among those so honored, as were Matt Rash and Isom Dart. The mysterious notes were taken seriously by the ranchers who were well aware of the goings-on up in Wyoming. None of them left the Park, but all of them were worried and waiting for trouble.

On July 7 Matt Rash stopped by the Bassett ranch on his way back from a trip to town; from there he went to his cabin for the night, then rode on up to a summer cabin he maintained on Cold Spring Mountain. It was there, on July 10, that George Rife and fourteen-year-old Felix Meyers found his already decomposing body lying on the bunk. The details in the *Craig Empire* are gruesome:

> Mr. Rash was lying on the bed partially turned over on his face, his head resting on his arm. Two bullet holes were found in his body, one through the back and abdomen, the other in the right breast. . . . On the floor, between the bed and table was a pool of blood which had thoroughly dried. A chair was at the table and the condition of the dishes showed that Rash must have been eating a lunch at the time he was shot. While eating he was facing a window in the west side of the cabin; behind him was the open door on the east side. . . . Evidently Rash had

been shot in the back and when he got up turned around only to be shot again through the right breast. He had fallen where the pool of dried blood was, then revived sufficiently to drag himself to his bed.

Rash had one boot off, which peculiarity is accounted for by the fact that he had always removed his boot as soon as he got into the cabin after he had been riding, the foot having been injured some years before and being sensitive, the rubbing of the stirrup caused him some annoyance.

Rash's saddle was on the ground near the entrance to the cabin, but his saddle horse was not in sight. Later the animal was seen at a distance dragging a new lariat rope. In the corral was a bronco which had been killed, having been shot just above the point of the nose. . . .

The murder stunned the community. Matt had been well thought of and was a leader among the ranchers, who had elected him president of their cattlemen's association. At the Bassett ranch they grieved as for a family member, for he had been a part of their lives for seventeen years. He had served almost as a father to the boys in the running of the ranch, and even after they grew old enough to act for themselves they followed his advice in managing the Bassett herd.

The most grief-stricken, however, was Ann, for Matt and she were sweethearts. She had been only four years old when he first rode through the Bassett gate; he had known her through her tomboy years and had been there to witness what she had become—a provocative combination of range rider and lady of fashion. No doubt when the young Ann practiced her new-found art of flirting he was amused and did not take her seriously. Each time Ann returned home, however, his interest grew, until the two of them were dallying with each other more seriously.

How deep or enduring their relationship might have been is unknown, but it is certain that Matt had been squiring her to parties in Craig as well as in the Park. Ann had just come home for what she said was the last time, her education completed and her eyes set on a future in the Park; but whether either one of them was ready for an immediate marriage is problematical. Matt was a bachelor in his middle thirties and he may have been hesitant about marrying the attractive but bad-tempered Ann Bassett. At twenty-one, Ann herself may have been more pragmatic than wildly in love, perhaps enjoying Matt's company but still willing to consider other men.

Whatever the situation had been before his murder, the thought of the slow death her lover had suffered, all alone on the mountain, was enough to make her feel that she had lost the one great love of her life. She mourned deeply, and vented her grief in wild anger and threats of revenge against the murderer who had assassinated her sweetheart. She had no doubt that the Two-Bar was the prime mover in this atrocity.

The ranchers agreed with Ann that it had been a "political" murder, because it was Matt Rash who had been coordinating the patrol of the dividing line between Two-Bar and the Park. Moreover, strange selections had been made by whoever had delivered the threatening notes. No notes had been left at Powder Springs, which everyone knew was the headquarters for any bona fide rustlers still in the area. Nor had a note been left at Charley Crouse's door, although, of all the men in the Park, he should have received one. If Matt Rash had once in a while appropriated a steer or branded a calf too young to be called a maverick, it was the common opinion that these actions were only an excuse for killing him, for Matt had too much to do in taking care of his legitimate business to be making a steady practice of stealing other men's cattle.

Ann told everyone who would listen that she suspected the so-called horse rancher from New Mexico, the Mr. Hicks who had left so abruptly. The ranchers listened and agreed that it was possible. Then a letter addressed to Matt came from Denver, postmarked on the day of Matt's murder. It was from Mr. Hicks, informing Matt that he would be returning soon. This seemed to exonerate Hicks, even though Ann and other less credulous people pointed out that the letter could have been sent as a smokescreen.

Matt had told several people that he was worried about the note he had received, and according to the *Craig Courier* "told one man that he expected to be killed and that it was unpleasant to be continually on his guard." His fears caused this man in the prime of life to make a will.

The will was probably written at the Bassett cabin in the presence of Josie, Eb, and Ann's friend from Craig, Blanche Tilton; it was probably witnessed by two disinterested persons who happened to be at hand, Longhorn Thompson and Larry Curtin; it probably left his estate to his sweetheart Ann. These may or may not be facts. What is incontrovertible is that *the will was lost*! Whatever it said, wherever it was written, whoever witnessed it, the will must surely have existed, or Ann would not have had the temerity to do what she did: she filed suit in court asking that Matt Rash's will be probated even though she could not produce it. The court records show:

> On or about the twentieth day of May, A. D. 1900, the said deceased Madison M. Rash did at the said Lodore in said county and state, write his said will in the presence of divers persons, and did then and there sign the same and deliver the same to petitioner for her to keep and that the same was in the possession of the petitioner from that time until the death of said decedent; and that since the death of said decedent, your petitioner has searched for the said will and that she cannot find the same, but that the same is lost. . . .

If nothing else was gained by this very unusual petition, it at least enlivened the settlement of Matt's estate. Matt's father Samuel and his brother James came up from Texas to arrange for settlement of Matt's affairs and to exhume his body for shipment to Texas. The relations between the Bassetts and Matt's relatives must have been amicable despite the suit, for the two opposing sides drove together to attend the trial at Hahn's Peak. On the way, they settled the matter over luncheon. Ann was given $250, no more than a moral victory considering the fact that Matt left a fairly sizable estate. Still, it justified her claims in the eyes of her friends, and she withdrew her suit forthwith.

Ann's lawsuit is the only comic note in a hideous summer. True to his promise in his letter to Matt, Mr. Hicks did return. When he heard what had happened in his absence, he let it be known around the Park that he thought it had probably been "the damn nigger" and gave an account of a quarrel he had witnessed between Rash and Isom Dart. Nobody believed his charges; Isom was too well known and too well respected for anyone to believe that he would shoot a man in the back. Hicks stayed in the Park only a short time before disappearing again.

The valley had not seen the last of murder, however. On October 3, in the early hours of dawn, Isom Dart was shot from ambush at his cabin up at Summit Springs. The circumstances were described in the *Craig Courier*:

> Another tragedy occurred in Brown's Park Thursday morning of last week, Isom Dart, a negro, falling victim to an assassin's bullet. The murder occurred on the Cold Springs ranch. Dart and George Bassett were walking together from the cabin to the corrall and when about twenty steps from the cabin door, a shot was fired from the direction of the corrall and Isom fell dead. Young Bassett ran back to the cabin, in which were Sam Bassett and Lew Brown, who saw Dart fall when he was shot. The young men were afraid to venture out after the killing and remained in the cabin for four hours. Finally they left the cabin and started for the Matt Rash ranch. . . . The murderer had stood behind a tree 120 yards from where Dart fell. His tracks where he stood were quite plain and it was evident that the murderer had his horse tied a short distance behind him. The horse was shod and his trail was easy to follow. Sam Bassett and Billy Bragg followed the trail eight miles and when they quit it was perfectly plain.

Isom's murder was just as heartrending to the Bassetts as Matt Rash's, and his murder seemed just as senseless. The affection the Bassetts all had for Isom was bone-deep. Josie described him as "just a good, honest old colored man who never hurt anybody." Even John Rolfe Burroughs, who gives full credence to J. S. Hoy's condemnation of most of the people in Brown's Park, says that "the Negro came by most of his cattle honestly."

The futility of Isom's murder led many people to speculate as to whom the real target had been. It had been early in the morning and the light was not bright, and the men had been in Jim McKnight's summer cabin. Had the killer been really shooting for Jim McKnight? Jim was already out of the Park, so that did not seem too probable. But the Bassett boys had been there, and Billy Bragg. Was one of them soon to be found dead when the killer realized he had made a mistake? There seemed good reason to believe that the Bassett boys were also targets. On October 20, the following item appeared in the *Craig Courier*:

> A report from Brown's Park states that a letter was found among the effects of Isam [*sic*] Dart, the negro who was recently murdered there, warning the Bassett boys and Joe Davenport to leave the Park inside of 60 days or suffer the same fate which befell Matt Rash and Dart. The boys are interested in ranching and stock in Brown's Park and were raised in that section. They have paid no attention to the warning and continue to attend to their interests.

It is surprising that such a letter, mentioning Dart's murder, was found among Dart's effects. This illogicality makes the letter suspect, and it is quite possible that it was fabricated perhaps by Ann, in an effort to spur the authorities to investigate more vigorously. In December the *Craig Courier* reported that Eb and Ann had each received a warning note suggesting they also leave the country. These notes may also have been spurious. Ann was determined that the authorities must not be allowed to close the books on the murderer of Matt and Isom, and may have used these notes to prod the sheriff's department into renewing their investigations, for fear of further murders. She was not alone in her demands. The entire countryside was in an uproar and feared what might come next, for during this period there were also two unexplained murders over in the Iron Mountain section, near John Coble's ranch where Tom Horn was known to have his headquarters. The small ranchers, feeling the authorities were too quick to ascribe these murders to retribution against rustlers and too slow to investigate thoroughly, were clamoring for action. Their protests grew to huge proportions after the following article appeared in the *Denver Post* on December 20, 1900:

> *WAR ON A WOMAN*
>
> NEW FEATURE TO THE ROUTT COUNTY TROUBLE
>
> **Outlaws Growing Bolder**
>
> They Warn Miss Anna Bassett to Leave The County Within Thirty Days or Suffer the Consequences

> *Hayden, Colo., Dec. 20*: The latest development in connection with the reign of terror in central and western Routt County is the publication of a warning letter to Miss Anna Bassett who has until recently been living with her father who is postmaster in Lodore and assisting her brothers in their ranch and range work.
>
> > Nov. 12—Anna Bassett, Lodore, Colo: You are requested to leave that country for parts unknown within thirty days or you will be killed thirty days for your life. "Committee"
>
> The note was enclosed in a letter bearing the postmark Cheyenne, Wyo. where it was mailed Nov. 15 and has just been made public by Miss Bassett who is now stopping with her friends in Craig. Had there been any vigorous effort by the authorities to hunt down the murderer of Rash and Dart the Bassetts would have paid no attention to the warning to leave, but the indifference of the authorities and the presence of suspicious characters in that section led them to believe their lives were in danger, hence all except the father left the country, together with Thompson and Joe Davenport who also had been warned to go by December 12.

The threat to Ann brought forth articles condemning the lack of action in both the Steamboat Springs *Pilot* and the *Denver Republican*. The county commissioners and the sheriff in Craig defended themselves in the columns of the *Craig Courier* by asking, essentially, "Where is the evidence?" The truth was, there was no evidence that would stand up in court.

Yet the people believed the big ranchers were guilty of the atrocities. J. H. Ratliff (mentioned earlier as the man who eventually saw the minutes of the Snake River Stock Growers Association referring to formation of a "cattleman's committee") had an experience at the time of the murders that convinced him that the Two-Bar was involved. He spent a night in the Two-Bar bunkhouse with another guest, Tom Horn. Isom Dart was murdered two or three days later. A. G. Wallihan also placed Horn near the Two-Bar ranch, and a Two-Bar cowboy told of Hi Bernard going out to the corral at night and cutting out two or three of the best horses for some unexplained reason, horses that were later found running loose in the sagebrush.

Another Two-Bar cowboy, E. V. Houghy, who later served as county assessor for many years, reminisced in the 1930s for J. Monaghan, compiler of the "CWA Reports," a Civil Works Administration historical project:

> The big cattlemen who were hiring him [Horn] would have a horse picketed every ten miles across the country for him and as he raced west he would change as he came to these fresh horses. He would tie up the horse he was riding and mount the fresh one. When he got to the western end of the county he would kill the man who was marked and come back along his string of picketed horses. On the way back he would turn each horse loose as he dismounted. . . . That fall I was rid-

> ing for the Two-Bar and as the roundup moved down the country we started picking up those Two-Bar horses every ten or fifteen miles. . . .

The possibility of more murders drove several people from the Park. Longhorn Thompson was shot at from ambush on Thanksgiving Day and promptly moved to Craig. Young Joe Davenport went to Missouri, and Sam Bassett went to Alaska. Sam, however, had been planning to leave the Park even before the shootings began, and had, in fact, sold his share of the Bassett cattle. An existing photograph shows him to be handsome like all the Bassetts, with large, candid eyes and a look of transparent honesty. Sam did not enjoy life with Eb and Ann, and he agreed with his father that the dog-eat-dog atmosphere on the range was not his idea of living. Sam spent several years panning gold in the Yukon; then he married and moved to a farm near Seattle, where he raised a family of successful children. Although he kept in touch with his kinfolk he never returned, even for a visit.

As for Tom Horn, his career lasted not too much longer. He had the unfortunate habit of drunken bragging when he was in his cups, and he incriminated himself in the fatal shooting of a teenage boy named Willie Nickells, whom he had mistaken for Willie's father in early-morning light. A Cheyenne jury convicted him, and Tom Horn—apparently expecting to be rescued by his powerful friends right up until the moment the rope went around his neck—was hanged on November 20, 1903.

HI BERNARD

Herbert Bassett was sixty-six years old when he finally fulfilled his dream of going to California. Although he may have considered a permanent return to Arkansas when he first thought of leaving Brown's Park, he did not settle there. Instead, he began making extended visits to old soldiers' homes from Los Angeles to Chattanooga, visits that would continue until he died. At times he would tire of the regimentation or of a particular climate and return to Colorado, but his children's inattention to spiritual matters distressed the old man, and soon he would slip away to sample the hospitality of still another of the government's refuges for old Union soldiers.

His greatest joy was going to Sunday school again, and he experienced a religious renaissance that left him more than ever preoccupied with man's sinfulness and need for redemption. Two of his letters to Josie have survived, and each one ends with a fervent and lengthy sermon about turning to God. They also mention happy things that happened to him, and it is evident that in his new environment this fine, honest misfit had finally found his niche. On May 30, 1903, he wrote to Josie from Los Angeles:

> This has been the best day to me for a great many years—Decoration Day—this is my first attendance on this memorial day and you bet I had a great big cry all alone. I was attending a Nazarine Meeting a few nights ago & sat in a draft & caught cold & was excused from marching in uniform & standing so long—all too much formality. So I took my time & went to the cemetary & out to a field of hay cut and cocked up & there I took in the whole proceedings. . . . The driveway up to the cemetary was between rows of pepper trees. . . . The old boys and the Marines formed two lines, one each side of the way. The flags from head of each column nearly touched & the procession passed under the flags & filed left & went to the flagpole. . . . I saw the old blue coats and gray beards and the canes to support them now—forty years ago they stood shoulder to shoulder fighting to sustain the best Govt on earth—today they are shoulder to shoulder again probably for the last time, to contribute to the memory of their dead comrades. Very few of those remaining are Soldiers of the Cross and ready for the last roll call. These few serious thoughts, together with the minute gun firing & the flags & flowers at all the graves gave me a good opportunity for a real genuine cry. . . .

With Herb gone, Sam in Alaska, and Josie in Craig, the Bassett ranch was left to Eb, now in his early twenties, and George, in his later teens, with the dubious assistance of their older sister Ann. She was filled with a hatred for Two-Bar that bordered on neurosis.

In 1902 the *Craig Courier* occasionally carried a little column headed "Brown's Park Rodeo" written by an anonymous Special Correspondent. In one issue that summer the columnist reported on the bad effects of a drought on the Brown's Park grasslands and commented that if "outside" cattle pushed in at the same rate as they had during the previous year, the graze might be permanently damaged. Then on December 19 the columnist submitted this plaintive little paragraph:

> A cattle roundup party spent about a month ending with November, gathering in northwestern Colorado, Utah and Wyoming, going nearly to the U. P. We hear of our cattle being as far east in Routt County as they can go. We hope hereafter people that "shove" their cattle down here from eastern and middle Routt county will do unto us as they would wish to be done by, and cut our cattle out and leave them on their home range and not drive them so far away that we never get them, or if we do get them it costs as much as the cattle are worth.

It is plain that with Matt Rash's murder the fight went out of the Brown's Park ranchers. Probably fearing that they might share Matt's fate, they had stopped patroling the Divide. The thousand dollars reputedly paid Tom Horn for the murders of Rash and Dart had been a small price for the cattle barons. Brown's Park was now open to them.

But Ann Bassett, raised in her mother's tradition and determined that Matt's death would not go unavenged, launched a vendetta against her enemy on as large a scale as was possible to her. She patrolled the Divide herself with a rifle slung from her saddle, and she shot any Two-Bar cow wandering over the line. When cows did make their way into Brown's Park she pushed them into the Green River to drown or to founder in the mud along its flats.

At about this time a new family moved into Brown's Park, by the name of Chew. The father, Jack Chew, was none too successful either then or later, but his family of fourteen or more children were raised by his wife Mary to be industrious and hard-working, and to avoid the alcohol that was their father's downfall. One of the girls had just entered her teens when they moved to the Park. Her name was Leath, but she was later to be called Avvon. She eventually wrote an appealing story of her early days called *The Chew Bunch.* In that book Leath wrote of an incident that happened when she was a young girl:

On a sunny day in June, I decided to shirk my share of the care of the fat baby Ralph, and go explore a trail that took off from Pot Creek, down a piece. I called Smarty, the little brown mare, slipped on a bridle, and mounting her bareback, I was soon single-footing down a "bran new" trail. . . .

The trail led down a gentle incline to a river about one half mile away, whose banks were thickly lined with cottonwood trees. . . . This I knew was the Green River. . . .

Across the river, in the low hills to the east, a dust began to rise. The cause of the dust was at first hidden. As I watched, a small herd of cattle came into sight and rushed for the river. They were followed by four riders, swinging bullwhips or lariats, whooping and yelling. The cattle rushed into the swift water of the river without slacking pace. They were soon in swimming water. Many were carried downstream a considerable distance before gaining the opposite shore. There were doubts in my mind that all would reach my side and I watched and wondered. Dad didn't handle cattle in that fashion. Greetings were called across the river. I impulsively decided to cross. Riding upstream about two hundred yards, I signaled that I was coming over. The game little mare stepped off into swimming water and I, holding the bridle rein and tuft of the mane in one hand, kept the other hand free for emergencies, floating clear of Smarty's submerged back. The current carried us downstream swiftly. We were almost even with those waiting on shore with lassoes ready. As the horse touched bottom, I was instantly astride her slippery back.

"Crazy stunt," was the greeting. "What's your name?" I felt the attractive young woman was unpleasantly abrupt. I grinned self-consciously as I retorted, "Smarty kin swim and so kin I." Then I said somewhat belligerently, "I am Leath Chew." I had long since found myself a much criticized child and I hated my name. Hated the accent the adults employed.

The woman said, "You are Mark's sister. I am Ann Bassett." She introduced the youngsters whose names I promptly forgot. They were visiting from Chicago and I never saw any of them again. I had heard of Ann Bassett and knew she was called Queen Ann, but I did not know then that she was attempting to put into action a plan to destroy all Ora Haley's Two Bar cattle, nor did I know that day of Queen Ann's uncontrollable fear of deep water. The Two Bar spread was on the Little Snake River, and Haley had been credited with trying to get possession of the range in Browns Park where the Bassetts lived. His method, we were told, was to put two or three hundred head over the divide into Boone Draw, about half way to the Bassett Ranch. Here they would be turned loose and allowed to drift along Vermillion Creek and into the Park. It was Ann's custom to collect these Two Bar animals and drive them into the Green River, using any help she could get, but generally the young folks with whom she was always a favorite. When crowded into the river, many of the cattle were swept into the canyon by the swift currents, and those that made the west and south bank drifted up Hoy Canyon to Wild Mountain and Diamond Mountain. Without any supervision, they soon fell into the hands of the riders, who used the "long rope."

. . . This was the beginning of a long friendship between Queen Ann and myself. She was the first woman I ever met whom I both liked and admired.

In *Where the Old West Stayed Young*, John Rolfe Burroughs gives another version of this story, quoting an unnamed girl who was most probably this same Avvon "Leath" Chew: "We were especially active during 1902 and 1903, and we cost Ora Haley hundreds of cattle."

These essentially ineffective tricks by which Ann vented her rage had a more destructive effect on Ann herself than on her enemy Ora Haley. In committing large-scale, illegal, vengeful acts, Ann lost her sense of proportion and stepped over the invisible and somewhat elastic line that the ranchers drew for themselves, behind which they could, with no qualms of conscience, take an eye for an eye, a horse for a horse, and an occasional beef for their table. In her outrage over the pattern of behavior of the cattle barons, Ann denied them any rights whatsoever to peaceful possession of their property. While she was not an actual rustler, she was indeed thinking like a rustler. Her sense of right and wrong had become completely distorted.

Ann had no intention of ever again leaving Brown's Park permanently. Her days at school and her visits to old school friends had never really accustomed her to city life, and she felt at home only as a proud "Bassett of Brown's Park." Perhaps Matt's attraction for her had been that by marrying him she could be assured of a life spent in her home valley.

Matt's death and her mourning period had prolonged her stay at the Bassett ranch, but Ann did not envision living there forever, whether she married or stayed single. With fifteen hundred dollars of her own cattle money she bought a place up on Douglas Mountain called the Smelter ranch, so named because of some long-abandoned smelters from a copper-mining operation started by Griff Edwards many years before. This gave her a home of her own, at least during the summer months. She divided her time thereafter between the Bassett homestead and the Douglas ranch, as she preferred to call it.

She continued to work with Eb and George, although the arrangement was not a happy one. George was mild-mannered, but Eb and Ann were always bickering and often battling. Eb resented Ann's dictatorial, queenlike attempt to assume management of their affairs; he accused her of laziness in doing her share of the housework and in shirking those ranch chores that did not interest her. Eb loved to dress well and was quite a ladies' man himself, but he was impatient with Ann's preoccupation with the gloves, hats, and bottles of cream with which she guarded her complexion, and considered her too self-centered to be a good member of a family undertaking.

Ann was completely unconcerned over Eb's opinion. She did things she considered important, and that meant taking good care of her appearance and her clothes, spending as much time as she chose with her friends in Craig, and riding for pleasure, as much as for business, up and down the valley.

Among the few oldtimers from Brown's Park still living is Rosalie Burton of Vernal, Utah. When she was a little girl named Rosalie Miles, her parents settled in Brown's Park. Her father was eking out a precarious living for his family by raising a few cattle and working as a blacksmith for the neighboring ranchers. Rosalie vividly remembers Ann riding up to the Miles cabin, her back straight and her head held high, singing as she rode, with a side of beef tied to her saddle.

"Maybe it was Two-Bar beef like they said," Rosalie said, "but we would have gone hungry without it. They were good to poor people, both Aunt Ann and Aunt Josie were. We'd be invited to pick apples in the Bassett orchard, and at Christmas they'd be the ones to fix up a tree at the schoolhouse. We wouldn't have had much of a Christmas if Josie and Ann hadn't been there."

Ann was a true Bassett. Even as she killed Ora Haley's stray cows, upstaged George, and fought with Eb, it would never have occurred to her to neglect the acts of thoughtfulness and generosity that were part of the Bassett tradition.

Ann did not want to drift along forever, working with her brothers in an uneasy partnership that was not hers to command. She saw herself as another Elizabeth, but even more successful. Unlike Elizabeth, however, Ann wanted—in fact needed—a man to do the work. For that matter, so did Eb and George. Matt Rash, Isom Dart, and Jim McKnight were no longer available to them, the boys were still inexperienced, and Ann had probably never been attentive to the details of buying and selling cattle. As she went on her visits to Craig and Rock Springs, as she flirted and dallied with one man or another, she was looking for another Matt Rash, someone with the competence to carry her along to where she wanted to go.

Ann finally settled on a man who could help her attain her goals: Hi Bernard. In doing so, she had to adopt Routt County's attitude that "Ora Haley had bought the bullets and let another man shoot them," and agree that when Hi Bernard cooperated with Tom Horn he had only been following orders. Once she had adjusted herself to this charitable attitude toward Hi, he became the logical choice for a husband, for of all the men in the area he was the one most capable of making his own fortune—and Ann's—if he were ever to strike out on his own.

In "Confidentially Told," Frank Willis describes Hi's courtship of Ann—or Ann's entrapment of Hi. According to Willis, Ann wrote a note to Hi, suggesting an interview at her cabin on Douglas Mountain. When Hi arrived he found the petite Ann, curved in all the right places, waiting for him in a pretty dress and smelling of a seductive perfume, with the light of friendship shining in her soft eyes. She proposed a partnership with Hi, using her Douglas Mountain range in the summer and joining with the Bassett brothers in using the winter range down in the valley. "Surely," she may have said, "a man of your ability needs to be building for himself rather than for another."

Hi had never been married, but he had always liked women. He had come to Routt County with a common-law wife who was generally accepted by the people as Mrs. Bernard, but she had disappeared after three years or so, and Hi was now alone. He purportedly told Frank Willis of his reaction to Ann's business proposal:

> She outlined the program in a very business-like way and said, "You are a cow man, and if you are interested just think the matter over and advise me of your decision at some future date." As simple as that. By that time cattle and range was the last thing on my mind. When we were called to dinner I had turned to ashes, and I did sure need a bracer of strong coffee to pick me up, for I had a counter offer to make and it needed a lot of backbone that I was unable to locate just then. So far the most important part of the contract had been overlooked. I did not intend to let that slip away from me. It was not Brown's Park and a jumble of sand hills I was after. It was a wife. I braced myself and boldly said so. It seemed the most natural thing in the world for a man to fall in love with a striking young woman and want to marry her.

So the forty-six-year-old man and the twenty-six-year-old woman were married. The *Craig Courier's* description of the wedding hints at the community's amazement:

> Yesterday evening, April 13, 1904, at the home of Mr. and Mrs. Frank Ranney, were united in marriage Miss Anna Bassett of Brown's Park and H. H. Bernard. Rev. Anderson officiated during the ceremony. The bride and groom are both well known residents of western Routt county. Miss Bassett's name has been heralded in many parts of the country as a member of the Bassett family of Browns Park, most of the stories however being imaginative newspaper talk and entirely unauthoritative. Miss Bassett herself is an amiable lady who has many fast friends in her home locality. Of Hi Bernard it is said he is first in one thing at least, and that is the management of cattle. Mr. Bernard has no equal in this line in Northwestern Colorado. Every foot of the range is familiar to him, and during roundup season he is king. His qualities in this line are attested by the position of foreman he has held with Mr. Haley for several years. The Courier extends to the new couple most sincere wishes for future welfare and happiness.

The canyons of Routt County rang with the news that the grief-stricken sweetheart of the murdered Matt Rash had married the man who had supposedly cooperated with Tom Horn. People waited to see what Ora Haley would say about his manager marrying a woman who had loudly condemned him as a murderer and who had been busily destroying his cattle.

The newlyweds returned to the Two-Bar ranch and the hands threw a party that lasted until dawn. A few days later a telegram arrived from Ora Haley. It may have started with some congratulatory message, but it undoubtedly ended with the statement that Hi was fired.

Ann Bassett had a certain contempt for men, springing possibly from the reversal of roles between her strong mother and her unassertive father. She looked at men as poor weak creatures, and found only in women the qualities of courage, intelligence, and good common sense. Ann believed that she could marry Hi Bernard and then, through her sexual attractiveness and her natural womanly superiority, bring him into harmony with her own plans.

To Hi, living with Ann and her two natures was as difficult as trying to catch a handful of quicksilver. She was cultivated and ladylike, yet bad-tempered and obscene; generous to children and to the helpless, yet arrogant with her equals and an enemy to those above her; ambitious but indolent; loving but imperious; seductive but manipulative. In speaking of Hi's marriage with such a creature, Josie said, "He was in his second childhood."

With Ann on her most attractive good behavior, life was good for both of them at first. Hi filed a homestead claim next to Ann's purchased property on Douglas Mountain—her water supply was more than ample for both—and raised cattle of his own for the first time in his life. The courthouse records show that Herb, probably during a summer visit, borrowed jointly with Eb and Hi Bernard, with a mortgage on the Bassett ranch as security. Hi and the Bassetts worked as a team, just as Elizabeth and Matt Rash had worked in previous years.

Ann had grown up in a house where friends and strangers alike had always been welcome, and she now greeted passersby on Douglas Mountain with the same hospitable warmth. In the summers Ann and Hi would often bring up one of the Park's children to keep them company, and not too long after their marriage Josie sent her son Chick over from Craig to stay with them on almost a permanent basis. To Hi, alone since childhood except for the men in his bunkhouse, the entertainers in Denver's dance halls, and a temporary common-law wife, the experience of being a family man was wonderful. He loved children and was good to them. (Rosalie Burton has remembered for fifty years the little white slippers and white stockings he brought her from Denver.) As for Chick, Hi informally adopted him, and had such a fatherly feeling for him that he made Chick the sole heir in his will.

The year after their marriage Ann undertook a job that was to keep her busy from the first of April well into July for the next four summers. Prudent ranchers allowed their cattle to mate only at a time that would produce calves in the spring. After the spring calving, the cows were segregated from the bulls until late summer. Ann's job was to herd the bulls, and in a letter to Esther Campbell she told how it all began:

> Speaking of wild cattle in Teepee and lower Brown's Draw reminds me of how I became a bull herder. Geo. and Bill Kennon were supposed to have that job. A number of our cattle, some of Sparks, Kennons and Lombards were left or missed on the fall shove off. They were there two or more years and became really wild, so instead of tending bulls at Teepee Geo. and Bill were catching wild cattle. The boys were having a lot of fun—so were the bulls, they were scattered from Lily Park to Cold Springs Mountain. I was not interested in wild cattle so I took over, made a career of it. . . .

Ann watched not only the Kennon bulls but also those belonging to many of the ranchers in the countryside, including Eb and George. All told, she herded around two hundred and fifty bulls; the ranchers paid her a dollar a head, and Eb and George gave her a token trinket, fancy spurs or the like.

Each night Ann left a horse saddled in the corral. As dawn approached and the bulls began to stir and moan, she would know they were getting ready to move. Snatching a handful of raisins to eat, she would ride out to be sure they were ready to graze quietly. Only then could she return to camp for breakfast.

Nobody really "herds" bulls; instead, one drives away any cows that seem likely to approach them. With such a sizable group of bulls, any cow who was in season could have suffered as much as a girl caught in a gang-raping. Ann's days consisted of riding a circuit to be sure that no cows wandered into the danger zone from their grazing in Brown's Draw, and then going to sit on a log high on a ridge with a view of the whole valley, where she could see her bulls below her. She kept a horse saddled in case she had to make a quick ride to drive away any unwary cows, but as long as everything was in order she was free to dream away her day.

In those long, lazy days, Ann began the writing that was to occupy her more and more with every passing year. On paper Ann found relief from the conflicts of her nature; on paper she could create a world, not as it was but as it ought to be. Just as her father Herb had found refuge and dreaming time in his little post office, so Ann now found refuge on her log from the growing unpleasantness of her marriage to Hi.

In the early days of his infatuation, Ann and Hi had formed the partnership that Ann had originally envisioned; its name, the Bassett-Bernard Cattle Company, is indicative of the position Ann meant to maintain in their relationship. Hi's secondary position became very irksome to him. He had been in charge of large undertakings since his twenties and he found it increasingly burdensome to be tied to a woman who, although neither as knowledgeable nor as industrious as he, insisted on being the boss.

Another source of friction must have been their disagreement on what might be called the politics of the range: the rights of big versus little ranchers; sheep versus cattle; stock detectives, rustlers, illegal mavericking, range butchering of stray cattle, and, most of all, Tom Horn. Ann could become enraged over injustice or cruelty, whether to a maltreated animal or oppressed Indian, but she would have had no mercy on Hi's feelings about the big ranchers to whom he had shown such loyalty. If the name Two-Bar was mentioned, Hi could expect an attack on everything that he had formerly stood for. He gradually became taciturn and spent as much time as he could in Denver.

Ann on her part was completely bored by this older man whose eyesight was failing, whose stamina was beginning to falter after an undernourished childhood and almost forty years of rigorous life on the range, and who preferred spending quiet evenings at home with Chick to attending parties in Craig or Brown's Park. She still felt she should do away with a few Two-Bar cows once in a while just as a matter of principle, and of course this would have been anathema to Hi.

They became increasingly disenchanted with each other. Joe Haslem, later a neighbor of Josie's, tells a revealing story about Ann and Hi that happened back in the days when Joe was punching cows for the big outfits:

> There was a helluva lot of rivalry between outfits in those days. Well, both the Sevens and Two-Bar had wagons up at the Smelter this one summer, and Ann and Hi were up there too of course. Well, this Seven cowboy caught a horse out of his string to ride, and he was a bucking horse. The kid was a tough rider, but that goddam horse was hard to ride! In them days when a man got on a horse he got on to stay. This old horse was just bucking around and around, and blowing his wind every time he hit the ground. Well, Ann was riding around behind Hi and kept saying, "I can do better than that, can't I! I can do better than that, can't I!" And old Hi finally said, "Yes, goddammit, I've heard you fart louder than that horse lots of times."

Hi's answer was obviously not that of a man still deeply in love, and what he said was punishingly humiliating to the proud but insecure woman who so passionately demanded recognition as a top-notch rider and cowhand. Hi came home to an increasingly indifferent Ann, who no longer tried to hide her disappointment in him.

The break finally came when Hi returned from an extended trip to Denver to find the cabin on Douglas Mountain occupied by not only his wife but also a woman friend she had brought in. More importantly, a good-looking young cowboy named Tom Yarberry was spending more time in the living room than in the bunkhouse. Hi returned to Denver. After six years, in the autumn of 1910, the ill-conceived marriage was over.

QUEEN OF THE CATTLE RUSTLERS

At the time Hi Bernard was fired from the Two-Bar for marrying Ann Bassett, Ora Haley and the other big cattle outfits were, although they may not have realized it, on the verge of losing their sovereignty over the range. During the years of Ann's marriage to Hi, the balance of power began to tip, slowly but inexorably, to the side of the small ranchers. A new force injected itself into the range wars, none other than the United States government.

Governments are notorious for responding to trouble rather than forestalling it, and this entrant into the battle came fifty years too late. It might have come later than that if the Senators from the cattle states had had their way. But the people of the United States had elected, finally, a President more interested in conservation than in continual expansion and exploitation of the land. Under the authority of Theodore Roosevelt, the government stepped in to bring order out of anarchy and to save what was left of the range from destructive overgrazing.

There is a saying in the west: "First grass, then sagebrush, then cedar." That explains, in a few words, what happened to much of the grazing land after the buffalo were exterminated. John Rolfe Burroughs gives a vivid description of the process:

> Old timers spoke . . . of when the mountains were rimmed with flames and they had run nervous fingers through the hair on their heads wondering how much longer it would be there. Although the country seemed on fire, oddly enough with the coming of darkness the ridges did not glow against the sky nor did trees, suddenly bursting into flame, flare torchlike in the night. But if, save only for the twinkling of stars, darkness prevailed, silence did not. Always and ever—muted by distance or raucously close at hand—the cattle made their presence known. Reddened by the rays of the sun, the columns towering hundreds of feet into the air that some people took to be flame-tinged smoke and others didn't know what to make of, were caused by immense steer herds that, trampling out the grass, none too gradually were pulverizing the country.

This was the cause of the devastation that was taking place on the free grasslands. Too many cattle on the land destroyed the capacity of the land to rebuild perennial grasses, and the grasses were supplanted by sagebrush. Cattle can eat sagebrush in an emergency, but it is such rough fodder that a steady diet can cause a cow to be "brushed." It will die within a few weeks unless its diet is supplemented by food of a gentler sort. Sheep, however, can subsist on sagebrush, and this is the reason why many a small rancher would have liked to turn to sheep. Even here, however, overgrazing by too many animals would eventually destroy the sagebrush and the hardier cedars would take over. The result was land worth nothing to anybody. Worse yet, as overgrazing destroyed the ground cover on the slopes, there was less water retention, more runoff and more erosion. Even the water sources themselves were damaged, which was disastrous in an already arid land.

People had been saying for years that the free range was overcrowded. As Burroughs puts it, "Even the cattle barons admitted privately that there were too many animals on the range and that something should be done about it. Something, of course, that would in nowise restrict their own operations or interfere with profits."

That "something" was begun in Routt County in 1908 when President Theodore Roosevelt established a "Park Range Forest Reserve"—known now as the Routt National Forest—to preserve and foster timberlands and to protect the grasslands within its boundaries from overgrazing. Thenceforth the free grassland was to be used in a manner that would protect it, and access to it was to be apportioned among its present users in ratio to the number of cattle which users had previously grazed there.

Unfortunately, this obviously fair method of allotting grazing privileges pleased neither the big cattlemen nor the small ranchers. A crusty Scotsman named Robert McIntosh wrote to the newly established Forest Reserve:

> I decline in part and in whole your permit No. 74 to graze seventy (70) heads of horses. . . . I came here in the year "one" succeeding the antelope. . . . I have lived on the edge of said reserve thirty (30) years and have yet to learn that sage, buck and service-berry brush will grow into forest timber. Some years ago my band of horses numbered 1,200 head. I then concluded as one of the sovereigns of the country that I had more than my share. I reduced the band to about 100 brood mares, which gives me between 300 and 400 horses, all ages, and now I come in supplication to you for permission to graze in part only 300 head of horses, and to be now by you allotted 70 head. I can stand it, but how are the scores of families going to stand it?
>
> . . . This country or range has been invaded by nonresidents with sheep and cattle, whose families live in cities and towns. . . . The cure for this is no more large herds of cattle or sheep for nonresidents.

The small ranchers, with their small herds and small profit margins, were enraged at what seemed large cuts in the number of animals they could graze, and they agreed with McIntosh that the large out-of-state owners were still getting the better of the deal. All existing users were given the same rights, but to the small ranchers the principal of equal treatment was not as important as the reality of how they were to keep their heads above water. There was a storm of local protest from individuals, from civic organizations in the towns, and from the *Steamboat Pilot*, which called the Forest Reserve "semisocialistic nonsense."

As so often it must when a new idea is enacted into law, the government squared its bureaucratic shoulders and proceeded to implement the new Reserve, knowing that ultimately everybody would benefit. Gifford Pinchot, Chief Forester back in Washington, hired a young, toughly competent local rancher named J. H. "Harry" Ratliff as supervisor of the new Reserve. Ratliff was honest enough, naive enough and stubborn enough to take on the influential townspeople (including his own banker), the big cattlemen, and the small ranchers.

The small ranchers protested loudly, but they could do very little; the big cattlemen were better equipped. When they learned that Ratliff could not be manipulated, they trumped up a false charge that he had sold a mortgaged horse. The first trial was conducted by Presiding Judge Shumate with such obvious bias that one fair-minded member of the jury refused to cast a "guilty" ballot, and a second trial had to be scheduled. For his second trial, Ratliff had additional support from two Forest Service lawyers supplied on orders from Pinchot, who also took the matter to the President himself. Ratliff was proud and deeply gratified when he later found the initials "T.R." on papers returned from Washington.

Perhaps because of Washington's interest, Ratliff's second trial was not marred by any more improper rulings from Judge Shumate. The second jury was chosen from the same community as the first, but by this time sentiment was beginning to change. People had seen members of the first jury riding horses given to them by grateful cattlemen. Although they did not like the Forest Service, their sense of fair play was outraged, and Ratliff was promptly acquitted by his second jury.

The big cattlemen were also fighting Ratliff on the line, bringing their herds up to the now-restricted Reserve. After the second trial, however, many large cattlemen withdrew from the contest or at least held themselves neutral. But one or two continued the battle, and the most vigorous opposition was waged by Ora Haley's Two-Bar outfit. One of its more aggressive acts was to start a stampede as the Two-Bar cattle approached the counting stations set up on the boundaries of the Reserve, hoping to make their frightened cattle charge through the line. Bill Patton, the manager who had replaced Hi Bernard, threw a can of pebbles in among the herd, disregarding the real danger that someone might be killed or maimed by the hooves of the charging beasts. When this attempt failed, other approaches were used, such as slipping the cattle through unguarded sections of the boundaries. Ratliff and his men stood firm, however, and met each attack with a counterattack. There was suprisingly little loss of life or limb even at the height of the animosity, although one young and healthy ranger named Johnny O'Connor died of unknown causes down in the Snake River country; it was hard to determine the cause of death since he was buried hurriedly, with no notification to the coroner and without a death certificate.

In the fall of 1910, while this reduction of the range was still being enforced and slowly accepted, Hi Bernard went back to Denver, leaving Ann in full control of her property up on Douglas Mountain. Ann then did something that perhaps Hi could have restrained her from doing. She added to the problems of the already beleaguered and constricted Two-Bar by closing off her water hole on Douglas Mountain. This was her legal right, but it becomes highly significant as a possible cause of the events of the following spring.

On March 18, 1911, a stock detective named Nelson reported back to his boss, Bill Patton. He had been sent up to Ann's Douglas ranch to see what evidence he could pick up of rustling. Posing as a prospector, he went off into the hills each day, supposedly looking for ore deposits; in reality he sat on a ridge overlooking Ann's cabin, watching what was going on. Within three days of his arrival he could report that some freshly butchered beef was hanging in Ann's storeroom.

On Nelson's report, Patton immediately went back up to Douglas Mountain with his employee and found the hide and entrails of a freshly butchered cow. These were not hard to find, for they were lying in plain view of the road. Although Nelson tried to restrain Patton until more conclusive evidence came along, Patton insisted on secreting the hide in the brush to show to the sheriff and filed an immediate complaint.

Patton's impatience was perhaps caused by the fact that he had some tall explaining to do, and quickly, about Two-Bar's unfavorable profit and loss statement. The local people did not have much use for Patton; his cowboys said that he was nothing like his predecessor, Hi Bernard, who was completely honest and would never have misappropriated any of his own boss's beef. Whatever Patton's reason for hasty action, Ann and Tom Yarberry, whom she had installed as manager after Hi Bernard left for Denver, were indicted and arrested for cattle thievery.

Was she guilty? Of course she was! She had been trumpeting her hatred of Two-Bar from one end of Routt County to the other since the deaths, more than ten years before, of Matt Rash and Isom Dart. She had been actively engaged in killing Two-Bar cattle in those years and had urged her fellow ranchers to do the same. As if that were not enough, it was being rumored that since Hi's departure her new manager Tom Yarberry had been taking small droves of cattle—cattle not belonging to Ann Bernard—down to a butcher shop in Vernal.

If that last accusation was true, then Ann had turned from acts of revenge in retaliation for suffered wrongs to acts of pure of thievery for her own private gain. However, if that was the case, why did Patton prosecute on such a flimsy charge as the one named in the indictment? If that flimsy charge was the only one available, then there seems a certain validity to Ann's contention—and the opinion of a good number of her neighbors—that this was simply an attempt to retaliate for the shutting off of her water hole to the big herds.

The truth is probably somewhere in between. Perhaps Two-Bar's growing concern about profits in this post-Reserve period heightened their concern about rustling. If this is so, then Ann Bassett Bernard was an obvious choice for surveillance, for she had indeed been a thorn in Two-Bar's side. The haste shown in prosecuting her on a shaky case may have been caused by a desire to indict her quickly, send her to prison quickly, and regain immediate access to her water supply on Douglas Mountain.

Ann's trial was a *cause célèbre* in Craig where the trial was held. She had gone to high school in Craig, and had visited friends and gone to parties there since her teenage years. All of Craig was well aware of her feud with Two-Bar and its tragic cause. She was the one who had married Two-Bar's Hi Bernard, arousing endless speculation as to her reasons. She had the glamour of the east about her, with her fancy clothes, her citified accent, and her educated air. Her accuser, on the other hand, was Bill Patton, whom nobody thought much of, the manager of a ranch belonging to a man who had become a hated symbol of everything that people thought was wrong with northwestern Colorado—the nonresident Wyoming cattle tycoon named Ora Haley.

The duel between Ann and Ora Haley aroused such a fever of interest that the citizens of Craig chipped in to rent the local opera house so that more people might cram in to listen to the proceedings. The case came to trial in August 1911, less than six months after Ann's indictment. The citizenry sat through the legal battles between the prosecution and defense, who challenged again and again as the jury was chosen, and through the evidence presented by the prosecution. The evidence was, substantially, that on such-and-such a date Bill Patton and two of his cowboys had examined a hide that belonged to a Two-Bar steer. How could they tell? Well, "someone" had cut out the right flank of the animal's hide, thus getting rid of the brand, but they testified that the steer was still recognizable as a Two-Bar steer because of the method by which it had been spayed. How did they know that it was Ann Bernard and Tom Yarberry who had butchered this beef? Because the hide was found near Ann's cabin and fresh-butchered beef was found in her storeroom.

Ann and Tom were defended by a very prominent pair of lawyers. According to John Rolfe Burroughs, Ann had asked Judge A. M. Gooding of Steamboat Springs to represent her. Not wanting to be embroiled in the affair, Gooding had set the very high fee of one thousand dollars, but capitulated when Ann coyly lifted her skirt and extracted ten hundred-dollar bills from the top of her silk stocking. Gooding subsequently engaged a noted defense attorney, Miles Saunders, to help him be sure that Ann obtained justice.

Saunders had made no objection to the prosecution's reconstruction of the killing of the steer. His contention, supported by the testimony of Ann's brother Eb, was that the butchered cow had belonged to Eb Bassett himself and bore Eb's brand. Eb also pointed out that he had made no attempt to hide the butchering but, innocent of wrongdoing, had left the entrails and the hide beside a commonly traveled trail. And why was the portion of the hide that contained the brand missing? Eb shrugged, as if to say that someone who wanted to frame his innocent sister must have been responsible.

Eb was not the only witness to come to Ann's defense. Two of her cowboys testified, but since both were known to be on the shifty side, they possibly hurt Ann's case. Next, however, came Emory Clark. He testified that, while on the Two-Bar roundup in the fall of 1910, Bill Patton told him that he intended to "get rid of those two s.o.b.'s," meaning Ann and Yarberry. As if Clark's testimony were not enough, a popular young cowpuncher named Chick Bowen testified that only a few days before Patton had filed his complaint against Ann and Yarberry, Patton had said to him that Two-Bar needed Ann's water on Douglas Mountain. Patton had told Bowen that Ann was in the way, and that "he would get rid of Yarberry even if he had to put a job on him."

Although the personal relations between Ann and Hi Bernard had been a continuing subject of gossip, Bernard came all the way from Denver to testify on behalf of his estranged wife, and to contradict Bill Patton's testimony that the spaying methods on Two-Bar cattle were so distinctive that through them a Two-Bar cow could be positively identified.

The final witness for the defense was the one they had all been waiting for. Ann herself, her hourglass figure beautifully dressed, her rich brown hair perfectly coifed, took the stand and answered the questions of her attorney and the prosecutor in perfect English and in well-modulated and clearly enunciated words. She presented a picture of a maligned and abused lady being persecuted by evil men.

It was a hung jury. Two jurors had held out for conviction but ten were in favor of letting her go. As one juror put it later, "We figured she might have done it, but they didn't prove it in court." There was celebration that night in Craig, even though the matter was not finally settled. A new trial was set for Ann and Yarberry for the following February.

When February 1912 came around, the trial was rescheduled for August. In August Ann sent word from Tucson that she was ill and could not appear. Yarberry was there, but the trial was postponed until Ann could participate. Ann's bail, put up by Eb, was declared forfeit. Not until a year later, in August 1913, was the case tried for the second time. Ann appeared in all her well-dressed femininity, but by this time Yarberry had jumped bail and Ann stood trial alone.

The choosing of the jury at this second trial was not as prolonged as in the first. The same evidence was presented, but with one notable difference: Chick Bowen, the well-liked young cowboy who had been such a convincing witness against Bill Patton, had been legally murdered the preceding January by a sheriff up in Baggs, Wyoming.

Back in the period around 1908, the big cattlemen had attempted to have a certain Bob Meldrum appointed deputy sheriff in Routt County. Meldrum had formerly worked with Tom Horn in chasing down rustlers, and had also been a strikebreaker for the mines in Colorado, when the miners had struck for the first time against truly deplorable conditions. The citizens of Routt County had been outraged at this blatant attempt to "legalize" an associate of Horn's by making him a deputy sheriff. Even the *Steamboat Pilot*, which usually supported the big cattle interests, said: "This paper will oppose to the last ditch the giving of any professional man-hunter a sheriff's deputyship, or anything else which would give him a badge of authority for shooting down any of Routt County's citizens. . . ."

Bob Meldrum moved up to Baggs, where he became sheriff and almost immediately he acquired the reputation of using his official position to shoot before asking questions. This was the man who shot Chick Bowen. The *Craig Empire*'s account of Bowen's death had been read by those now attending Ann's second trial:

> As Bowen was leaving the hotel after supper, Meldrum told him he was under arrest for yelling while crossing a bridge on the way home ten days before. All except the marshall considered it a joke at first, but when Bowen's hat blew off and he attempted to recover it Meldrum commenced shooting. The first shot entered Bowen's left leg while the second struck the top button of his overalls and glanced off.
>
> At this stage of the game the cowboy realized that Meldrum was in earnest and proceeded to use nature's weapons on the bad man. With his fists he broke the

> officer's nose and pummelled him until he yelled for mercy. Deputy Sheriff James Davis pulled Bowen off and as he did so Meldrum fired again, the shot taking effect in the groin. . . .

Meldrum's last shot went true. Chick Bowen died the next day and was buried with church services attended by all the law-abiding people in the community. Ann's most valuable witness had been eliminated.

Whether they were justified in their belief or not, the people of Routt County, remembering the attempt to have Meldrum installed legally as sheriff and now witnessing the worst of the local cattle barons accusing Ann of rustling, decided that there might very well be a connection between Ora Haley and Bob Meldrum. The atmosphere at Ann's second trial was even more tense than at her first.

The prosecution and the defense droned on with few dramatic moments, since the evidence had been heard two years before and was thoroughly familiar to the close-packed spectators. One interesting bit of showmanship was displayed when defense attorney Saunders insisted that Ora Haley, then sitting inside the railing next to Patton and the prosecutor, be removed to the spectators' side of the bar for fear he might intimidate the jury. Aside from that, the trial was without many fireworks until Ora Haley himself took the stand.

After the prosecutor's questioning, Saunders took over. Offhandedly he led Haley through the usual questions about his name, his occupation, his place of residence and his position in the proceedings. Still in a routine manner, Saunders asked Ora Haley, "And how many cattle have you in Routt County?"

Haley thought for a moment and replied, "Ten thousand head."

For sixteen long years Haley had been engaged in a legal duel with Routt County, designed to cut his taxes. He refused to accept the county's assessment of the size of his herds, and the county, exhausted by spending scanty tax money on expensive legal action, finally capitulated.

Now Defense Attorney Saunders wheeled suddenly and confronted the witness. "You have ten thousand cattle? Then why, Mr. Haley, did you file a statement just four months ago, stating that you had five thousand, six hundred cattle in this county. *Did you lie*?"

Haley turned red and then turned white. The prosecution entered objections, but they did not matter. Haley stood condemned in the bright light of open court of being a small-minded, money-grubbing rich man who had cheated his fellow citizens of his fair share of tax monies to administer the land that had made him millions. From then on, the course was all on level ground for Ann. After eight hours of deliberation, the jury acquitted her of all charges.

Craig's newspaper brought out the first "extra" in its history, and the *Denver Post* described what happened when the jury's verdict became known:

> BUSINESSES CLOSE, BANDS BLARE—
> TOWN OF CRAIG GOES WILD WITH JOY
>
> After deliberating over eight hours, the jury in the "Queen Anne" cattle rustling case reported at 7:10 this evening. The verdict was not guilty.
>
> This is the third time [*sic*] this case has been tried and the trial has attracted the attention of the entire Northwestern Colorado. The courtroom was packed when the jury's decision became known and the crowd poured into the streets, shouting and throwing their hats into the air.
>
> Cowboy friends of Mrs. Bernard were out in force and the air rang with their revolver shots. Mrs. Bernard was placed in an automobile and paraded through the main streets of the town receiving the congratulations and well wishes of her friends.
>
> This evening Mrs. Bernard rented the motion picture show and invited all to attend. She also is giving a free dance, and a monster banquet is being prepared at the leading hotel.
>
> The business houses of Craig are all closed and a brass band parades the streets in honor of Mrs. Bernard's release. . . .

So it was over. Ann was vindicated before the court and received the adulation of her neighbors. Her vendetta against Two-Bar had been given almost an official blessing. During the trial a Denver reporter had called her "Queen of the Cattle Rustlers" as payment for her rudeness to him but that night Ann indeed felt like a queen and was certainly treated like one. From then on, throughout her home country, people called her "Queen Ann." Each time she heard it she stood a little straighter and held her head a little higher, sensing that her triumph in Craig would become a legend in the country's stories of how the big cattlemen had been finally vanquished by a slip of a woman from Brown's Park. On that night in Craig she took the congratulations of her friends not only for herself but for her mother Elizabeth as well. She was truly "Queen Ann."

Of course Ann exaggerated the importance of her actions in the ultimate withering of the cattle barons. They were all rich men and knowledgeable in the ways of earning riches. When Ora Haley died he left a huge estate, all of it in negotiable securities and none of it in cattle. When the days of the cattle barons came to a close the rich men wisely bowed out, and it was not because of the defiant challenges such as those Ann Bassett had flung in their faces.

Eb was the one who had posted the bail which was forfeited when Ann did not appear because she was ill in Tucson. It is said that Eb drained his personal resources in Ann's defense; the Bassetts stuck together no matter how much they bickered among themselves. Faced with insolvency, Eb went south and waited on tables at a rail stop on the Rio Grande Railway. Since he was as personable as his sisters, it is said that he earned enough money on tips from traveling females to accumulate a stake to start again. He returned to Brown's Park and purchased the nucleus of a new herd—a herd that was purportedly augmented by cattle rustled from Ora Haley.

THE DRIFTING YEARS

One of the cultural opportunities in Craig, Colorado, was its literary society. Among the activities at its weekly meetings was the reading of a handwritten newspaper called "The Budget." On December 8, 1893, the following news item appeared in it:

> There is one general supply store and bank combined; one Drug Store and Post Office combined; two hotels; two livery, feed and sale stables; two blacksmith shops; two lodges; one dramatic company; two saloons; one tonsorial room; one lumber office; one harness shop; one meat market; one printing office; one taxidermy; one flour mill; two carpenter shops. There is several buildings under way of construction. The one attracting the most attention is the new church.
>
> There are in this town about 15 town cows who understand how to steal hay in the cutest manner. Ain't it queer how people will keep so many seemingly worthless dogs.

When Josie McKnight moved to Craig in 1900 and leased the Elmo Hotel, the town had had seven more years in which to grow, but it was still unpretentious, and the Elmo Hotel was just as unpretentious as Craig itself. It was located on the unpaved main street of the town, flanked by modest frame buildings that housed most of the town's businesses. Its first floor consisted of a small office and a large dining room. A steep staircase led to the bedrooms of the permanent guests who boarded there, to others reserved for transients, and to the quarters in which Josie lived with Crof and Chick.

Josie was accustomed to cooking for large numbers of people, but this was her first experience in slinging hash for strangers and she did not like it. Later in life she described a disagreeable chore as being "as bad as cooking for a bunch of schoolteachers." The old lady who helped her was clumsy and slow; the place was hard to keep clean because of the dust kicked up by the horses on the dirt road outside; and when one of the cattle buyers or sales drummers came home late from the saloon and stumbled noisily up the stairs she would be homesick for the peace of Brown's Park and the once-unappreciated luxury of having her home to herself.

Still, there were compensations. The boys were doing well in school, and she could assure Herb that she was taking them to Sunday school every single week. She had many friends in Craig from her school days, and the ranchers from outlying areas who came to Craig for supplies often stopped for a meal and to catch her up on the news, just as her neighbors had done when she lived on Beaver Creek. There was also Charley Ranney to take her fishing and escort her to parties. While he was not an exciting man, he was a welcome change after her battles with Jim McKnight.

Pictures of Crawford and Chick when they were youngsters show two handsome, blue-eyed little fellows dressed in good tweed jackets, each with the bland look of a choirboy. The similarities between them stopped at that point, however. Crawford was almost a complete replica of his Grandpa Bassett; he was mild, peaceable, quiet, loving, rather a dreamer and completely docile. Chick was another Queen Ann. He was an engaging little boy and so amusing that Josie's paying guests enjoyed listening to him and watching his antics, while little Crawford stood by quietly by. Josie believed that children should be busy and occupied and that they should behave themselves. She did not indulge Chick or put up with misbehavior, but he fought her every step of the way.

A born rebel, Chick would not have been an easy child to raise under the best of circumstances. With Josie he was incorrigible, and for one of those sad, strange reasons that so often result from a broken home: he neither liked nor trusted his mother. Chick's widow, Edith Jensen, says that Chick had not liked his mother "since she went away and left him when he was just a little fellow, not even five years old." With the illogic of babyhood, he had distorted the strange disappearance of his mother from his life when Jim McKnight had taken him to Salt Lake City, and when he was returned to Josie physically she had already lost him psychologically.

Perhaps it was the difficulty of raising her boys in a boarding house and her inability to handle Chick that made Josie even consider marrying Charley Ranney. She had first known him when she was in Craig's high school. He had been principal at that time, and she, always an eager and appreciative student, had admired his ability to keep his classes interested in what he was saying. She now became fond of him, respecting his honesty and his uprightness. He had many of the good qualities of Herb Bassett.

Charles Ranney was the town's druggist when Josie moved to Craig. He was an active civic leader, Grand Master of the Masonic Lodge, and member of one of the town's leading families. (One of Craig's principal streets is Ranney Street.) He was a thirty-three-year-old bachelor, only seven years older than Josie. There is a photograph of Charley with his brothers Frank and Louden and Ann and Josie. Charley looks pleasant enough in the picture, though not very prepossessing. Josie would have seen him at better moments, and would have appreciated his good humor, his gentlemanliness, and his obvious adoration of her.

To a woman with small children to raise and the notoriety of a divorce on her record, a well-to-do druggist from a prominent family must have been considered a more than suitable husband. Still, Josie's consent to marry him was ill-advised.

Louise Miller of the Moffatt County Historical Society, who knew Charles Ranney, has said, "It was a marriage between a racehorse and a plughorse. I knew Charley later; we were living near his ranch at Fortification Creek and he was running a filling station then. We would stop, in a hurry perhaps, to get some gas. He would dilly-dally, and wash the windshield and check the oil and finally get gas in the car; but then he would stop to talk and by the time we got out of there we would be in a *lather*. It would have taken us twenty minutes to get a few gallons of gas."

However unwisely, Josie did marry Charles Ranney. In its April 26 issue in 1902, the *Craig Courier* reported that Chick McKnight sang "Dem Goo-Goo Eyes" at the school closing exercises, and in the following week ran the account of the wedding:

> C. A. Ranney and Mrs. Josie McKnight were united in marriage Thursday afternoon by Rev. H. E. Anderson. The wedding occurred at the Tucker residence which Mr. Ranney recently purchased and refitted in anticipation of this happy event. The marriage was strictly a home affair, only relatives of the young people being in attendance. . . .

Josie was freed from her hotel, with a nicely furnished home for herself and her sons, and had the love of a good and honest man. She moved into "the old Tucker house" and, according to a booklet celebrating Craig's Centennial, installed the first windmill ever seen in Craig and planted Craig's first plum trees. Her life was finally settled and secure, and it would seem almost idyllic except for one dreadful but incontrovertible fact: Josie's sons detested the man she had married.

Crawford MacKnight, the docile and gentle boy, was to say of him: "He was not malicious but he was hell on discipline. He was a schoolteacher and we kids had to stay in line. Like the Army, you ask? Hell, it was worse than the Army. In the Army there's a certain slack but there wasn't any slack around him! If he said 'Bounce!' you'd better bounce. He'd been a strict old bachelor too long. I minded my mother because she made you *want* to mind her, but he was cold to everybody, with a not very definite sense of humor."

If peaceable Crof could feel oppressed and miserable, imagine the feelings of the tempestuous Chick! He disliked his mother; he had contempt for Crof because he was a "mama's boy"; and he hated his stepfather and fought him with every weapon he had. He was rude, inattentive, disobedient and openly defiant. Whatever peace the family could have had was destroyed by Chick and his open warfare against them all. The boy's only adult friend was a teacher who took an interest in him and gave him singing lessons.

At the age of eight Chick decided he had had enough. After a severe whipping, which he no doubt deserved, he saddled his pony and ran away from home. He headed for Brown's Park and had gone a good number of miles when darkness fell. There were coyotes out on those lonely stretches, and their howls, plus his hunger, sent him back home again. Josie then bowed to his needs and those of his suffering family, and wrote Ann to ask if Chick could stay with her and Hi on Douglas Mountain. From that time forward, Chick went back and forth, living with Josie during school terms, then in Brown's Park with Hi Bernard and Ann, and later even with Eb, until he was finally grown enough to leave Josie behind him permanently.

When Chick arrived in the Park he was such a hellion that Rosalie Burton remembers with a shudder how he bossed and bullied the children in the school during the terms he spent there. He even attacked the teacher, who was doing what she could to tame the wild bear cub Josie had returned to them. Sending him back showed real wisdom on Josie's part, however, for his Aunt Ann understood him and they enjoyed one another. As for Hi, he treated Chick like the son he had never had. He outfitted him with good boots and saddle, and as the child outgrew them they were replaced again and again. The two of them would ride up to Rock Springs or over to Craig, and since Chick always had money in his pocket for candy or whatever else he wanted, his less fortunate friends would follow him around town, hoping to share in the bounty.

Hi's cowboys had always admired him because he was a leader rather than a driver, and now he handled Chick with the same skill. Although Chick always had money in his pocket, it quite probably was money he had earned, for Hi treated Chick like a man and expected a man's response. He started Chick in the cattle business when he was only ten years old. There was a boggy place down by the Green River where the cows would become mired. Hi helped Chick rescue the calves of doomed cows and gave him dogies to raise for his own. Chick responded to authority for the first time in his life.

Evidently Chick took his manhood seriously. An old-timer told of an incident: "He was taking some horses to the high country. He stopped at the store at Hayden, said, 'Gimme a couple of packs of Bull Durham and a couple books of white paper.' When refused, Chick commented, 'This is a hell of a town, a man can't buy a smoke in it!' " Chick was not even eleven at the time.

Josie had solved Chick's problems, but Crof and she were still chafing under Charley's heavy-handedness. Although she was not a woman to let conventions hamper her, she had been strongly influenced by both her father and the nuns at St. Mary's. If she thought of another divorce she possibly rejected the idea, since her husband was a man against whom she could have none of the complaints that she had had against Jim McKnight. Emotionally and physically, however, she must have been existing in a vacuum under the pressure that Charley put upon her.

Charley was under pressure too. At the time they were married in 1902, a new drugstore was being built in town. Charley's drugstore was possibly out-of-date and may still have held the post office. It was also the office for F. C. Nichols, M.D. The competition from a shining new drugstore must have been overpowering, judging from its advertisements in the Craig newspaper. Even though Charley ran his own ads and, according to the paper, put in a "handsome hot drink fountain," eventually he traded his building for a ranch on nearby Fortification Creek. The new owner of the building converted it into a restaurant-bakery.

A move back to the country may have pleased Josie. But Charley seems to have been more interested in real estate ventures at that time than he was in farming, and it may have only aggravated her further, for Josie was primarily a rancher. One night, it is said, Charley Ranney came home to find that Josie was gone. It may be that she had packed up and left in one of her celebrated storms of temper. Josie always said very little about her marriages, but she did tell a granddaughter, "I would have stayed with Mr. Ranney—he was a fine man—if he hadn't been so hard on the children." It is equally possible that Josie Ranney had met Charles Williams and had, for the first time in her maturity, fallen wildly in love. Chick told his wife that Josie ran away from Charley Ranney with "a man who came to town." If this is the actual truth of it, this would be just as characteristic of the imperious, self-willed Josie as leaving in a temper over Charley's domination.

Although no court record of Josie's divorce from Charley has been located, it is almost certain that she left him in early 1906, just a little less than four years after she entered the marriage. When she was giving her taped interviews she was vague and perhaps intentionally misleading about her marriages.

It is almost impossible to exaggerate the indignation Josie's *second* divorce must have aroused among many of the "good women" who heard about it.

She affronted them even more by moving to Baggs, starting another boarding house, and marrying again as soon as she was legally free. The rapidity of the marriage confirmed the gossip as to why she left Charley. Strangely (and yet perhaps not strangely, considering Josie's charisma) Charley himself does not seem to have held a grudge against her. Nine years later, at Christmastime 1915, Charley wrote Josie a letter, apparently in response to a Christmas letter she had written to him in which she chided him for not coming to see her when he had been in Vernal for a Fourth of July celebration.

> My dear old sweetheart;
> Being particulary sociable tonight (as I am all alone) I'll write you a few lines in answer to the great kick you put up. None of us knew where you lived; Lymon said "in a canyon away over in those mountains along Green River." I believe everyone in the party would have been pleased to have seen you. I looked every day for you as it was big doings in Vernal. I worked my best to gauge the trip so we would spend the 4th in Vernal. Wonder why? Maybe you were not very much put out for it took from July to December to work up that grouch. Now let's be good for you are the only wife I ever had and I don't want to quarrel and I don't believe you do. I expect *always* to think lots of you. . . . Give Dad [Herb Bassett] my kindest regards. I believe he is my friend. I got a dandy [election] vote from Brown's Park and I credit much of it to him. . . . Give my best to your boys. I would like to see them. Tell them to come and see me if they ever get up this way. And now, wishing you a merry Xmas and everything good for the future I remain the same old scout only a little older. My hearty good will and best wishes be with you. Chas to Josie

Josie's new love—Charles Williams of Baggs—was a different man entirely. Crawford MacKnight describes him as "a railroad man and a prizefighter who was also a pharmacist." Ann told Esther Campbell that he was a "sports promoter." In the "Baggs Budget" column of the *Craig Courier* on October 16, 1905, it was noted that "Charles Williams, Snake River's favorite 'pug,' will go to Craig and Hayden to fight a match with someone who has been sending challenges from that country."

Nothing else is known about Charles Williams. He and Josie were married on July 12, 1906, and by November of that same year the marriage was over. Crawford MacKnight, always close-mouthed about his mother's marriages, said only that they lived in Brown's Park for a while, that he had been good to Chick and him, but that he was "a city man who didn't like the country."

Josie filed for divorce in 1908, giving the cause as "desertion" in November 1906. There is a flaw in her petition for divorce: she gives marriage date as February 11, 1906, when in reality the license was issued July 12, 1906. Most probably the February date was when she left Charley Ranney.

Exactly how and where Josie spent the years after her separation from

Charles Williams in 1906 is unclear. In her tapes, Josie herself gives a poignant glimpse of the dissatisfactions of that period:

> I wanted to do something, to get away off somewhere. I wanted to be in the hills—I didn't know what I wanted! I didn't want to be in town; I knew I had to at school time. And every year as long as the boys went to school I went with them, I went and located right there so I knew where they were every night. They finished school in Craig, and then they finished high school in Baggs. And then they were ready to go to Rawlins, so we moved to Rawlins, and they finished high school in Rawlins, the both of them. Then Crawford went to Mary University in Rock Springs [where again she ran a boarding house] and Chick "outlawed" on me and went home, back to Brown's Park, and went to work with the cattle. He wouldn't go to the university, said, "I'm not interested and I'm not going to stay." Then he went home to my father. Then Crawford finished in the university [one year] and we both went back to Brown's Park.

Josie returned to Brown's Park with a new husband, Emerson "Nig" Wells. Finally, in the summer of 1911, she could look forward to staying in the Park permanently and to resuming the ranch life she had left so many years before.

Everyone who has talked of Nig Wells has spoken highly of him. He was an all-around good rancher—Crawford said it, Joe Haslem said it—and "a helluva nice guy." He had only one problem: he was a serious alcoholic, and every so often would drink to the point of delirium tremens. Between binges he was a "peach of a fellow," well-liked and competent.

To Josie, the move back to Brown's Park must have seemed like the end of a ten-year bad dream. Nig and she rented the old Davenport ranch from the bank which then owned it, and she was once again back into the rhythm of ranching that she knew and loved so well. Nig himself had been range foreman for big cattle outfits before he decided to try ranching on his own, and was highly proficient.

Everything was propitious except for his drinking problem, which the doctor said was beginning to affect his health. Josie hated whiskey and despised drunkards, but Nig was too fine a fellow to walk away from and she was not going to give him up to alcohol without a struggle.

In those days (and well into the 1920s at least) one could purchase substances advertised as guaranteed to kill the craving for strong drink, which could be put into a man's coffee without his even knowing it. Josie decided to use "the Keeley Cure" on Nig Wells. The Keeley Cure was advertised in the local newspapers as "a positive and permanent cure for Liquor and Drug Addictions," and was administered through the Keeley Institute in Salt Lake City, part of a widespread network of such establishments. Evidently a person with a problem could go away for "the cure," but it is probable that there was also something that could be administered at home, for both Esther Campbell and Josie's daughter-in-law specifically refer to the Keeley Cure as a medicine Josie was using for Nig.*

The New Year of 1913 approached, and a big dance was planned over at Linwood, on the Utah–Wyoming border. Utah was a dry state, but Wyoming was wide open, so a dance hall had been built in Linwood just over the Wyoming line.

Josie told the story on one of her tapes:

> He [Nig] was a good man, a good farmer and as good a man as ever lived, and he got on those whiskey drunks and went like foolish people. I didn't want to go, but the Rifes came—Guy Rife and his new wife and another Rife boy and his wife—and they wanted to go to Linwood. . . . I didn't want to go. I thought, now if we go there they'll all get drunk. Wyoming was a regular honky-tonk . . . and those men proceeded to go to that honky-tonk and get drunk.
>
> Well, there was a dance and I stayed at the hotel with Mrs. Rife—we had rooms at the hotel [Minnie's hotel]. Mrs. Rife's husband, Orrin Rife, he didn't drink at all, but he couldn't get those fellows to the room to save him.
>
> Mrs. Guy Rife wanted me to go with her to the saloon to get the men. I said, "I didn't take them there and I never went to a saloon, ever, and I'm not going. . . ."
>
> I knew an old Mexican. He worked in Brown's Park—forget his name, old Joe something, an old man. He came over and told me, "I hate to tell you, but Wells is terribly drunk. They're running a game and I stole his watch away from him and his money and I brought it to you." I said, "Why, that was a wonderful thing for you to do. That wasn't stealing at all, you were just protecting him, and me too."
>
> . . . Well, I didn't know what to do. I couldn't get him away from there. We danced the first night. I went to the dance and tried to stand it all I could. I couldn't do anything else! I went with Minnie and a whole crowd of women and went to the dance. . . . That was New Year's Eve and they danced all night till sunup. I didn't. I went home and went to bed. The next night they danced again. I went for a little while, and went back and went to bed.
>
> The next morning there was a man from Kansas City—a horse buyer, I forget his name. He was a very nice man, and he came to see me and said, "I think your husband is ready to quit drinking." He said he hadn't had a thing to eat, not a thing but whiskey, and he said, "He's down in the living room." It was just kind of a bunkroom–living room . . . a cot over here and a cot over there and a big stove in the middle. I went, and he was there.
>
> I said, "Wells, I brought you a cup of coffee. Do you think you can drink it?" He said, "I'll try. I feel like hell this morning." I said, "As soon as it comes sunup and

*If this particular concoction was similar to another famous "cure" widely used at that time, it probably contained caffeine and strychnine, or at least tartar emetic, which was supposed to produce vomiting if a man drank. Tartar emetic is also a heart depressant, according to the book *Nostrums and Quackery*, issued by the American Medical Association in 1912 in its campaign to discourage the use of patent medicines.

> time, we'll start for home." We had a team that wasn't very safe, kind of a tricky outfit. But I thought, I can drive anything to get out of here.
>
> So he drank a little of the coffee and he didn't drink any more, and I helped him get his shoes on and helped him get his sweater on; then I got a basin of warm water for him to wash his face and I said, "Now, if you can eat some breakfast, I'll bring it over here. I think you're too shaky to go up that hillside with ice on it, back to the other hotel." . . .
>
> He said, "I won't want any breakfast, I feel like hell." He kept saying that to me and I said, "I'm awfully sorry, but I can't help. You did it yourself." He kept acting like he was sick to his stomach, and I said, "Are you going to throw that whiskey up? I wish you would." So I got a slop bucket and set [it] there by him on the bed, and I saw that he was wrong. Something was wrong. . . .
>
> The horse buyer said to me, "If I was in your place I'd give him a drink of whiskey. He needs it." And I said, "I think he needs anything *but* a drink of whiskey, but if you think that's all right, I will get it. . . ."
>
> I gave Wells a drink . . . then I combed his hair and put the bottle back. . . . Well, he kept turning—kind of twisting around like he was in misery somehow, I don't know what. But I knew he was wrong. And finally he just straightened right back and died. He threw up a little kind of foam, right from his lungs of course. . . . Well, I laid him down and I didn't know what to do. I was stranded. I was just— I might as well have been drunk. . . . There I was, clear up in Linwood thirty miles from home. . . .

A cowboy from Brown's Park named Charley Olmey was there. He went up to Green River City with Josie's team and buckboard to buy a casket. The women laid Emerson Wells out as best they could and put him outside in the freezing cold. Josie talked to the local constable, but there was no one to sign a death certificate or hold an autopsy. When Charley Olmey came back the next day, they put Wells' body in the buckboard and took him back to Brown's Park.

> We took him back there, and then the next day I took him down and buried him by Uncle Sam, down in that cemetery. It was on the— he died on the third day of the month of January and was buried on the seventh. We didn't get around with all that performance before the seventh. And the whole country was there. There were lots of people in Brown's Park then, lots of people.

Josie was not a crying woman. It would have been characteristic of her to go to the dining room and announce calmly that Nig was dead. But such behavior would have added fuel to the fire of rumors that started almost before Nig's dead face was covered with a sheet. People were astonished that a comparatively young man had died so unexpectedly, and for no apparent reason except for a ripsnorter of a three-day drunk. The town of Linwood had seen a lot of men go into the saloon and stay there until their money ran out. Drinking even huge amounts of whiskey was not accepted in Linwood as a cause of death. In addition, Linwood soon heard that Josie had been angry with Wells and that on that last morning of his life someone heard her say, "If I give you this drink it will be the last one I ever give you!" It was more believable to lots of people that Josie had poisoned Nig Wells than that he had died of acute alcoholism.

Consider Josie's position: Both Ann and she had been so popular with the men when they were girls with their free and easy ways and forceful personalities that the more proper women had whispered, "Those girls are fast!" Josie's "early pregnancy" and hasty marriage to Jim McKnight must have given credence to this opinion. Then had come divorces from McKnight, from Ranney, and from Williams. Nor was it forgotten that she had shot Jim McKnight. Now she was back in Brown's Park and a fourth husband had just died under mysterious circumstances.

It does not matter whether the women of Linwood were morally outraged or merely envious of a woman who had four husbands while most of them had been limited to one. The wolf pack fell upon her, and the leader of the pack, its prime instigator, was Minnie Crouse Rasmussen.

Of the two hotels in Linwood, one was run by Minnie, a daughter of Charley Crouse of Brown's Park. (She was later widowed and remarried; now she is known locally as Minnie Crouse Rasmussen after her second husband.)

Minnie had been sent to school outside of the Park, and her education was as good as that given the Bassett girls. When she finished her education, her father Charley had sent her over to the Linwood area to homestead a particularly nice meadowland, planning that both his sons and he could join Minnie in using the graze for their horses. The site of that homestead is still known as "Minnie's Gap." By the year 1912 she had married a carpenter named Knud Ronholt and had moved in to Linwood, where she had built a social position as strong as that of the Bassetts in Brown's Park. She was young, sprightly and very popular in the area. Minnie's strong position in Linwood explains why she could play such an important role in the aftermath of the events surrounding the New Year's dance.

In recent days, when Crawford and Flossie MacKnight were asked about Minnie, Flossie spoke up very quickly, saying that Minnie had spread a terrible story about one of her aunts. "She's a liar, isn't she, Crawford?"

Crawford, as temperate and tolerant as his Grandfather Bassett before him, thought a moment before answering. "Well, I wouldn't say she is a *liar*." He hesitated again. Then, in a burst of candor he said, "But she was a hateful, spiteful little piece of furniture. If she didn't like anybody she'd pour it on 'em. I never did see eye to eye with Minnie." He hesitated again. "I liked her. . . ."

That, indeed, was the problem Josie was to face. Everybody liked Minnie Crouse Rasmussen.

Minnie reported that she had heard Josie and Nig arguing and had also seen Josie prevent a woman from taking a glass of milk that she had prepared for Nig on one of the nights during his three-day drinking bout. To the question, "Could it have been poison?" the popular verdict was, "Of course! It must have been poison!" When a more realistic person reminded the gossips that Josie had been questioned by the local constable, Minnie retorted that "Josie wrapped him about her little finger!"

Minnie was so sure Josie was guilty that she prepared an article for publication in the *Green River Star* that hinted heavily at dirty dealings and said, "It is the opinion of those who saw Wells just before he died that he swallowed poison, perhaps strychnine, as his actions were similar to the actions of men who had been known to die of the effects of an overdose of that drug." The article also stated that "the man and wife are said to have had a fuss."

The *Green River Star* evidently refused to print the accusation, but Minnie kept a copy of what she had written until her old age; then she turned it over to Dick Dunham for use in his book *Flaming Gorge Country*. Dunham presents the unprinted article in such a way that a careless reader could overlook the fact that it was never published. In her later years, Minnie also gave a little vial to a local man for his personal collection of memorabilia, stating that she had found that bottle in Josie's suitcase. When she was in her nineties she was still accusing Josie of having poisoned Nig Wells, and by this time was also accusing her of stealing a buttonhook and a piece of embroidery from one of Minnie's baby dresses.

Minnie's absolute certainty that Josie was guilty carried many people along, and soon the whole mountain area was ringing with the tale, which grew to ridiculous proportions. A story was told that some cowboys had dug into Nig Wells' grave only to find an empty coffin; this was expanded into a version that said the Vernal sheriff was the one who dug up the grave and found no corpse. It was easy for them to explain what was done with Wells' body—obviously Josie had thrown it into a deep ravine on her way home from Linwood.

Dick Dunham cites one fantastic tale in *Flaming Gorge Country*—and he stresses that it is fantastic—that Josie, summoned for questioning, faced down her accusers by appearing with a six-shooter strapped to her waist and a rifle in her hand. The author of this book was told emphatically by one woman that Josie had killed *all five* of her husbands, getting rid of one by sending him out on the ice on the Green River when she knew it was too thin to hold him.

The people who knew her must have pooh-poohed the idea that a woman as smart as Josie would have gone to Linwood armed with poison to kill a man while half the country was there to watch her. They also would have agreed, knowing Josie's temper, that if she had been angry enough she would have killed Wells, but that her style would have been to grab a gun and shoot him, right there on the night they were fighting about his drinking, rather than to wait until morning and sneak poison into a glass of whiskey. As for the Vernal sheriff's finding an empty grave? Neither the Brown's Park people nor the Vernal sheriff would let murder go unpunished if they could help it. Murder was different from minor cattle thievery.

That Josie felt real grief for Emerson Wells is unquestionable. He might have been her fourth husband, but he was closer to a compatible match than any of the other three, and she had cause to mourn him. As she lived and relived his sudden and inexplicable death, her mind may have gone back to the Keeley Cure. Could it have thrown his system off? If so, she must have suffered remorse as well, reflecting ruefully on her foolishness in trying to make a good man perfect.

A. H. "Herb" Bassett: husband of Elizabeth, Ann and Josie's father.

Josie Bassett McKnight Ranney, at left, with her second husband, Charlie Ranney, at far right. Ann Bassett is seated in front, with Louden Ranney, and in center back are Esther Davenport and Frank Ranney. (*Flossie MacKnight*)

The Bassett cabin in Brown's Park, located near the spring and sheltered by cottonwoods, overlooked the Bassett orchard and hay fields and the valley below. Herb Bassett stands outside the fence; some McClure in-laws of son George Bassett stand within. (*Flossie MacKnight*).

"Queen Ann" Bassett around the time of her marriage to Hi Bernard. (*Denver Public Library, Western History Department*)

Hi Bernard was a good rancher but was fired as manager of Ora Haley's Two-Bar Ranch for marrying Haley's archenemy, Ann Bassett. (*Flossie MacKnight*)

"Uncle Sam" Bassett: miner, prospector, government scout, and an early resident of Brown's Park. He beguiled his brother Herbert into forgetting California and settling in Brown's Park with him. (*Flossie MacKnight*)

Elbert "Eb" Bassett, Herb and Elizabeth's son, brother of Ann and Josie. He ranched in Brown's Park and was a "fancy roper," but took his own life when its problems seemed too burdensome. (*Flossie MacKnight*)

View of Brown's Park from the Bassett cabin. (*Esther Campbell*)

Crawford and Flossie MacKnight circa 1917. (*Flossie MacKnight*)

Ora Ben Haley, Wyoming cattle tycoon and owner of the Two-Bar Ranch near Brown's Park. (*Archives and Western History Department, University of Wyoming Library*)

W. G. "Billy" Tittsworth, whose reminiscences in *Outskirt Episodes* caused the Bassett women much distress. (*Utah State Historical Society*)

Tom Horn, the stock detective who instilled real terror in rustlers and honest men alike, throughout Wyoming and Colorado. (*Ms Wilmot McFadden. Rock Springs Public Library, Rock Springs, Wyoming*)

Butch Cassidy in a "mug shot" taken at Wyoming State Prison shortly before he became known to the Bassetts by his real name, Bob Parker.

below, Isom Dart, a master cowhand respected by all who knew him, was another victim of Tom Horn. (*Denver Public Library, Western History Department*)

Madison M. "Matt" Rash—rancher, president of the Brown's Park Cattle Association, and Ann Bassett's sweetheart—was ambushed in his cabin by Tom Horn for alleged rustling. (*Flossie MacKnight*)

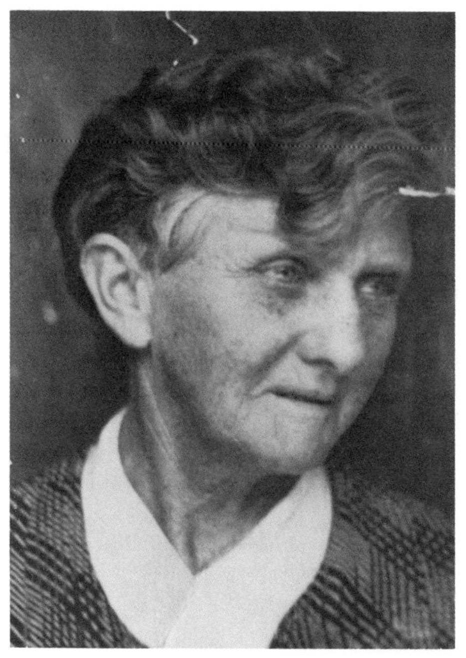

Josie Bassett in her middle years, when she was Josie Morris. ("*The Jensen Book*," *Jensen, Utah*)

Josie with her granddaughter Amy around 1920, when she still wore skirts and her hair was long.

Ann and Frank Willis. (*Esther Campbell*)

Ann Bassett Willis in her middle years. (*Flossie MacKnight*)

Josie still chopped her own wood when she was more than 80 years old. (*Flossie MacKnight*)

Josie with Ann and Frank Willis at her cabin on Cub Creek and *below,* inside the cabin. *(Esther Campbell)*

Josie Morris and Esther Campbell taken when Josie was queen of the Vernal rodeo. (*Esther Campbell*)

Flossie and Crawford Mac-Knight, and Josie with Chick and Edith McKnight, who were visiting Josie after 38 years' absence. (*Flossie MacKnight*)

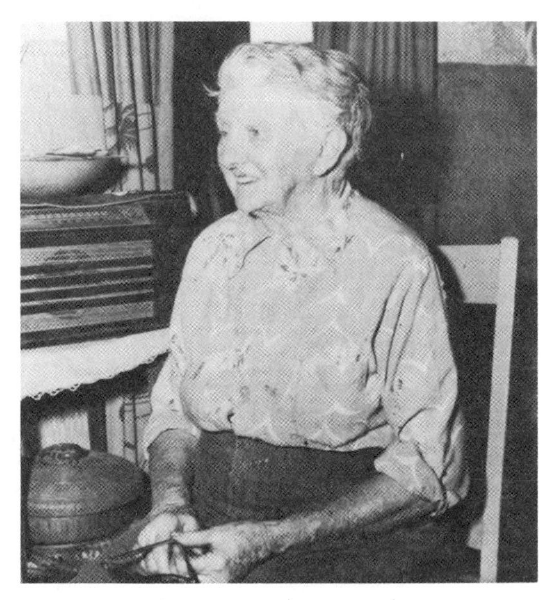

Josie Bassett Morris in her 80s.

CUB CREEK

Nig's death left Josie at loose ends, living on a rented ranch which she had no money to buy. Her boys were grown, and although this released her from town boarding houses it also meant the loss of their companionship. Nig Wells had replaced her boys in her life, but he was dead, and even her grieving for him was affected by the poisoning story. Moreover, she was thirty-nine years old, an age when most women start looking for gray hairs as they stand before the mirror. She must have felt an urgent need to continue living in the quiet of the country and establish herself before she got any older. Yet without money to buy a going ranch, the only way open to her was to find a homestead and pull herself up by her bootstraps, building as her mother had built before her.

The only land then available for homesteading was down near Vernal, Utah, so to Vernal she must go. No doubt she felt a strong wrench at leaving what had always been her real home, even during her years of living in town, yet the old patterns had already been broken. Ann, whether she won or lost her second trial, to be held that summer, had no intention of returning to Brown's Park. Herb would never again stay in the Park permanently; he was too happy in his old soldiers' homes. Her brother George had married a schoolteacher named Ruby McClure, who was polite but certainly not cordial to her husband's notorious sisters. Although Eb would have welcomed her at the Bassett ranch, Josie could not have considered becoming a satellite to anyone, especially to her brother Eb. The changes brought about by tragedies and the passing years had blunted any sadness at her leaving.

She planned to leave for Utah in the fall when her lease on the ranch expired. In the meantime, she managed the ranch with the help of Ben Morris, a cowhand who had been working with Nig Wells before his death. Ben Morris was an Oklahoman who had drifted into the Park like so many cowhands before him. At the age of thirty-four he was still a drifter, but he was a good cowpuncher, capable and very strong.

Ben was also a handsome man who knew how to talk to women. He had a good sense of humor and was a nice enough fellow to have around. Perhaps because of an overriding need for comfort in her bereavement, Josie overlooked other facts about Ben: he was uncouth and shiftless, and eventually he proved to be downright dishonest.

Josie's affair with Ben Morris destroyed whatever vestiges of affection Chick might have had for her; more importantly, she almost lost Crawford too. Josie's boys had lived a pillar-to-post existence in Craig, Baggs, Rawlins and Rock Springs, in years that had lost them their father Jim McKnight and given them a succession of stepfathers. Chick was evidently unforgiving, but Crawford had at least tried to understand his mother's needs. When she settled down with Nig Wells he must have been happy that his mother had a good man whom he could like and respect, and he grieved along with Josie at Nig's death. He found it hard now to sympathize with her new attachment.

Chick had not lived with Josie since he had refused to go to college. Now Crawford also tried to find other places to be, and went over to Craig to work for a while. When his job was over, he came back to Josie's for a visit. As he rode past her corral, he noticed twenty or thirty sheep with a nose-brand he recognized as belonging to Henry Nebb, a sheepman on the other side of the mountain for whom Crawford had sometimes worked in the summers. "He was a nice old fellow and an honest one," Crawford later said. "If he owed you a nickel you'd get it."

Crof looked at the sheep and went on into the house to talk with Josie about them.

"I really know nothing about them," Josie told him. "They're Morris's business, not mine."

"They'd better be your business, mother! Those sheep don't belong to Morris and they can get you in a helluva lot of trouble."

Crawford was disgusted at Ben for stealing the sheep and at Josie for not being aware of it. He rode over the mountain and talked to Mr. Nebb, telling him that he figured that sooner or later the matter would come out if the sheep had not been acquired legally. Mr. Nebb told him he already knew where his sheep were. "I hate to cause your mother trouble, Crof, but something will have to be done about it." Crof agreed, and promised to drive the sheep back over the mountain himself, a promise which he kept.

Crawford hunted up Chick, and the two teenagers went back to confront Ben Morris. Surly and abusive, Morris told them to leave him alone, that it was nobody's business but his own. Chick and Crawford then jumped him. Morris was a powerful man and it took both of them to beat him, but beat him they did. Chick was so furious that he hit Morris on the head with the butt of his gun and raked him with his spurs. The boys vented on Morris all their stored-up anger and embarrassment, and left him lying on the ground, bleeding and unconscious. Josie was frightened at that merciless beating they had given Ben and started to berate them, so they exchanged a few words with her, too. Then both of them left, after telling Josie what they thought of her choice in men.

At that particular time Josie may not have cared too much what her sons thought of Ben Morris. She had her own future to worry about and she knew very well what grueling labor was ahead of her, once she found her homestead. Possibly she recognized Ben's failings but overlooked them, knowing that he could give her the help she would need.

Ben was still with her when, in the late fall of 1913, after the hay had been harvested and part of the cattle disposed of, Josie emigrated to Utah. Crawford came back to help her and Ben, and together they herded the stock (one hundred and fifty sheep and fifty head of cattle, Josie was to recall) over Blue Mountain to Jensen, a small Mormon settlement about fifteen miles east of Vernal. Crawford then left to join Chick, who had already gone to work for their father, Jim McKnight.

Soon after Josie and Ben reached Jensen, Josie must have decided that she should legalize their relationship. Perhaps she felt it prudent to conform to the standards of her new Mormon neighbors; perhaps she wanted to pacify her sons or relieve Herb's anxiety at her irregular relationship; perhaps she was really in love with Ben Morris; or perhaps she was too obstinate to admit she had made a mistake. Whatever her motivation, marry him she did. On November 24, 1913, a marriage license was issued to Josephine Wells, age thirty-nine, of Brown's Park, and M. B. Morris, age thirty-four, of Jensen, Utah. It is highly doubtful that any of her family gave them a wedding celebration.

They put their stock with Joe Haslem to be pastured for the winter. Ben got a job at the gilsonite mine near Jensen, and they lived in rented quarters while Josie searched for a likely place to settle. Just west of Vernal, a portion of the lands reserved for the Utes had been opened up for settlement a few years before, and it was Josie's hope that she could still find a good homestead. She spent most of the winter riding the area, almost convinced that she had come too late and that any desirable land, meaning land with water, had been taken. Then someone suggested to her that there might be something available nearer to Jensen, down along Cub Creek, near Brown's Park and Vernal. She remembered traveling the area once on a ride from Brown's Park, over Douglas and Blue Mountains before dipping down into what was generally called the Gorge.

When Josie rode out to explore, the Green River was too dangerous to ford because of the spring breakup of the ice. She therefore crossed the Green by way of the bridge at Jensen and backtracked through two steep, narrow canyons. For ten miles she followed a primitive trail, no more than a wagon track, before she reached her destination. But once she arrived, she forgot all about the long hard ride.

At the base of a high ridge, which was actually the last shoulder of Blue Mountain, she found land heavily covered with a tangle of brush fed by strong springs, signifying that crops and pastures would flourish there once the ground was cleared. Except for one ranch halfway back along the trail to town, there were no settlers for miles around. This meant that, in addition to the one hundred and sixty acres she could claim, there would be space for livestock to graze in the surrounding public lands. Most pleasing of all was the beauty of the area, with its huge bluffs towering over the spot where she would build her cabin. This was not just a place that could be made into a paying ranch—it was a piece of land that she could grow to love. It was another Brown's Park, another beauty spot.

When Josie put her signature on her homestead claim, she was making a commitment that she intended to keep for a lifetime. As Ben and she started clearing brush for her first vegetable garden, she knew she would be sowing seeds in that garden for countless springs thereafter. She set out the saplings of plum and apple and apricot trees and knew she would still be there when they bore their fruit. They lived in a tent that first summer and carried their water from the spring, and only as autumn approached was Ben able to build two one-room cabins, one for them and one for Grandpa Bassett on his visits to them. They were small and barely adequate, those first two cabins, but Josie was content, for once again she was living on her own ground. All things would now be possible to her, given time and a willingness to work, and these two things she had in endless abundance.

Not long after Josie settled on Cub Creek the second Bassett arrived, none other than Queen Ann herself. Ann had been as much at loose ends after her victory in court as Josie had been when Nig Wells died. Now Ann decided that she also would move to Utah. She bought an already proved-up claim on South Fork in the hills across Cub Creek, about five miles or so from where Josie and Ben were located, and supplemented this purchased land with her own homestead on an adjacent piece of ground. Herb Bassett came home for the summer and at least supervised the building of a cabin. (Flossie MacKnight remembers Herb building with his own hands a "two-holer" that was an engineering marvel.) Ann stocked the ranch with sheep, not too many but enough to satisfy any grazing requirements. Josie was chopping brush to establish fields, but Ann had no such plans.

The enthusiastic celebration that had greeted Ann's "not guilty" verdict must have left her feeling that she was destined to be the Robin Hood of northwestern Colorado. She still intended to continue her battle against the cattle barons, and soon it was rumored in the countryside that she allowed her ranch to be used as a waystation for rustlers bringing cattle into Utah from the north. It is not likely that the flamboyant Ann would have been accepted as the leader of a group of men who needed secrecy, but her ranch could have been a "safe" place and Ann could have shared in the profits. She would have needed money to satisfy her expensive tastes and to hire men to make improvements on her property, for Ann never worked as Josie was working. Her primary need, however, if she did indeed work with the night-riders, was to act out her fantasies of herself as another Elizabeth. However, the title "Queen of the Cattle Rustlers" was a shabby distortion of her hard-working and basically honest mother.

At this time a fifteen-year-old youngster named Duard Campbell was working on Willis Johnson's summer ranch on Blue Mountain with his friend Azur, one of Johnson's sons. When the father would head for Vernal on business, the two boys would watch him start down the trail on his high-stepping pacer and then immediately head out to visit Queen Ann. There was an element of hero worship in the affection Duard would always have for the glamorous Queen Ann; he and Azur listened to her tales of her travels and her battles against Two-Bar with open mouths and uncritical ears. Sometimes, as a gift for their hostess, they would steal a couple of watermelons as they passed the Daniels ranch on their way to South Fork; or they would go by Josie's place, grab a goose, take it to Ann to cook, and then invite Josie herself to come dine with them. They were full of high spirits, and they loved the equally high-spirited Ann.

Duard later told his wife Esther that Azur and he once went to Ann's ranch and found a large group of strange men there, surely from another part of the country. "They were probably some of Ann's riders," said Duard, "maybe from as far away as Montana."

The story seemed believable to the boys and would have been credible to many of the Jensen people, for they looked with suspicion at the two Bassett sisters who had invaded their God-fearing community. Life in the Jensen area was nothing like what Josie and Ann had left in Brown's Park. They got along well with most of the other ranchers—Joe Haslem was to say that Josie Morris was the best neighbor he had ever had—but they were alien to the Mormon townspeople. Josie may have missed the dances and the sociability of the Park, but she was too busy to bother too much about it. It was Ann who became easily bored; Josie once said that Ann could never be satisfied if it were too long a ride to town. Ann left periodically and spent time in the cities. When that world proved even duller than South Fork, she returned either to her own ranch or to stay with Josie. She was a bird of passage, going and coming with the seasons like a migrating swallow.

As could have been predicted, before two years had passed Josie was thoroughly sick of her marriage to Ben Morris. He was essentially a crude man who increasingly annoyed the well-bred Josie. She herself was relaxed and colloquial in her speech and she had an earthy sense of humor, but she had been reared in a cultured home where courtesy and good manners were taken as a matter of course. Josie's family tells the story of one suppertime when Ben stopped shoveling food into his big mouth long enough to tell Josie that her gravy was lumpy. She had been clearing brush all day and her temper flared. She grabbed the bowl of gravy and poured it on him, saying, "Then wear it, you son of a bitch!"

His mistreatment of a horse brought on their final separation. Ben used a spade bit, guaranteed to control any bucking or misbehaving horse but cruelly and painfully. Josie came in one night from the corral in a fury because she had found one of their horses with a pitifully ripped and bloody mouth. That was the end of the marriage as far as she was concerned, and she stressed her point by running him off with a frying pan. Later at the Jensen store they asked Ben what had happened. "She gave me fifteen minutes to get off her property," he told them, "and I only used five of them."

Once Josie no longer had to live with Ben she could afford to get along with him, and they became friends of sorts. Ben would drop by to see her, bringing his new wife along, and once in later years Josie helped him in a way that must have made him forget any lingering resentment at her attack with a frying pan.

Ben had been up on Diamond Mountain and, as was the custom of the country, unhitched his horse in front of a small cabin and prepared to spend the night. The cabin was unoccupied but several bags of grain were stored there. Ben had already settled himself for the night on those bags of grain when some Greek sheepherders, owners of the grain, flung open the cabin door and shot him, no doubt thinking he deserved it for trespassing. Although he had been shot in the side, Ben managed to get his gun out and kill one of the herders, whereupon the other two fled. Ben then plugged up his wound temporarily, saddled his horse and rode on down the mountain to Vernal, where he turned himself in to the sheriff.

The sheriff put Ben in a cell, apparently planning to keep him there until his case came up for trial. Josie heard of this treatment of a wounded man who should be in the hospital, and was as enraged as she had been over the horse with a torn and bloody mouth. She marched down to the jail, bandaged his wound properly, bought him a new shirt to replace the one stiffened with blood, gave the sheriff a piece of her mind, and then borrowed money for Ben's bail so that he could be taken to the hospital for proper attention. Josie never bore a grudge against any of her discarded husbands.

During the approximately two years that Josie and Ben had spent together,

Crof and Chick had been living at Jim McKnight's ranch. Chick was especially happy there, for Jim had Arabian thoroughbreds and Chick loved to work with horses above all things, unless it was displaying the fancy roping he had learned from his Uncle Eb. Eventually Chick headed for the ranches in Nevada; while his family usually knew where he was, they seldom heard from him.

Crawford, however, when he heard that his mother was alone again, showed the deep and faithful love he would always have for her. He came back to live with Josie, who was delighted to welcome him and immediately included him in plans for her future. As far as Josie was concerned, Crof and she were full partners in her homestead; however, she pointed out that their potential on Cub Creek could be made even better if they obtained summer grazing rights up on Blue Mountain. So Crawford went up to Blue Mountain in 1915 to homestead his own piece of ground. Josie continued to chop brush and dig irrigation ditches to enrich the home place in the valley, while Crof made his contribution to the partnership by homesteading.

Crawford spent as little time as he could on the cold and lonely mountain. He sometimes came down and worked with Josie, but since she was as good a ranch hand as any man she often handled the work on Cub Creek while Crof earned needed cash by working for other ranchers. He was working in Jensen when he went to a Mormon dance and met Flossie Murray.

Flossie was the daughter of one of the established and more well-to-do farmers in Jensen. Her family was staunchly Mormon. On her father's side she was the granddaughter of Jeremiah Hatch Murray, who had come to Utah as a child, and Karen Maria Nilsson, who had come from Denmark and made the hard journey across the plains to Salt Lake City on foot as a member of the "Handcart Brigade." Her credentials on her mother's side were equally impeccable, for her mother Emma was a daughter of Nathan Hunting, the first bishop of the Mormon church in Jensen.

Flossie was a tiny girl and almost beautiful, with dark hair, black eyes that were brooding even as they were bright, and a classically proportioned profile. From the moment she set eyes on Crawford MacKnight he was practically married, for her teenage prettiness covered a strength of will and a determination that nearly equaled Josie's.

Crawford was unlike anyone Flossie had ever known. He was soft-spoken, well-mannered, well-educated, with the Bassett courtliness and sparkle, and there was a relaxed easiness and good humor about him that her own family completely lacked. Flossie's mother was a highly religious woman who kept an immaculate but cold house, directing any warmth she possessed to the Lord in prayer rather than to her children.

Mrs. Murray had taken Flossie out of school at the end of the eighth grade, declaring that her help was needed in feeding the ranch hands and keeping the house. Living as she did in a constricted, moralistic, and humorless home, and helping her mother in a dull routine of household duties, Flossie must have looked at Crawford almost as a being from another world. Fortunately for her and for Crawford, the strength of her will withstood the efforts of many of her family to dissuade this good Mormon girl from marrying a "gentile" who was also "an outlaw from Brown's Park." Such was the Park's reputation among these pious people.

Crawford introduced Flossie to his mother and his Aunt Ann, and they welcomed her warmly. Ann decided that Flossie must be taken to Brown's Park to be introduced to the rest of the Bassetts. She therefore directed Flossie to meet her at Josie's cabin, from whence they would ride over Douglas Mountain to see George and Eb.

Ann arrived at Josie's cabin riding a troublesome stallion with a tendency to balk. She was accompanied by a cowhand named Frank Willis, who had been living at her ranch on South Fork. The three of them set out for Brown's Park, spending an uneventful night on Douglas Mountain and arriving the next day at George's cabin, where he lived with his wife Ruby, his daughter Edna, and whichever of Ruby's relatives were still in the area.

When Eb heard that Crawford's fiancee was in the Park, he rode over and, with all the imperiousness of his sister Ann, promptly appropriated Flossie and took her back to the Bassett homestead where he was living. He intended to prepare their meal and become acquainted with her, but then Ann arrived and announced that she herself had come for dinner. Eb was not pleased for he had wanted to talk to Flossie without Ann's overpowering presence. Giving Ann permission to cook whatever she wanted, he took Flossie down to the old apple orchard. There he grilled some beefsteak for just the two of them. Flossie was enjoying her conversation with Eb when Ruby McClure Bassett arrived to complain that Flossie had not come back to her place so that she herself could get to know Flossie better.

After this confusing visit with the various factions among the Bassetts, Flossie started out on the return trip with Ann and Frank. As they reached the top of the mountain, they were caught in a storm. It was cold and raining, almost sleeting, and at one place the trail was so narrow that all three dismounted and led their horses rather than take the chance of being hurtled over the cliff. When night came, they sheltered themselves in an abandoned cabin, and Ann directed Flossie to feed the horses while she herself started to cook a meal.

Flossie was slipping the feed bags over the horses' noses when she looked up to see three wolves on the slope above her, watching her interestedly. With quivering legs and trembling lips she ran back to the cabin and blurted out that there were wolves outside. Queen Ann replied, "Don't be so cowardly! They won't hurt you."

The trio continued their ride home the next day. When they came to the place where the river must be forded, Ann decided that Flossie had the most trustworthy horse and should lead the way. It was almost winter, and ice had already formed at the mouth of the creek that was the entrance to the ford. Frank chopped the ice away to make an access hole, and Flossie plunged in, swimming her horse when the water became deep, while Queen Ann shouted instructions to her all the way across the river. Her horse reached the other bank, followed by Ann's balky stallion and Frank's small buckskin, and at Jack Chew's camp up on Blue Mountain they stopped to dry their wet clothes. Strangely enough, Ann and Frank seemed to find nothing out of the ordinary about their adventure.

Until that time Flossie had lived almost a town life on a farm on the outskirts of Jensen, and her riding had been no more adventuresome than going after the sheep her father pastured on the river bottoms a few miles from home. This wild ride was her introduction to what the Bassetts took as a matter of course. These outgoing, articulate people, with their warmth toward each other that could change to bickering in a flash, were as foreign to her experience as feeding horses while watched by fire-eyed wolves. But nineteen-year-old Flossie had a streak of adventure in her own makeup, and she found that she was enjoying herself. More than ever she defended these "gentiles" against her family's criticisms, even pointing out that Grandpa Bassett preached just as much religion to her as she heard while sitting in the Jensen Ward church on Sunday morning, and that Crawford MacKnight was just as fine as his Grandpa Bassett.

It was 1917 and the United States was sending its boys to Europe to make the world safe for democracy. Crawford was drafted, and despite her family's objections Flossie married him the day before he left for the Army. Rather than live with her disapproving family, Flossie went to stay with Josie until she could learn exactly where Crof was to be stationed; then she announced that she intended to join him. She left Josie's ranch and took the old wooden horsedrawn stage to Salt Lake, where she could board a train heading for Washington state.

On the first part of her journey she had the company of Grandpa Bassett. Disapproving of his daughters' ways, Herb never wanted to stay permanently with them. Josie insisted that he stop his wanderings and stay with her permanently, letting her take care of him in his old age, but Herb had had enough of living in the back country, and he wanted to return to his old soldiers and his Sunday school. To avoid argument he packed his bag, saddled a horse and rode on down to Jensen. There he left the horse with a farewell note for Josie. He was headed for the home at Tracy, Illinois, which he had visited before and which was one of his favorites, since he had found there a couple of old soldiers he had known in his days in the Army band.

He returned to Josie's the following summer, for he could not stay away long from this daughter whom he loved despite his disapproval of her, but at the end of the summer he insisted on returning to Tracy. When Herb reached the home in 1918 he was more than usually tired, for a heat wave had followed him across the country, and his journey in the open-windowed railway coach had been hard on an old gentlemen of eighty-six years. Soon after he arrived he was talking quietly to someone when, just as quietly, he died.

In one of Herb's letters to Josie he had mentioned that as he wrote he could hear the gun salute and the bugle playing taps for a departed soldier. Now taps was played for him, and he was buried there in Tracy. His family never disturbed his body to bring it back to the graveyard in Brown's Park. This would not have displeased Herb, for Brown's Park had never been his true home.

THE LAST LOVE

Soon after Josie moved to Cub Creek she had the annoyance of a lawsuit filed against her by Ben Daniels, owner of the one other ranch on Cub Creek. Ben's grandfather had homesteaded the ranch, and until Josie's arrival no neighbor had settled near them. She had claimed on ground that Daniels was accustomed to thinking of as his own, but he had no legal quarrel with her right to homestead. Water was more precious than land, however, and he could properly be concerned over the water rights to Cub Creek.

Ben took her to court, and the verdict was that he was entitled to all water rights on Cub Creek. This was not enough to force Josie to abandon her homestead, however, because she was able to retain the use of her strong and reliable springs. She was warned, however, that if the water from her springs overflowed into Cub Creek they could then be considered tributaries and could therefore be claimed by Daniels. From then on, especially during the early spring months when runoff from the cliffs was at its peak, Josie would flood her own fields rather than let any of her spring water drain into Cub Creek.

When Ben Daniels sold his ranch in 1917, Josie was not at all unhappy to lose her inhospitable neighbor. The new owner first leased and then sold the ranch to Ed Lewis and his father, a well-to-do banker in Walsenberg, a southern Colorado town.

Ed Lewis was a bachelor in his mid-thirties when he moved to Cub Creek, a tall, strong man with a quarter-strain of Indian blood that gave character to his darkly handsome face. For the first time since she had left Charley Ranney, Josie found herself interested in a man who was not only a rancher and an outdoorsman but was also on her own cultural level. Ed came from a well-educated family and shared her enjoyment of good literature. They were once found reading poetry aloud to each other, both of them visibly moved by the beauty of Tennyson's imagery. Aside from a five- or six-year discrepancy in their ages, they seemed to match perfectly.

Josie developed an easy intimacy with Ed as they lived apart on their separate ranches but spent as much time together as they could, oblivious of the local gossip about their obvious attachment. This comfortable relationship developed while Crof and Flossie were away from home, and might have continued indefinitely except for the complications caused by their return.

Flossie had not wanted to come back to Utah after the Armistice. She had been given training as a nurse's aide in an Army hospital and had worked happily and effectively all during Crawford's Army service. She had wanted to stay in Washington after the war ended, for she loved its damp greenness and its cities, which offered undreamed-of glamour to a young girl from Jensen, Utah. She returned only because of Crof, who not only missed the openness and arid grandeur of his home country but also wanted to continue ranching with his mother.

Crawford was let out of the Army almost immediately after the Armistice, and they arrived home before Christmas. Flossie was then far advanced in pregnancy with her first child, who would be born in February. Crof and she took over Grandpa Bassett's little cabin, which gave them a certain amount of privacy, but the family all ate together in the "kitchen cabin" where Josie slept. When it became obvious to Flossie that she could expect Ed Lewis to be staying for breakfast more often than not, she was both embarrassed and ashamed. Surely she did not openly challenge Josie, but her disapproval must nevertheless have been obvious. It was an uncomfortable situation for both women.

It is easy to sympathize with Flossie. She had been raised to believe that the neighbors' opinions were almost as important as those of the angels in heaven, and Josie's disregard for convention was outside Flossie's experience. She had no defenses against the embarrassment she suffered when her Mormon family condemned her scandalous mother-in-law. It is also easy to sympathize with Josie, whose pleasant love affair had been disrupted.

The presence of Ed Lewis at the breakfast table was not Flossie's only difficulty. She now says, "Josie was just as good to me as my own mother was," but one kitchen is too small for two strong women. No matter how makeshift their life in Washington, Crawford and Flossie had been in charge of their own household. Now Flossie found herself living with a woman whose will was even stronger than her own, who assumed the direction of Crawford as a matter of course, and who treated Flossie herself as a beloved but immature daughter rather than as a grown woman with equal status.

Flossie was accustomed to boiling her clothes over an outdoor fire, taking care of chickens, and working in the garden, but she had never before milked cows, chopped wood, or done the heavy labor considered man's work in ordinary households. This set her apart from Josie, who could dig post holes, string barbed wire, rope a calf and brand it if there was no man around to do it, and who thought nothing of butchering a cow or a deer and carrying it home on her horse. Crawford was much like Herb Bassett, who had always worked better with someone else in charge. Josie directed Crawford's days, working just as hard as he did, if not harder, then returning to the cabin to announce what they would cook for supper. Flossie felt resentment against the unaccustomed labor and even greater resentment at being treated like a child.

Flossie's position in the household is almost pitiably summed up by the fact that, as the children were born and started to talk, they called Josie "Mother" and called their own mother "Flossie."

Flossie found life in the isolated cabin boring and lonely compared to life in Jensen. Huge demands are made on Mormons. Their lives are regimented by their church, which expects its members to respond to a church request as if it has come down from heaven. By no means, however, are Mormons naturally puritanical. Dances, socials and community celebrations are actively sponsored by the church, and these intensify the feeling of fellowship already strong from common work and common worship. Serving the Mormon church is a pleasurable way of life. Flossie was not a devout Mormon (although she always sent her children to Sunday school), but now, marooned in the back country, she missed the activity and sociability she had known in her girlhood. It would have been more bearable for her if she had shared the love of the outdoors that filled many needs for both Crawford and Josie. They loved to go fishing, hunt arrowheads, or take a ride up the mountain to shoot a deer. Flossie found her pleasures only on her infrequent trips to town, and even these were marred by her mother's near-estrangement from this prodigal daughter.

Perhaps because of such strained conditions, Josie moved over to Ed's ranch and left Crof to handle things at home, although she still came back to help with the work and still expected Crof to follow her instructions. Crof himself expected this direction and did not chafe under it. Possibly to soothe Flossie's feelings, Josie told her that she and Ed had gone to Salt Lake City and been married there, but Flossie was to say of this, "I never saw a marriage license and I never quite believed her."

The relations between Flossie and Josie remained strained. Flossie's unhappiness might be eased by having a kitchen of her own, but nothing could reconcile her to the hard work and isolation of Cub Creek, and she still resented the mother-in-law who was responsible for keeping her there. Josie, unable—or unwilling—to understand anyone who preferred town life to the country, discounted Flossie's complaints as childish and unimportant.

Flossie's dissatisfaction was caused partially by exhaustion, since she no more than weaned one baby before another was on the way. Josie made no effort to hide her disapproval and genuine concern, and pointed out that Flossie was not only wearing herself out but was quite likely to produce unhealthy babies if she continued to be so prolific. Josie contended that cows cannot produce good calves season after season, nor could Flossie. Flossie, determined to adhere to the religious convictions of her church, looked on Josie's advice as unwarranted interference and enticement to sin. She continued to live as she believed all decent women should, and was to have five children in eight years.

Flossie had gone to her mother's home to have her first baby, a girl born February 24, 1919, whom they named Amy. By the time her second child arrived in November 1921, a boy they always called Boon, Josie was living with Ed Lewis. Flossie went up to his ranch for the delivery, with Josie as her midwife. Belle came along less than two years later in January 1923, and was born in Grandpa Bassett's old cabin. Josie came over from Ed's to deliver the baby, but the tensions between the two women were so great that she went back to Ed's immediately after the delivery and left Crawford to care for Flossie and the new baby.

If these two women could not get along when they lived five miles apart, one can readily imagine the strains when the affair between Josie and Ed ended abruptly and Josie came to live again in the impossibly crowded cabin on Cub Creek. Her return must have created havoc. Flossie might have preferred that Josie live in open sin rather than have her back in the house again.

The problem between Ed and Josie probably arose from the obvious difficulty of two strong-tempered people attempting to live together. If Ed Lewis had expressed his anger in the same way as Josie, life might have been easier. Josie would flash off quickly, usually for a good reason, but once her anger had been vented she became her sunny-tempered, courteous self again, never holding a grudge. When Ed's anger was aroused (sometimes because of jealousy, founded or unfounded in fact) he brooded and withdrew into a silence that lasted for days. It is a pity they could not resolve their personality differences, for the separation left them both the poorer.

Ed had become almost a grandfather to Crof's children, and that relationship was never severed. When Crawford and Flossie finally moved to Vernal, Ed stayed at their home when he went to town, for a day or two or for a month, depending on how he felt. The children continued to think of him as their grandfather and he continued to act like one, even feeling privileged to complain when the girls got to the age when they experimented with lipstick. When the children were at Josie's place in the summer, they would ride over to see Ed. Josie's granddaughter Betty says they used to steal Bull Durham from his tobacco can and go up in the woods to smoke it.

After their separation, Josie and Ed were politely formal to each other; he addressed her as "Mrs. Morris" and she responded with "Mr. Lewis," making it clear to everyone concerned that there was no longer anything between them. This made it embarrassing for everyone when they happened to meet at Crawford's house; but Ed was tactful enough to take himself off when Josie came to visit, and everyone grew accustomed to the situation.

But bitterness could not continue forever between two neighbors. Soon it became "Jose" and "Ed" if they happened to meet each other out on the trail, and although they did not "visit" each other, each turned to the other in need. When Ed broke his leg he managed to ride down to Josie's; she splinted it and took him in to town. Another winter, Ed was in the hospital with a lung punctured by a fall from a horse. It happened that it was a bad winter when the trails were impassable, and Josie knew that his horses must be hungry. She had no hay to spare, but she hitched up a bobsled and managed to get down to a place where there were young cottonwoods along the creek. She cut them down, then rounded up his horses and took them to the cottonwood grove where they could eat the tender bark and survive until Ed's return. In later years Ed would stop for supper if he happened to be near her cabin. In other words, they became neighbors in the Brown's Park sense of the word, salvaging at least something from the wreckage of their intimacy.

When Josie returned to those two one-room cabins on her homestead, Flossie already had three small children and was well advanced into another pregnancy. A new cabin had to be built; in truth it was long overdue. Pig Canyon (as the family called it) was a three-sided box and the cabins at its mouth were flooded by every heavy rainstorm and even by the runoff from melting snow. The ground on which they stood had to be shored up continually to prevent gullies from undermining them. Now Crawford and their ranch hand Dan Nelson finally got around to building a new cabin, this time at the foot of another box canyon on the property with an equally good spring. In addition to a living room and a kitchen, there were three bedrooms: a large one for Flossie and Crawford, one for Josie and one for the children. When the new baby Frank was born in December 1924, the family had already moved into it.

Again there was the backbreaking labor of clearing dense thickets of brush for new pastures and gardens. Josie worked with the axe and the hoe while Crof and Dan Nelson erected the cabin. It was while she was hacking at the brush that Josie made a revolutionary about-face and abandoned one of her firmly held principles.

The day of the flapper had already begun in the big cities of the east, but Josie had her own standards of what was proper behavior for a respectable woman. She had been disapproving when Ann had taken up smoking, rolling cigarettes from her own sack of Bull Durham, and even more so when Ann switched from riding horseback in a respectable divided skirt to riding in *pants.*

Josie herself had always done her rough outside work in long skirts she made for herself of old-fashioned blue and white mattress ticking. They were cumbersome and ugly, but indestructible. She now came to realize how much more practical pants would be. Once she had donned her first pair of bib overalls for work in the brush and had experienced her first freedom from long, bulky skirts, it was no time at all before she decided it was equally practical to wear pants for riding into town—neat pants, well-cut pants, but pants nonetheless. And once she had appeared on the public streets in those pants, in spite of the furor she had thought they would cause, she never went back to dresses. Except perhaps for an occasional wedding or funeral, she would always wear twill breeches with a western cut. Pants became her uniform.

As she chopped brush in her new bib overalls, she still wore her curly hair piled in a knot on top of her head. One day a particularly vicious thorn branch entangled her knot, and Josie was forced to cut her hair loose with her axe. That was enough! She marched into the house and finished the job with a pair of scissors.

Putting on pants and cutting her hair may have been symbols of a change in Josie's thinking that grew out of her breakup with Ed Lewis. Josie had never been promiscuous but she had always wanted a man beside her; and she was, in her own way, conventional enough to want to be married. (Actually, her reputation suffered from this; she might not have gained such notoriety had she been content with a succession of illicit but discreet affairs.) When she left Ed's ranch she was in her later forties but she had the vitality and appeal of a much younger woman. She scorned the cosmetics that Ann used so lavishly, but she groomed herself well and consistently used cold cream and lilac water. Physical labor had kept her lithe and supple. (Even in her very old age she carried herself with a relaxed straightness.) She certainly should have had no trouble finding another husband, had she wanted one.

But Josie said once to Joe Haslem, "I'm a good judge of men, Joe, but a very poor judge of husbands!" It seems as if she now decided that she could not live with any man who had the strength of character she admired because of her compelling need to manage her own affairs. She may have made a conscious decision to live without a husband, alone if need be. She in no way became a man-hater, but her family all agree that there was never another man in Josie's life who mattered to her. If she ever again took a lover it was to be transitory, an impulse of the moment—and so discreet that her grandchildren all seem sincere when affirming that they had never known her to have a man at her ranch who did not bed down in the barn or in the children's bedroom.

Josie continued to amaze the women in Jensen, who normally stayed in their houses or their vegetable gardens, seldom visiting the barnyards or corrals. As Josie's granddaughter Betty puts it, "They didn't want the embarrassment of seeing a stallion mount a mare." It shook their sense of decorum to see Josie ride up, speak pleasantly to them—she was so pleasant they could not really dislike her—and then go out to lean on the corral fence as she transacted her business with their husbands, as comfortable as if she had been sitting in a parlor. From behind their curtains they watched this strange, free woman, with pants covering her trim body and a broad-brimmed hat on short curls only sprinkled with gray, as she stood in the sunshine with a straightforward smile on her freckled face, talking of crops and cattle and horses. To Josie it would have seemed natural, as a rancher, to talk with other ranchers.

The opening months of 1925 found the family in serious disagreement, with two strong women pulling in different directions and Crawford trying to please them both. The future of the homestead was not in raising large numbers of cattle; those days had passed forever as the range filled up. Instead, they were concentrating on a small herd, probably never over two hundred head, of registered white-faced Hereford cattle, serviced by their own bull, a massive creature named Prince Albert. These and a small flock of sheep were all that their graze would maintain.

Since Crawford had given up his claim on Blue Mountain when he had been called into the Army, they had no summer range and had to use their valley property for summer grazing. This made it necessary to buy hay to supplement what they had raised for winter feeding. The years 1920 and 1921 had been terrible in the cattle market; prices had dropped out of sight at the end of the war. While the market was gradually recovering, even 1924 was not a banner year. Times were hard, and since they could not afford to eat up their "capital," the family lived on venison and pork sideback from their own pigs.

Josie was as optimistic as ever, telling them, with truth, that times would improve. Crawford himself was not sure they would ever be able to make a decent living without a summer range, and there was absolutely no possibility of obtaining one. They had no money to buy ground, and Flossie absolutely and passionately refused Josie's suggestion that they try to find another homestead on the mountain. Life there would have been so completely isolated, so bleak and rough during the winter months of the claiming period, that she could not and would not consent to it.

Flossie was doing her best to persuade Crawford to move to town, citing the obvious fact that soon Amy must start school. Josie resisted their move, believing that they could eventually turn the ranch into a profitable operation. She pointed out that the children could be taught at home in their younger years and be prepared well for high school, just as she herself had been prepared by her parents. All it would take was a little effort, and it was an effort Josie was capable of making successful.

But Flossie was adamant. Now, if ever, she could escape from the life so intensely distasteful to her, and could again become mistress of a home of her own. The peaceable Crawford was pulled first one way and then the other, but the battle between his wife and his mother could have only one outcome, given Flossie's determination.

They moved in to town and Crawford got a job clerking at Kelly's Mercantile. Later he was to work as a blacksmith, a carpenter, a sheepherder and a cowboy, on road construction crews and on surveying parties, even on WPA during the Depression. He always looked for the job that would bring him the most money to support his ever-growing family, and was never able to do more than live at a subsistence level until World War II finally brought a measure of prosperity to the country. He spent the war years in Salt Lake City as a guard at the big Bingham copper mine, and used his talents as a cook by working at a restaurant.

Flossie worked too when they moved to Vernal. She had a job for a time in Vernal's hotel, and later took in old Jack Chew, whose family had sent him down from Blue Mountain on the excuse that he was too fat to ride a horse any longer, but the real reason was that his wife and grown children were happier without him. By the time Jack reached Flossie's home he was an innocuous old man who caused no trouble and spent his time playing cribbage and checkers with other old duffers or with the children. The money received for his board and room was a help in their hand-to-mouth existence.

They lived in Vernal, then moved to Jensen and back to Vernal again before finally settling down on a piece of land left to Flossie by her father. But there was peace between Flossie and Crawford, and he was as acquiescent and good-natured as his grandfather before him, content as long as Flossie was happy and the children were fed.

Josie kept right on running the ranch with some help from Dan Nelson, who had been working with her for quite a while. Crawford's leavetaking made no difference in her plans; it only made them harder to accomplish. She accepted her defeat without bitterness and wasted no time in bemoaning it. Crawford still came out, when he could find time, to help in the seasons of heavy work, and she still considered him her partner, for they had shared in building up the ranch, erecting the new cabin, raising cattle and planting crops. Nothing had really changed as far as Josie was concerned, until Crawford dealt her a blow that was more disastrous than his moving to town.

It might have been avoided if Crawford and Flossie had been better managers. Unfortunately, Crawford could deny Flossie nothing that he could possibly give her, and Flossie herself was childlike in handling money. Flossie was an energetic worker and an expert at making something out of nothing when money was tight (it has been said of her that "she could make a Sunday dinner out of flour and water if she had to"), but when money was available, it seemed to vanish. Bananas, oranges, marshmallows, breakfast cereals, and all sorts of factory-made goodies were then appearing on the shelves of the stores, even stores out in the country. Flossie could not resist them, nor could she resist giving lavish presents at Christmastime when the stores were full of toys. Crawford's wages trickled through her fingers; money was spent on a pretty plate or a trinket for one of the children or patent leather slippers for Amy to wear to Sunday school. When they moved to town, Josie had given them a down payment on a piano so that Amy could have music lessons, with the understanding that Crawford would then be responsible for the monthly payments. It was only one of several monthly payments that had to be met.

When they had returned from World War I, there had been only one automobile in the whole town of Vernal; now times had changed, and ranchers were buying cars and trucks. Crawford and Flossie had real need for a car of some sort, because the days of a wagon pulled by a team of horses were almost gone.

Pressed for money, Crawford thought of his shares of the cattle out on Josie's ranch. He was not optimistic about Josie's chances of permanent success. Even though 1927 was a good cattle year, and prices were better than since the end of the war, he knew that one summer of drought, one hard winter when cattle froze on their range, one year when cattle again sold for less than it cost to raise them would ruin them. He therefore did not feel he was doing his mother any great disservice when he told her he intended to sell his share of their stock to settle a huge bill at the grocery store, to regain the repossessed piano, and to buy himself a car.

The grandchildren will remember forever the scene that followed. Josie was frightening in her violence, and even grabbed a kitchen chair and brought it down with such force that it shattered. Josie understood the economics of small ranching even better than Crawford, and she knew that bad times could ruin them. However, she also knew that to diminish the herd now, just as it was of a size to provide cattle for sale each year without undermining its basic integrity, was to give up before the battle had even been started. Crawford and Flossie had dealt a crippling blow to her plans for growth, and she raged at them as she had never raged before. She screamed at their short-sightedness, their shiftlessness, their lack of faith in what was possible now that times were better, their rejection of her chance for a success that would make them *all* secure.

But in the end she was forced to accept what she could not change. From then on she kept a few dairy cows and a small number of heifers to fatten through the summer in hopes of a good fall market, but her great plans of attaining long-term financial security were over. Prince Albert, the magnificent bull, went up for sale with Crawford's share of the herd.

Amy remembers the years when neither woman had a good word to say about the other, the years when a truce had been declared but the weapons still kept polished. Their attitudes softened in time, and each learned to live with the other. Josie was always to be upset by what she called Flossie's "childish ways," but she learned to stop trying to make her over and accepted her as she was.

Young Flossie, so defiant and unforgiving when her mother-in-law was the dominant force in Crawford's life, later found Josie to be as loving as she was demanding. For example, when Betty was born in 1927 in Jensen, Flossie's own mother did not come to visit the new baby until it was three weeks old. For the first time Flossie could look back on the times that Josie had delivered her babies at the detested Cub Creek ranch and remember their warmth and gaiety as well as their frustrations.

Perhaps the most significant turning point came in 1930 when Flossie suffered a near-breakdown from too many babies, too much work, and too many adult responsibilities. Crawford took her up to the Black Hills and into Wyoming while Josie kept the children at the ranch. They worked together in Wyoming, Crawford as a salesman for a woolen mill and Flossie as helper to a woman who ran a restaurant and gift shop. They reexperienced their first days of marriage when they had been alone and together at Camp Lewis in Washington, and then came home renewed and relaxed, with Flossie again able to take up her responsibilities.

Flossie knew that Josie had given her this chance. Her resentment melted away, and the normal annoyances between a woman and her mother-in-law were offset by her respect for Josie and her debt of thanks. Flossie learned to be generous too.

After the birth of Betty Ann, in 1927, it had seemed that five children were to be enough for Crawford and Flossie MacKnight. However, in 1935 they started what was almost a second family with the birth of another girl, Jane. She was followed in 1937 by Dorothy, and in 1940 by a sickly little girl named Wilda. The birth of a stillborn boy, who died before he was named, brought Flossie's child-bearing to a close.

ANN AND EB

Josie had lost Ann as a near neighbor even before Crawford and Flossie left the ranch; however, Ann was to come back so regularly throughout the following decades that she was still a continuing presence in everyone's life. Her reason for leaving South Fork was a cause for happiness to them all, for Ann Bassett Bernard had, at the age of thirty-six, decided that she could sincerely love Frank Willis, her intimate friend for several years, and that a marriage to him would be successful. The years were to prove that Ann chose wisely.

Frank had been born in Reeceville, Tennessee, in 1883, four years after Ann's birth in Brown's Park. He had come to Colorado in 1900 to work as a surveyor on one of the engineering marvels of that period, the road leading over Rabbit Ears Pass on the western face of the Rockies just before the mountains give way to the Yampa Valley at Steamboat Springs. When the road over Rabbit Ears was finished, Frank adopted the life of a miner and then of a cowpuncher, wandering around in Wyoming and western Colorado. He worked for a time at the Two-Bar when Hi Bernard was its manager. It is said that Frank was once offered five hundred dollars to get evidence to convict the Bassetts of rustling, but that he had refused because he thought Two-Bar was trying to "set them up." During another period he lived at the Bassett ranch with Eb, and also had lived with Hi Bernard for a time when Hi returned to run cattle in Brown's Park after his divorce from Ann.

Frank was married at one time and had a daughter (who became a Catholic nun and corresponded with Frank until the time of his death). The marriage was an unhappy one, for his wife was harsh and domineering. While Frank was living with Eb his wife came there, either for a visit or an attempted reconciliation, and made Frank so miserable that Eb considered he did Frank a kindness when he insisted that she leave.

Frank was a self-educated, keen-witted man, keen enough to keep the interest of the intelligent Queen Ann. He had a witty sense of humor and a fund of good stories from his years of roaming the cattle country. He never worried about making a lot of money, and on occasion he liked to drink a little too much. He was more or less like the character in the song he used to sing to Crof's children when he got out his old banjo—a "Rovin' Gambler."

Considering Ann's need to dominate, Frank Willis was indeed good material for marriage, for all he needed was direction—something Ann was able to give in abundance. He sincerely loved Ann, and was more than willing to be "straightened out" if it meant that he could marry her.

He came home tipsy one night when Ann and he were visiting Crawford's family, and Ann beat him over the head with a broom, shouting, "You worthless, no-good drifter! You *shall* not behave this way!" Frank seemed to thrive on such treatment. He was always perfectly willing to do what Ann told him. Josie said to him once, "The Devil has it in for you, Frank, and is paying you back in wives." But if marriages are ever really made in heaven, this was one of them. Ann would rage at Frank and then throw her arms around him, saying, "Oh darling, I've been so cruel! How could I do this to you!" And Frank lived through her tantrums for the pleasure of her company.

Their marriage was a stable one, but its stability was gained in many different places and many different occupations. Childless, they could afford to adapt themselves to Ann's restlessness and her need for variety. They spent many summers with Josie, Ann simultaneously delighting and exasperating the whole family with her "Annisms." Then they would be off again for a new job in a new environment.

They married in 1923 and moved to California shortly thereafter. Just before they left, Ann made one last, audacious gesture, perhaps to settle an old score with a disliked neighbor, or perhaps to remind people that she was still queen of the cattle rustlers. The story was uncovered in the files of Glade Ross, and while it is unconfirmed, it sounds typical of Ann:

> Wylo [MacKay] was sixteen when 400 of their yearling ewes disappeared in the area of Dragon, Utah where they'd wintered. That spring his father and partner gave a check to Ann Bassett for 400 head of yearling ewes and sent Wylo up to Josie's place on Cub Creek to pick them up. When he got up there he found that the sheep still had MacKay-Bender brand on, and the ear notches hadn't even been changed. Ann had the check already and skipped for California with it. . . .

Ann gained a loving, down-to-earth man who steadied her and gave her a much-needed stability. Her brother Eb was not as lucky.

Eb's eventual downfall and disintegration had its beginnings as far back as 1914, the year after Ann's trial for cattle theft. The court records show that in 1914 Eb received a United States land patent for 159.99 acres of ground on which he had filed three years previously. These acres were in reality the original Bassett ranch. Evidently some flaw in the original survey on which Herb had based his claim back in 1884 had necessitated a new claim being filed, and this new claim had been filed by Eb rather than Herb, since Eb was to be the eventual owner of the ground.

The land patent was granted on March 14, 1914. On December 26, 1914, Eb deeded the land over to George, who by this time had acquired his own acreage and built his own cabin for his family. Judging by what happened later, Eb signed his land over to George to escape a forced sale, either to satisfy taxes, his obligation to pay Ann's forfeited bond for nonappearance at the second trial, or even some other judgment levied against his property.

Eb's transfer of ownership did not save him. His land was sold by the sheriff of Moffat County (Moffat County had been created from the western part of Routt County by this time), and the land was bought by Ora Haley. Within a short time, Ora Haley liquidated his Colorado holdings, and his land was sold to Clay Springs Cattle Company.

George Bassett, the owner of record of Eb's land, filed suit, claiming that the sheriff's sale to satisfy a judgment against Eb could have been held on cattle and horses rather than land, and that the land was not offered for sale in parcels consistent with the size of the judgment, but was sold in mass for a grossly inadequate price.

Considering the influence that Ora Haley could have exercised if he saw a chance of picking up the Bassett property, it is possible that these facts were true. However, the court ruled against George, partially basing its decision on the grounds that Eb's transfer to George had been only for the purpose of evading the judgment, which of course was true.

By a stroke of good fortune, the Bassett cabin and orchards had been found to be outside the actual boundaries of the homestead established by survey and granted to Eb in 1914. Since the land was still in the public domain, Eb could continue to occupy his cabin as a squatter, and he still had summer range in Zenobia Basin. But that was not enough to save him from financial ruin.

He continued as he had before, raising what cattle he could, riding in local rodeos and exhibiting such skill with a lariat that he equaled some of Buffalo Bill's professional performers, and enchanting various women with his good looks and Bassett charm. He never married any of these ladies, but he began corresponding with Mattie Hughes Edwards, an old girlfriend who had married, moved away, and eventually been widowed. Eb asked her to return to the Park, and she consented. She was either on her way to join him, or had just arrived, when, on November 19, 1925, the *Craig Courier* burst the bombshell:

LADORE RANCHER SUICIDES

EBEN [*sic*] BASSETT OF BROWN'S PARK TOOK
POISON AT HOME OF FRANK LAWRENCE ON BIG
GULCH EARLY THURSDAY MORNING

Was One of Pioneer Cattlemen of Northwestern Colorado

Was to Have Appeared in Court Today
to Answer Charge of Killing Cow

Nobody ever knew exactly why Eb "suicided." He was on his way to Craig, it is true, to answer a charge of killing a cow, but that was a minor matter. Crawford said that there was a woman he loved whom he could not have. Others say he was in trouble for making an insurance claim on a cabin that had burned down under suspicious circumstances.

He left the Lawrence cabin during the night, went out to the granary and swallowed strychnine, which Lawrence kept for coyotes. He left a note that said only, "No one but me knew or suspected what I was going to do, no one. Eb Bassett."

It is possible that Eb had a streak of volatility from his mother that was not sufficiently tempered either by Herb's more imperturbable genes or by the environment in which he had been raised. Ann suspected foul play, but Josie understood him and never doubted that he just grew tired of living.

He left his property to Josie and Ann, and named Josie executor. Josie went up to Zenobia Basin in the November cold and rounded up his cattle and horses. She later told Esther Campbell that it had been a dispiriting trip for her, mostly because a local rancher or two had followed her around, seemingly for fear Eb's cattle might include some of their own. It is obvious that Eb's reputation among his neighbors had not been good.

George Bassett's daughter Edna, in reminiscing about the relationship between her father and Eb, said, "As far back as my knowledge goes, . . . [Eb] did many things, terrible things, that were extremely hurtful and expensive. Dad seemed to take it all stoically, trying to smooth things over, make amends. They were friends . . . they worked together some, saw a good deal of each other, and I know Dad was fond of Eb, making it that much harder for him to bear Eb's transgressions."

No doubt, George mourned Eb. As for little Mattie Edwards, she moved into the old Bassett cabin and continued to live there. Eb was buried in the Bassett cemetery, and Mattie erected an elaborate tombstone bearing the words, "Dear Old Pal."

AN UNCOMMON WOMAN

The descendants of Josie Morris tell tales of living with their grandmother that are like a kaleidoscope in which the same colorful bits and pieces are formed and reformed into patterns of unbelievable beauty. Each one speaks of a childhood so enriched by summers out on Cub Creek that town dwellers listen with a wistful envy. "We knew there was never much money," Betty said, "and I suppose we were poor. But we never felt poor, our lives were so very happy."

When Crawford and Flossie moved to Vernal, it was only for the winter months as far as the children were concerned, for Josie took it almost as her right that their summers belonged to her. At first Flossie fought it, for she wanted to repossess her children and gain her proper status in their eyes. Crawford sided with his mother, however, saying that Josie should have the children "for company" when they were out of school. As each child became old enough to let go of Flossie's skirts, Josie took joyful possession for the summer months.

As time passed and Flossie learned to trust and respect Josie, the two women shared responsibility for the children amicably. Flossie became "Mama," who disciplined them, saw to their schooling, provided their winter-time holidays and was their in-town mainstay; Josie, "Mother" to the older children and "Granny Jose" to the younger ones, gave them a summer life so filled with excitement and hilarious fun that not until they were grown did they realize what lessons she had been teaching them all the while. It is plain that their relationship was extraordinarily close, and the personality of this unusual grandmother influenced them deeply.

Josie did not believe in unproductive idleness. "Idle hands are the Devil's playthings," she said, and she kept herself and her grandchildren busy from sunup until bedtime.

Their days started at dawn, when Josie sometimes woke them by saying, "Oh, do come look at this beautiful sunrise!" Their beds were on the porch which was covered with "moon vines" (morning glories), which Josie watered as one of her first tasks of the morning. If the children burrowed into their pillows and pretended not to hear, she would sprinkle water on their faces as she passed, telling them that it was time to be up and doing, and sending them all to the spring to give their faces a "dippy-douse" in the ice-cold water.

They worked—oh, how those children worked—even the smallest ones. Dottie must have been barely out of the toddler years when she used a hoe with a short red handle to dig up a whole row of pepper plants in the garden, proud as a little peacock that she was old enough to help her granny. Josie kissed her and thanked her sincerely for helping, only then explaining to her the difference between a weed and a pepper plant.

They hoed the garden and they pulled weeds and they learned to handle the floodgates of Josie's intricate irrigation system for her fields. They gathered eggs and they cleaned the chicken house, and they went out to the pasture to bring in the dairy cows when it was milking time. They helped Josie stir the dirty clothes set to boil in the big copper kettle, and watched as she made lye soap. They helped her fill the same big copper kettle with glass jars of vegetables, or of beef or venison that they had helped her cut up for canning.

They hung thin strips of raw beef or venison on the barbs of the wires she had stretched between cedar trees, and learned to pepper them heavily and cover them with cheesecloth to keep the flies away as they hung drying in the sun until crisp and brittle. Josie liked the taste of this sun-dried jerky better than the smoked. It was the way the Indians had taught her mother when Josie was a little girl. The children watched Josie pound this jerky into small pieces and fry it in lard, thicken it with flour and flavor it with milk for a gravy good enough for the President of the United States when spooned out on Josie's marvelous biscuits. Each child remembers those biscuits as the most delicious food of their childhood.

They watched for chokecherry time. When the birds' droppings turned blue, they knew that the berries were ripe up on the mountain. Then Josie would pack a lunch and they would all go cherry picking for the day. There were Josie's own raspberries and gooseberries to pick as well, and then they would help stir the jam as it bubbled on the old range and strain the jelly juice through a flour or sugar sack.

After their noon dinner they were required to rest for a while in the cool cabin, but then they were free to go swim in the duck pond, and Josie never said a word about how muddy and sandy they might be, as long as they cleaned themselves up before bedtime.

Josie herself would rest by bending over her sewing machine, making dresses for the girls out of Aunt Ann's discarded clothes, sent when Ann went either up or down in the hundreds of pounds she gained and lost in her lifetime. All of the children's clothes were homemade. Flour sacks in those days were printed in bright flowers so they could be made into clothing. Flossie and Josie would decide jointly which of the flour-sack patterns was the prettiest and buy their flour accordingly; then Josie would turn the sacks into shirts or dresses, or the bonnets which the girls hated but which Josie insisted they wear in the hot sun. She made shirts for the boys too, and patched their pants, and when Frank objected to wearing patches he wore them anyway. "Better a clean patch than a dirty hole," Josie told him.

They remember her as a strict disciplinarian and not one to put up with wrangling or fighting. She had papered wooden apple boxes with wallpaper scraps, and when they were naughty they sat on those apple boxes until they could behave themselves; she called it "still time." She also kept a red stick, an old umbrella handle, for spankings, and sometimes she might use it or give a child a sharp rap on the head with her thimble. Usually it was not necessary, for they obeyed her out of respect for the sheer power of her personality. "She radiated power," Jane said of her.

Josie was never dour or dull. Once she had resigned herself to the fact that she would never be rich from cattle, she relaxed into pure enjoyment of the life she had chosen, and she shared that enjoyment with the children. They would be weeding in the garden, perhaps, or the older ones working with the butter churn, when Josie would look around and say, "As soon as that turns to butter, why don't we go fishing?" Then they would pack a lunch of biscuits filled with jam and a bottle of water and walk down to a good fishing hole she knew of in Cub Creek, to catch the descendants of the fish Crof and she had stocked when they had first homesteaded there. The best fishing, however, was down on the Green River itself, and they would often walk the seven miles to get there, Josie walking at a steady pace and the children dashing and running until they were so tired they stopped to rest before running again to catch up with her. On the way she would call them over to look at a strange rock or a pretty flower. The opportunity to walk and to look was one of Josie's pleasures on these fishing expeditions. Other times she would spread straw in the wagon and they would spend the night down on the river, fishing in the good hours of dusk and then sleeping under the stars.

Josie loved to fish. One year an invasion of Mormon crickets ate everything in sight. The crickets were excellent fish bait and since the crops were ruined anyway, that summer they almost lived down on the Green, thus turning a disaster into a vacation.

There were other expeditions. When the chores were done, they would take a walk up onto the rim of the canyon to spot likely cedar trees for her winter fuel, or they would go over to Hieroglyph Rock to hunt for arrowheads. Then they would all straggle home for supper, and there would be stories and quiet things until bedtime, when they all had to take a final wash in the spring. As they finally lay in bed waiting for sleep, they could see Josie reading a book or her father's old Bible by the light of the kerosene lamp.

She taught them to ride almost as soon as they could walk. They were started out bareback so that if they tumbled off they would not be caught by the saddle. When they had learned to ride like young Indians, they were graduated to a terrible old wooden Army saddle with huge stirrups; it was uncomfortable and gave them saddle-sores, but the stirrups would not catch them if they were thrown. Only later were they promoted to regular saddles, and it was a great day for each of them when they reached that stage, for then they could ride in comfort whenever they chose.

Frank and Belle used to ride up on Blue Mountain during lambing time with cloth sacks tied to their saddles to carry home "bum lambs." A third lamb in a litter is pushed away by the mother ewe because she has neither the milk nor an extra teat to feed it, and the sheepherders abandoned these lambs, leaving them for the taking of anyone wanting to care for them. The children would carry them home, then stick a finger down into a pan of warm milk so that the lamb would suck on the finger and in time learn to drink unassisted. Sometimes those lambs would bite, but rubber nipples cost money.

As the children grew older she taught them to shoot. They learned to squeeze carefully as they looked down the sights of a rifle so that the shot would not be wasted nor a wild creature left maimed and suffering. Josie helped all of them when it was time to shoot their first deer, and then showed them how to dress it out. She told them of their father Crof's pet deer, who had followed them down from Brown's Park when they came to Jensen and who had been a faithful pet until he died from eating poisoned fly-paper; and how, for years thereafter, she could not bear to shoot a deer, as long as Crof had been around to do it for her. They learned from her a respect for all living things, who were to be unmolested except when food was needed.

To Josie's way of thinking, to waste anything of value was a sin, and wasting food was a deadly sin. She and Dottie were riding their horses back from town one day when Josie spotted a herd of deer grazing not too far away. "We're almost out of meat, Dottie, I think I'll shoot one for us." She directed Dottie to tie up Helen, Josie's mount, and to hold tight to her own horse Peanuts because he was flighty and might bolt. Josie unhooked her rifle from her saddle, took aim and shot. They heard a crash, and Josie went into the brush while Dottie stayed with the horses. She heard her grandmother give a dismayed cry, then call to her to come quickly. By some chance, Josie's one bullet had downed two deer, and she was deeply distressed instead of pleased at her prowess.

"All this good meat will be going to waste! Oh, how awful this is. We must do something!" Dottie was sent back up the road to Doug Chew's house and told to fetch him with his truck. She was also told to talk to nobody but Doug, since it was not deer season and there was no use spreading the word that the law had been broken. Josie had to take that risk, however, for it was unthinkable to waste the meat. By the time Dottie had fetched Doug Chew, Josie had the deer dressed out, and Doug took some down to Crawford and saved some for himself. Josie took her own portion home, at peace with herself.

Josie would not have been in real danger from the game wardens even if the story had come out. They were good honest men with a job to do, but they seldom bothered any of the country people who, they knew, were not going to shoot deer merely for sport and waste the meat. Betty tells a marvelous story about Josie and the game wardens:

> I remember one time she got picked up for poaching, and it scared me half to death. I thought they were going to take mother off to jail for sure. I wasn't a full-grown woman, but I was about fifteen. The game warden just loved mother. I went out there with Neldon—the man I would eventually marry—and she had killed a deer just before we got there, and we were ready to eat. Well, the game warden and his friend walked in the house and said, "How about some supper, Jose?" She said, "Fine, I'm getting it cooked," but then she looked at us, for we were going to go help her get this deer in. It was just down the road a way in the brush, but of course we couldn't with the game warden there.
>
> He said, "Jose, I hate to eat your supper and do what we got to, but we've caught you." She said, "You caught me what?" He said, "We know you killed a deer a while ago—we were sitting up there watching you. We'll have to arrest you."
>
> Mother said, "Well, I guess—if that's what you have to do—" He said, "Why don't you take us to the deer and get it over with? There's no use letting good meat spoil." And mother said, "All right. If I'm caught, I'm caught, and I'll just have to take my medicine."
>
> She got in their car and they drove down and she took them right to it. It was all gutted out and ready to bring home. They got out and went to it, and—I'll never forget it!—he looked at the deer and he looked at her and said, "My God, Jose, we were only kiddin' you! We thought you were just going along with the joke!"
>
> She said, "Well, what are you going to do to me?" And he said, "Well, if you'll cook us a good supper with some steak and potatoes and gravy we're going to turn around and go home! What the hell else did you think we were going to do!"

She taught the children to be unafraid, insisting they could do anything that needed to be done as long as they were careful. One day she needed to transfer a mean and dangerous old sow from one pen to another, and she gave Betty detailed instructions as to what to do: she was to lean over the rail of the sty and poke the old sow as Josie herself held open the gate. Betty was afraid and said she did not want to do it. "Oh pshaw!" said Josie. "I've told you what to do, and it's all thought out, how to do it. Now do it!" So Betty did it.

When Frank was not more than eleven years old, she sent him on a two-day trip over Blue Mountain and back. She always did a lot of trading with the ranchers, swapping excess hay for a calf or some pigs. That was the way she had acquired her thoroughbred horse Helen, by taking the colt as payment for some hay. Frank's trip involved a trade she had made for some pigs with a rancher clear across Blue Mountain and down the other side to the Yampa River at Pool Creek. She sent Frank to get those pigs even after he had said, "Gran, I don't know how I'm going to do it," for pigs cannot be driven like cows.

"Don't worry, Frank," Josie reassured him. "I've done it myself and you'll have no trouble. All you have to do is saddle up your horse and I'll give you a bag of food and a sack of corn, and you *lead* them back—you don't have to herd them. Just tempt them along by feeding them a trail of corn. If they get tired and want to stop, just sit under a tree and rest right along with the pigs until they're ready to go again."

It took Frank all day to get across Blue Mountain and down to Rial Chew's place. Frank stayed there overnight and then started out the next morning, leading the old sow and her five piglets across the mountain following a trail of corn. Rial went the first mile with him to get the pigs well away from their home place. Then he said, "You're on your own now." Frank had started at daylight, and it was getting dark when he finally delivered the pigs to Josie, feeling quite proud of himself.

He had done so well that the next trip Josie sent him on was to pick up some horses over in Lily Park. He was gone six days that time, camping out at night and fixing his own meals over a campfire. He felt like a man able to do a man's job before he ever reached his teens.

Not only did she teach them to be unafraid; she also taught them optimism in the face of danger and light-heartedness in the face of discomfort. Two stories are told of mishaps on that ten-mile wagon trip through two canyons to reach her home on Cub Creek. She was bringing two of the little girls home in the spring when a freak storm hit, sending down sleet and heavy rain and chilling them to the bone. They stopped at Hieroglyph Rock that time and crept in under a ledge. Josie built a fire of cow chips to warm them for the last lap of their journey, and turned it almost into a picnic. They sat there, giggling and singing songs and telling stories, congratulating themselves for having a dry match to light the fire, happy that things had turned out so well.

On the second occasion Josie faced real danger when a cloudburst sent a flash flood down through the second canyon. She had Amy with her, still small, and Belle, who was then a toddler. This time Josie had to unhitch the horses and let them find their own way to safety. She put Belle on her back, and instructed Amy to walk just a little higher then she on the slope of the canyon while Josie held her hand. The three of them went through the water with Josie probing her way over the rocky, uneven terrain with a long stick. Amy wanted to be terrified, for she was old enough to know that they were in danger, but "Mother's calm was so contagious" that she felt almost as matter-of-fact as her grandmother seemed to be.

Betty makes light of Josie's temper and insists she was angry only for good reason. Once the little girls were in the wagon with Josie on a long steep decline when suddenly the old mare sat down in her traces. Josie jammed on the brake and told the girls, "Get out of the wagon! Put rocks under the wheels! No! Bigger ones! There, that's better!" She snapped out orders like a drill sergeant until the wagon was secure; then she got out of the wagon and knelt by the old mare, stroking her nose and telling the girls to walk on down the trail, that the horse would get up when she felt better. "If mother had such a bad temper," Betty said, "that's one time she'd have used the whip."

The children were not isolated with only their grandmother for company, for in a smaller way Josie's cabin was as much a stopping-place as the Bassett cabin in her childhood. Folks riding over the trail from Brown's Park often stopped for a visit. Her cabin was on the direct path of the ranchers who summered their herds on Blue Mountain, and most of them planned to lay over at Josie's cabin on their way up or down. Josie would brew pot after pot of coffee and make pan after pan of biscuits and feed them all, and if it was getting on toward evening they were welcome to stay the night and then sit down to breakfast.

Josie was a good neighbor, and they appreciated it. As autumn approached and nights got cool on the mountain, cattle would often start straying down to warmer ground before the time of the fall "push." Josie kept her eyes open and checked out the brands on the strays so that she could tell their owners that some cows had come by that they might want to hunt for. If a good number seemed intent on losing themselves in a remote area, she had even been known to drive them back up or ride up the mountain to tell a friend that he was losing an important number of cattle.

The ranchers knew these things about Josie, and if by chance they overlooked a cow at roundup time and it later strayed close to Josie's corral, they did not grudge her a beef for her own winter supply, feeling well paid when they ate jerky and gravy at her cabin on their next trip through. They all followed the old country rules of behavior, like the game warden's eating her venison stew without batting an eye, and telling her what good mutton it was.

Josie would grin and say that the mutton had been especially plentiful that year, and neither one thought much about it. Josie once killed a pesky steer that kept breaking through her fences and ravaging her pasture, and later had no hesitation at telling the owner of the steer just exactly what she had done.

The cabin that Crof and Dan Nelson had built when they moved from Pig Canyon was getting rickety in the 1930s from heavy snows and poor foundations. It had wooden floors, but the spring runoffs and the rains had rotted them, and the place was almost ready to fall down. Still, it was livable enough for Josie to lend it for a year to a family down on its luck, while she herself built a dugout with two rooms and a porch and moved her things over there. When the family moved out, Josie tore down the old cabin and used the logs to build what Frank described as a dormitory—several beds and no kitchen. It was Josie's version of a bunkhouse, and the children slept there, along with anyone else who happened to be staying at the ranch.

When she could afford it, however, she built a new cabin, the one still in existence at Dinosaur Monument. She built it herself around 1935 or 1936 with help from twelve-year-old Frank and two of his friends. Josie meant this cabin to be a fine one, and she took special care over it. It had large windows overlooking her gardens, and she went over to Ann's old place on South Fork and carried home petrified wood to use in the fireplace. Remembering how the wooden floors had rotted in the last cabin, she poured a concrete floor; but, since she had no experience with cement, she used the river sand, and the floor cracked, powdered and crumbled as the years went by, becoming more and more uneven under the rag rugs she had braided. She was rueful about her mistake, saying she would have been better off to stick to good hard dirt floors instead of trying to be so fancy.

When the cabin was finished, she moved in and hung her pictures and her hand-painted plates, her stuffed heads of an antelope and a four-point buck she had shot in her Brown's Park days. She spread her crocheted and braided rugs on the floor and covered the beds with her hand-made quilts. The rooms were not large—they must be kept warm in the winter—but the bedrooms had space for hanging clothes neatly and enough room for her old "shirtwaist box" in which she kept her treasures, and a cabinet for vases and other pretty oddments. The living room held a square walnut table that could be expanded to seat eight people, a writing desk, and a cabinet with full-length glass doors in which she kept her hand-painted teacups and pieces of old cut-glass. Among her glassware was a set of fingerbowls her mother had brought out from Arkansas. Josie insisted on good table manners, and when the children showed curiosity about the little bowls, she introduced them to how they were used, "so they would know what to do if the occasion should arise."

Curtains did not cover windows in her living room. In the winter she wanted to look out and watch the deer browsing on the snow-covered pasture and in the summer she wanted to see her flowers. Josie had flowers as profuse and as varied as she could make them. There were poppies and iris and asters and cosmos and marigolds. Her flowers were more important to her than the vegetables. Pictures of her garden show a riot of color.

During most summers Aunt Ann would write to announce that Frank and she were coming for a visit, and then, Betty remembers, the "whole place would be spiffed up as if for the second coming of Christ." The children would watch wide-eyed as Uncle Frank pitched a sleeping tent and set up card tables to hold Ann's two suitcases full of cosmetics. Ann still dressed in high style and always brought an extensive wardrobe. She might wear bib overalls at the ranch itself, but she still made up her face carefully each morning, and she had clothes with her in case of unexpected company or a trip in to town. She added a touch of glamour to the children's lives, and her arrival was always an excitement.

Soon the children would begin to wish that Aunt Ann and Uncle Frank would leave. Uncle Frank was always fun, always good-humored. He played cards with the children, took them places in his car, and got out his long-necked banjo and sang cowboy songs to them. But they loved Aunt Ann only because they were supposed to love her. As Amy said, "Mother made us behave ourselves but Aunt Ann preached!"

Ann meant well and she was kind to the children, but only in her own way. She would take one or two of them in to Vernal and buy them striped tee-shirts and treat them to a malted milk. Betty remembers these purchases as symbols of Aunt Ann's lack of empathy, for Betty had told Aunt Ann that she did not like striped tee-shirts and that malted milks made her sick. Ann still bought Betty a striped tee-shirt and handed her a malt to drink, and then could not understand why Betty threw up on the way home. Ann corrected the children on every possible matter, trying to undo all of their supposed faults in a three-week visit. She corrected their grammar, their accents, their table manners, their posture, and their shrill children's voices. She even tried to correct the way the young Indians rode horseback, and spent fruitless hours insisting that the girls learn to "post" in eastern finishing school style.

It was a pity that she received more dutiful politeness than love, for she was fond of the children, and had a special love for Frank, who had been named for her own Frank Willis. When he was a little fellow, not more than five years old, she had gone to Crawford and Flossie and begged to adopt him, promising he would be given chances far beyond what he could normally expect and sent to a military school that might eventually lead to West Point. They naturally refused to give up their child, and Ann cried bitterly. When Frank grew up and went into the Army without benefit of West Point, she wrote him faithfully, and Frank just as faithfully answered her—until, that is, she sent him a dictionary and told him he must work on his spelling. Poor Ann!

As Ann's visit lengthened, Josie would inevitably become irritated. Ann was well informed about current events and was an articulate, interesting conversationalist. Unfortunately she could not resist taking the opposite side of a question and brushing aside anyone else's opinion. This, coupled with her nagging at the children and her ingrained habit of baiting Josie, would bring on a fight. The children could see one coming a day or two ahead of time by the increased combativeness of Ann's comments and the increased irritability of Josie's responses. Once Josie became so angry that she shouted at Ann, "Now that's enough of your nonsense!" and hit her over the head with Jane's doll. They always made up—and this time they apologized to Jane as well for her broken doll—and they always parted friends, with Ann breathing a sigh of relief at her escape from the primitive cabin in the middle of nowhere, and Josie breathing a sigh of relief at regaining her peace and tranquillity.

APRICOT BRANDY AND CHOKECHERRY WINE

During all the years after Crawford and Flossie moved to town, Josie never considered her own needs as separate from theirs. The food from her garden, the heifers that she fattened, the venison that she shot—all were used to keep food on Crawford's table as well as her own. It took cold, hard cash to put shoes on the children's feet and gasoline in the car, however, and necessities became luxuries because there was so little money to pay for them. Josie desperately wanted a "cash crop."

It was Frank Willis who found her cash crop for her, providing Josie with one more skill she could pass on to her grandchildren. Frank ordered a copper still and some oaken kegs out of Chattanooga, Tennessee, gave Josie lessons on how to distill corn whiskey, and told her how to age it. Josie became the most ladylike bootlegger in the whole state of Utah.

Neither Josie nor Ann ever drank anything except perhaps for a glass of "holiday cheer" at a family celebration. (In their youth a woman did less damage to her reputation by having a love affair than by taking a drink of strong liquor.) Still, each was independent enough to share the country's general outrage at the loss of individual liberty when the "Drys" managed to ram Prohibition down the thirsty gullets of their fellow citizens. Josie knew, of course, that making whiskey was illegal, but she saw absolutely nothing immoral in it, as long as she made honest whiskey and aged it properly.

Crawford and Flossie disapproved of Josie's bootlegging, but they could scarcely complain too loudly when the money went to pay rent, buy shoes, and furnish what food supplies they could not grow themselves. They never joined Josie in brewing her liquor, but their children helped with the distilling just as they helped with weeding the garden.

Amy giggles when she tells of the day that Boon and she were helping "Mother" and emptied a kettle of used mash into the chicken yard where they were accustomed to dumping table scraps. By the time Josie saw what they had done, the chickens were all drunk as cowboys on a Saturday night. One old turkey gobbler was barely on his feet; he would take a few uncertain steps, then spread his wings as wide as he could, let out a raucous "gobble gobble" and try to fly. Work stopped as Josie laughed as hard as the children over the orgy in the chicken yard.

Josie hid her still in a gulch below the cabin and covered it with growing vines so that it was completely invisible from above. Betty remembers crawling through a tunnel of sunlight green to reach the still and check the temperature gauge for her grandmother. She also remembers the day Josie rode her horse to Jensen, leaving the older children to watch the little ones. The older children decided that it would be fun to see if whiskey affected pigs as much as chickens, so they fed fermented mash to the old sow. The results were completely satisfactory—the children rode the old sow around the barnyard, and it was too drunk to complain.

Josie started her career by making corn whiskey, but she soon branched out and specialized in brewing an excellent apricot brandy; even she herself enjoyed a sample taste. She put the finished product in the wooden kegs provided by Frank and then would hitch up the wagon and take the kegs down to the second canyon, where she would hide them for pickup by whoever "wholesaled" it for her. She also had a few customers whom she supplied personally, making deliveries in her wagon, with one or another of the grandchildren along for company. She became as famous locally for her apricot brandy as for her baking-powder biscuits.

Although the grandchildren helped Josie by checking the gauge on the still and emptying the mash, there were lines beyond which they knew they should not go. Therefore, when Josie told Boon and Belle to empty out some bottles of chokecherry juice because they had started to "turn," both of the children knew that they were doing something wrong when, instead, they kept the juice and added sugar to it until they had turned it into a halfway acceptable chokecherry wine. The summer rodeo was coming up, however, and the two of them were already making plans for earning some money there. They had been hunting and killing rattlesnakes, and had accumulated quite a good supply of belts and hat bands made from the skins. It seemed to them that bottles of wine would be just as saleable.

Josie drove them all to the rodeo in her wagon, and Boon and Belle hid their wine bottles in the straw. Crawford came over to the fairgrounds each night and drove them to his house to sleep. Thus the wagon, unattended during the three-day festivities, made a perfect place for Belle and Boon to set up shop. By the end of the rodeo they had made thirty dollars on their snakeskin handicrafts and the chokecherry wine.

Crawford's children knew the value of that much money and they decided to give it to their dad for the school shoes they knew they all would need in September. But they had a problem: how to explain where such a huge amount of cash had come from. They were still trying to decide how to approach their father when Crawford came to pick them up on the last day.

They still had a bottle or two of the wine, and they placed these in the trunk of his car. On the way home, the wine exploded with such a noise that Crawford stopped the car to check for a blowout. Finding nothing wrong, he drove on, but by the time he reached the house the smell of the wine was permeating the car. He took Belle and Boon out to the barn and said, "Now let's hear what you have to say for yourselves."

As they confessed to Crawford, they were too proud and excited to act ashamed; and when they pulled out their profits, that unbelievable thirty dollars, and said, "It's for you dad, for our shoes," Crawford had tears in his eyes.

Josie made whiskey right into the 1930s, even after the Eighteenth Amendment had been repealed. It all came to an end when Boon came galloping up to her cabin with the news that the revenuers were on their way out to the ranch. Boon had been tipped off by some official (perhaps one of Josie's steady customers?) who knew of the impending raid and had told him to ride out fast and warn his grandmother.

Together they carried the vats of mash from the second room in the springhouse down to the place where the still was hidden; then they pulled even more vines over the spot so that it looked like an impenetrable thicket in a deep gully. When the revenuers arrived, Josie was calmly working in her garden. She greeted them courteously with an offer of coffee, and when they told her she had been accused of running a roadhouse and manufacturing whiskey she was properly amazed at such an outlandish idea and invited them to look anywhere they wished. The men searched the area and then told her that obviously their information had been untrue, for there were not the usual broken bottles associated with a roadhouse and certainly they had found none of the equipment used by a bootlegger. They accepted her offer of coffee, and they all parted friends.

But Crawford finally put his foot down. "For God's sake, mother, you'll get yourself put in prison!" He vowed he would come out and break up the still with an axe if she continued to flirt with danger. Josie agreed, for she wanted neither a prison term for herself nor disgrace for her family. Her only problem was where, now, to find another cash crop.

THE CATTLE TRIAL

Except for a few good years in the late 1920s, the cattle market had been so depressed, and people had scratched so hard for a living, that they hardly noticed the difference when the Great Depression struck the country. Then, to add to their troubles, there were extreme and persistent droughts from 1930 until 1933. Ranchers who had earlier bought new cars and mechanized farm equipment could not now replace their worn-out machines because there was no market for their beef. Along with Josie, they lived by barter because they could not sell for cash. They cut back on their herds, and even ground up wild thistles for feed because their crops had failed and they had no money to buy hay. The merchants suffered along with the ranchers, and when what few industries there were in that area practically closed their doors, wages fell as far as cattle prices.

The people in Vernal and Jensen took care of each other. An old man who owned a little coal mine would fill his wagon with coal and take it around town, filling empty coal bins without the poor people asking for it. If they had a dollar or two they would give it to him, and he would buy himself a bottle of wine and then go back to dig more coal. Nobody actually starved. The Mormons took care of their own, as well as some who were not their own, and the other churches were also distribution points for food and clothing donated by people fortunate enough to still have something to spare.

While Josie was selling her apricot brandy and helping Crawford make ends meet, she was also running her own personal relief organization. In the crisis of drought and depression she was as open-handed as her parents had been when hard times had hit Brown's Park. Her food and her roof were at the disposal of anyone who needed help. Strangers stayed at her ranch during this period—an old cowboy down on his luck, a young couple evicted for lack of rent money, a little girl whose parents had too many mouths to feed. When she went to town her wagon held meat and chicken and butter, and fruit and vegetables from her garden, and these were distributed to anyone known to be in need. Betty remembers that once Josie piled her wagon high with haunches of illegal venison and supplied almost every house in Jensen, friend or stranger, "including a Mormon bishop with eleven little bare-assed kids."

In those times of privation, Josie would have had no qualms about considering her neighbors' property as equally available for distribution as her own. Josie had no strong sense of property rights, and would have killed someone else's beef without thinking twice if she knew it would feed hungry people. It is almost surprising that it was not until January 1936 that she was indicted for stealing cattle belonging to the ranchers who grazed their herds on Blue Mountain.

Josie and her family always claimed that she was framed by a more or less shifty acquaintance by the name of Jim Robinson. Jim had used her ranch as headquarters for a while some years previously when he was running sheep nearby, and they had had a falling-out then. Later they clashed again so seriously that Josie took Jim Robinson to court and had him put under a peace bond.

The second clash arose from a confrontation when Josie and young Belle were riding across Blue Mountain to see a rancher named Charley Mantle who lived on the other side. The trail passed through a section called Red Rock Canyon, which was close to the holdings of Jim Robinson's relatives by marriage, the Chews. As they got well into the canyon, they realized that someone was in the high "sarviceberry" bushes that lined the trail. It was Jim Robinson. Without actually coming out of the bushes, he shouted to them that they were not welcome there, that they could not go further. Josie told him that indeed she would continue, that it was public land and they were following a public trail. Jim Robinson insisted, and brandished what Josie took to be a long stick; but Belle saw the sunlight glinting from the "stick" and realized it must be a steel rifle barrel. Belle turned her pony around, telling her grandmother, "He's going to shoot us!" Josie decided to be prudent, and they retreated down the trail.

After questioning Belle further, Josie was convinced that the little girl really saw sunlight glint on steel. But even if Robinson had only threatened them with a stick, Josie felt that they could have been harmed, and at the least their freedom of access had been hindered. She went to Craig and filed a complaint. After the judge had heard the testimony of both Belle and Josie, he put Jim Robinson under bond not to molest them again.

With this background of dissension between the two of them, it is understandable that Josie felt Jim instigated her arrest for cattle theft out of spite. She also contended, with probable justice, that Jim wanted her homestead (she had never filed her final papers) and that he planted cow hides on her property to send her to jail so that he could take over her land.

In the years 1933 and 1934 the new Roosevelt administration had been paying money for horses, and the unemployed of Jensen had been chasing down wild horses and selling them to Uncle Sam. The government was also slaughtering Iowa pigs and western cattle to destroy the glut of livestock that had depressed prices to unbelievably low levels. Ranchers had been paid to slaughter their cattle, and there were piles of dead beef to bury up on Blue Mountain and down at the stockyard. Not everybody agreed with this waste of good cows, and sometimes a rancher who was cutting his herd would give a cow away or sell it for five dollars to someone who asked for it. (Josie's grandson Frank acquired a cow this way, and it was the start of a small herd he built up in the years before he went into service in World War II.) Fresh meat derived from the slaughter found its way to local tables, and hides were left all over the country. Josie and her lawyer were to declare that some of these hides had been hidden on her ranch to incriminate her.

A fascinating story can be pieced together from the trial transcripts and from the recollections of Hugh Colton of Vernal, who calls himself the "persecuting attorney" at Josie's trial.

It all started when a posse consisting of Elmer and Newel Snow, Andrew Dudley, Harley Wilkins, Jim Robinson himself, Deputy Sheriff Frank Swain (Jim Robinson's son-in-law), and his brother Garn Swain went out to see what evidence they could find on Josie's ranch. Hugh Colton went along as county attorney so that he would be fully informed as to what evidence was gathered. His recollections, preserved on tape and edited for clarity and reconciliation with the facts brought out in sworn testimony, begin the story:

> There was an old boy named Jim Robinson who was tainted with the past along the lines you say [less than unblemished reputation]. He had married one of the Chew girls, which is quite a family too, and another story. He ran a bunch of sheep at this time, although he was an old-time cowboy, and leased a homestead as kind of a headquarters. They had quarreled, Josie and he, and he had squealed on her.
>
> He [went to] people in Jensen who ran their cattle on Blue Mountain and said, "Josie's been sellin' beef." The sheriff investigated, and she had delivered six in the last three months or so to this meat shop [in Vernal]. It looked like a good case—and it was!
>
> Anyway, the cattlemen in the area rose up and said, "We've got to stop Jose," so the sheriff assigned his top deputy, Frank Swain, to investigate, and he told me, "You've got to get with this." I was sort of a drugstore cowboy myself, reared on ranches and growing up in the livestock industry. So we talked this over and Elmer Snow decided that we should get a search warrant for her place. Everything was legal.
>
> We [Swain and Colton] got to Jensen and here were *six* of these people who had missed cattle. Way back then, we had nothing but a little Model T Ford, but we got two carloads—a deputy sheriff, the "persecuting attorney," and these six locals. Now Jim Robinson was six feet two, two hundred pounds; Elmer Snow was six feet four, two hundred pounds; the only one my size was a fellow named Harley Wilkins. These fellows were all ready—they came out with rifles! We asked what this was for, and Jim Robinson said, "Well, she's a dangerous woman."

I had never met her—I had heard about her—and I thought, Well, we'll have to see how it happens. So we went up the east side of Cub Creek—there's a ridge there about a quarter-mile from Josie's cabin. They stop and dismount, and I said to the deputy, "What's this for?" He talked to them, and they said, "Well, we don't want her to get the drop on us."

We cautiously crept up the slope with all our military brass—I know they had at least two rifles, maybe more—and we looked over the brow of the hill. Down there was this little old cabin and out in front was this little old lady feeding her chickens. So we peered over the military crest of this ridge and watched her for oh, maybe thirty minutes, and she was just taking care of her normal chores.

I think it was this Jim Robinson who had 'em all spooked, saying, "She'll shoot you if she sees you coming," and all that. Finally I said to the deputy, "What the heck goes on here! I can't take this. Let's go down and talk to her." He said, "That's the way I feel." We called all the boys together and said, "We're not for this sort of thing; we're going down." After telling them how we felt they said, "Well, if you go, we'll be on the ridge here to cover you."

The deputy and I walked down [at this time cars could not negotiate the road farther than the ridge]. He knew her well enough to call her "Josie." She said, "Good morning, gentlemen, how are you," and that whole thing. Then he introduced me to her. Josie said, "Won't you come in and have a cup of coffee?" So we did—she served us coffee and we talked, and finally Frank said, "Well Jose, we got some sad news for you. We've got a search warrant here and you've been accused of butchering cattle." She took the paper and asked what she could do to help out, just as cooperative as a person could be—unflustered, white-haired. . . .

She said, "Well, how do you want to do it?" Then, for the first time, she got a little sarcastic and she said, "Why don't those others come down here with you?" They were lying up there on the hill, thinking they were hiding from her, and she had known everything that was going on! She said, "Especially this Jim Robinson—if there's anything here, he did it." So Frank Swain went out and waved them down; and they came, still with their rifles at half-mast.

The available trial transcript is not complete, but it includes the testimony of Deputy Sheriff Swain and two other members of the posse who agreed that Josie told them that she had butchered only three beef the preceding summer, which she had sold to the butcher in Vernal; that she never buried hides but sold all of them to get the money; that she had been pasturing some cows for a man named Henry Rasmussen and had butchered one of them, taking him half of the meat; and that her son Crawford had only been to see her twice, once on July 24 and again on Thanksgiving Day.

There is a conflict here between her statement and that of Henry Rasmussen, who testified that she had not brought him beef until *after* her arrest. Her statements about Crawford were undoubtedly true, for Crawford was working and had not too much time to come out to the ranch. The prosecution had no quarrel with her on this, witnessed by the fact that the original complaint had included Crawford only because he had helped her deliver beef to the butcher shop, and that all charges against him were dismissed before Josie's case came to trial.

All three witnesses told the same story of how eight full hides and a piece of another one had been discovered. (The prosecution based its case on only one of these.) They knew exactly where they must dig in the frozen January ground, for Jim Robinson had told them where he had seen hides not completely covered by dirt; in fact, when the posse reached the spot he took them to, they could see for themselves where the hides were buried.

First with a shovel and then with a pick-axe, they unearthed the hides, all of them in various stages of decay and covered with mud and with dirt. Each hide had been carefully rolled in as small a package as possible, but inside one hide were some willow shoots and some wild hay which Josie said was from her haystack, fifty yards or so from where the hides were uncovered. The hides were "ripe"—too filthy and nasty to handle on the spot—so they were put on poles and the posse carried them to town, where they were turned over to the Newton Company, a dealer in hides, for cleaning and verification of the brands.

The prosecution eventually made its case on a partial hide that had been unearthed which, they claimed, matched another piece of hide hanging on Josie's corral fence. Josie had stated that the piece on the fence was from Rasmussen's cow, which she had admitted butchering, and claimed that the remainder had been cut up for rawhide strips by her grandson Boon for fence-patching and for lariats. Rasmussen's brand was not found on it, however, and although the defense denied it, the prosecution strove to prove that it was a perfect match with the unearthed partial hide bearing Elmer Snow's brand.

Although Hugh Colton believes that he had an iron-clad case, the evidence does not seem completely conclusive, especially if the jury were to accept the contention that the hides had been planted. The most damaging witness for the prosecution was young Roy Gardner, Amy's high school sweetheart, who had helped Josie butcher a beef on one of his visits out to the ranch. However, the cow he helped her corral and butcher was not the cow on which the prosecution based its case, and his testimony was thrown out and the jury ordered to disregard it.

Colson's description of Josie's behavior during the posse's search is classic:

> Her profession—her trade—had been making moonshine, and there was a little log cabin maybe a fourth the size of a room, with a sloping roof and room for a still and a couple of barrels to brew her mash in. [Probably her springhouse.] On top of the roof were some cleats, and over these there was a cowhide covered with willows, and with dirt shoveled on to keep the willows down, just to make a shelter. Robinson had been a neighbor, living and running his sheep right in that area, and he knew all about it and he told them what to expect.

[While searching there] we found a bull whip, maybe twenty feet long with a long handle of braided rawhide. They were used a lot in the old days in driving cattle, and the cowboys became expert—and, as you will hear, Josie was too. Josie said, "Well! I wondered where that was!" and picked it up. This one was all rolled up, as the cowboys generally carry them on their saddles, so she carried it with her. She was becoming less talkative as we went along. She knew she was caught. . . .

The posse went down to the gulch where they found the hides.

Josie was still carrying this bull whip. As we started digging those eight hides out of the gulch she let that bull whip go! And she popped that thing—it sounded just like a revolver! Then she lit into this Jim Robinson and said, "And you're the dirty so and so who turned in this whole story to these people! *You're* the one who buried these hides!" Then she said, "You haven't got guts enough to come close enough that I can reach you or I'd cut your blankety-blank throat!" I think she could have done it too—she could throw that bull whip and make it sound just like a gun.

I can remember her like it was yesterday, poppin' that whip at this guy. And he *didn't* come too close, and he *didn't* say, "That isn't true." She was very definitely in a rage and she knew all the words. Then she told something about his life history with the Chews, in the presence of all these men.

When she got over her rage she cooperated in every way. The deputy said, "Well, Josie, we'll have to take you in to town." And she agreed, saying, "Do you mind if I change clothes?" Somebody piped up and said, "Yeah, and get a gun?" Frank said, "Look, I'll handle this!" because she didn't show one act of hostility to any of us except Jim Robinson.

So she came out after she changed her clothes and had fed her chickens again, because she wouldn't be back that night; and we took her to town and took her to the J. P. and filed a criminal complaint. The J. P. gave her a preliminary hearing and bound her over to the District Court.

Her good neighbor Joe Haslem and her old lover Ed Lewis went Josie's bail. When she appeared in court at the end of February she was wearing a dress instead of pants, looking for all the world like exactly what she was, a nice little gray-haired lady of sixty-two who had been accused of stealing cattle.

Her family came with her, Crawford and Flossie every day and occasionally one of the children. They were all frightened for Josie and defensive for her. Amy was embarrassed when she faced her high school friends, and was torn between fondness for Roy Gardner and anger that he was testifying against Josie, even though she knew he was under pressure from his family and from the prosecution. Her ambivalence probably broke up their romance.

Betty remembers going to court one day and hearing Josie protest loudly at some testimony or other, and the judge telling her to be quiet or he would have to find her in contempt. Josie answered him, "That is what this whole procedure is—contemptible!" Betty laughed because everyone else laughed, but Crawford told Josie later, "Mother, keep quiet! You'll only hurt yourself."

Hugh Colton's recollections continue:

We had a District Attorney then named Marcellus Pope, a very sedate gentleman who lived in Provo, and I was the county attorney. My duties were to prepare the case and he would try it. Together we tried it—we would take turns in questioning the witnesses. Due to my investigation I knew the case very well. We had another lawyer here in town [Wallace Calder] who was the stake president in the LDS—the Mormon Church—and she convinced him that she wasn't guilty and so he represented her in these trials. He was a very conscientious, humble sort of person, very righteous and upright.

The day of the trial was set and in walks Josie. She said, "Good morning, Judge," smiling in her gracious way—a very gracious, gray-haired lady. So the jury was chosen and the rest of the jurors dismissed from court. I think we were three days presenting the evidence.

Each morning she would walk into the court room and first turn to the jurors. "Good morning, ladies and gentlemen." Then, "Good morning, Judge; good morning, Mr. Pope," and then say "Good morning" to me. She would sit there, a pleasant woman, and here we were, in the back of our minds always thinking how distasteful it was to accuse a lady as gracious-appearing as she was of stealing cattle, which is a penitentiary offense. But I mean, we worked at it! Because this whole community makes its living on livestock and the whole community was wrapped up in it.

We thought we had a cinch case. But we had one person from Jensen, a man on the jury, whom we had thought would be a cinch, principally because he knew all these men. I guess they deliberated maybe five, six hours, and came in with a hung jury, and investigation showed that this neighbor down there—his name was Joe Paulson—had led all the opposition!

Well, then the district attorney said, "Something's wrong here, we're going to try her again." And we did. We went through the same thing, only this time she was perhaps a little more pleasant, each morning as she came to court. This time we were real careful about choosing a jury, because it was a cinch case! We went through that whole thing again for two or three days, and we argued a little more convincingly to the jury, we thought, about the facts of the case, to where there should have been no question that she was guilty—and there wasn't!

So we wait for the jury again, and they come in a second time with a hung jury. It was about evenly split—I don't know who led the opposition, and frankly didn't care. After the trial Mr. Pope said, "Well, we'll just have to try again," and I said, "Look, here's this old lady, and we've done the best we can with two juries. And she's beat us! Let's be sports enough to forget it." He said, "I agree with you," so we didn't try her again.

But this is in keeping with her nature and disposition. She had to be a very smart woman. Some time later she walked into my office and said, "Good morning, Mr. Colton!"

I hadn't seen her since the trial, but she couldn't help but know that I had done everything I could to convict her. I was then, and still am, in the cattle business and

I was concerned about this. I represent the people of this county which is one hundred and fifty miles north and south, and sixty miles east and west. And there's maybe one hundred thousand cattle here. A lot of these people are concerned about this. I was the only protection they had—when you turn cattle out on the range, anybody can steal 'em or shoot 'em, so when you get a prosecution they're all with you.

So she greeted me very cordially and said, "I want to ask you a question. I want to know if you would represent me in a case, and work as hard for me as you did against me in that cow-stealing case."

I looked at her and laughed and said, "What do you think?" She said, "I think you will." I answered her, "Well, you can be assured I will!" And I did.

The facts in the matter were these: At that time she had a neighbor, Harry Aumiller, who had employed her. He had about twenty or thirty horses to winter, and had these stacks of hay, and asked her to feed these horses during the winter, which she agreed to do. Aumiller spent his winters in Jensen. And that old lady—that was one of the hard winters here, and the snow was so deep that from January until the next April no one even saw her—that old lady stood out there and shoveled the snow off these haystacks—which is a hard job— and fed those horses. Along in April they got worried about her, and her grandson Boon flew over and saw her forking hay to those horses. He waved at her and she waved back.

When spring came she said, "I want my money," and he said, "Well, I'll see about it," and wouldn't pay her. So she came in and had me represent her in suing him for that winter's work.

I thought at first he would pay it without any question, because she was right—she had it coming, and more too. Anyway, he didn't pay her, so we sued and got a judgment against him. He was kind of thumbing his nose at her, saying "Try and get it!" So that was my job again. I waited until he had a bank account big enough to pay it, and executed on it, and got her the money.

Thank God! I never handled a case that pleased me quite so much as to make this guy—trying to beat this old woman—pay her.

Joe Haslem says that the reason Harry Aumiller would not pay Josie was that he hadn't asked her to feed his horses in the first place. Josie would have responded by saying that there was no way she would let good horseflesh starve, and that if Harry hadn't asked her he should have. Ordinarily she would have fed his horses with no thought of pay, just because he was a neighbor, but as will be later learned, Josie had no reason to work free for this particular man.

Joe Haslem also says, "Nah! I didn't go to her trial. Nobody had minded when old Jose would take a beef once in a while, but when she started selling them she had to be stopped. But I knew they wouldn't convict her."

And Duard Campbell repeated what he had always said: "You can't beat a Bassett in court!"

A NEW CRUSADE

Frank Willis and Ann tried both El Paso and Kansas City when they left Utah after their marriage, but found neither city to their liking. They went on to California, drawn by the work Frank could find in the oil fields. After a short stay in Bakersfield they moved to Huntington Beach, where Ann ran the small Cooper Hotel and Frank worked for Richfield Oil.

They were soon joined there by Josie's son Chick and his wife. Edith Embry had met Chick back in Brown's Park where she had taught school for a year and boarded with George and Ruby Bassett. Even then there had been a mild attraction, but it was only years later when they met again in southern California that the attraction became strong enough for marriage.

After working for Jim McKnight, Chick had "cowboyed" in Nevada for a while, and then headed for Hollywood, where he did stunt riding in the movies before hiring on to train polo ponies. By 1928 Edith and Chick were in Huntington Beach and Chick was driving a truck.

The restless Ann could not settle permanently to life in town. An undated article from Huntington Beach's local newspaper, headed "Local Woman Will Manage Sheep Ranch in Nevada," reads:

> Here is a surprise for Huntington Beach. For some time this city has been the home of a quiet [sic] matronly woman whom no one suspected was a capable sheep raiser. For years she tried to be domestic—and now she has returned to her native calling.
>
> Mrs. Frank Willis, who for several years has so efficiently managed the Cooper hotel, has recently formed a company of three women for the purpose of going into the sheep business. The corporation has leased 480 acres at St. Thomas, Nevada, with a wider range of government land adjacent. Mrs. Willis is leaving on Saturday to become active manager of the business. She has purchased five hundred sheep, but contemplates adding a hundred more to the ranch soon. . . . Mr. Willis, who is with the Richfield Oil company, will remain here for a time. . . .

The Nevada enterprise was evidently not successful, for by 1931 Frank and Ann were living in the Walapai Valley near Kingman, Arizona, and had purchased a cattle ranch at Hackberry on which they built a home. Chick and Edith followed them, and although the two couples had separate property, they worked in concert in the raising and selling of cattle. Edith and Ann worked on the roundups, helping herd the cattle and running the cookwagon.

On one of these roundups, Chick and Ann had a good old-time fight that noticeably cooled their friendship for a fairly long period of time. Chick watched Ann ride one day, billowing over her saddle, and said, "Hey Ann, you ought to put a rumble seat on that saddle!" Perhaps this inspired Ann to reach for the carrot sticks again, for a picture taken not much later shows her to be rather svelte and still a decidely handsome woman.

Not too long after the move to Arizona, Chick—the veteran of hundreds of falls from wild horses and untrained polo ponies—broke his neck in three places in an automobile accident. It eventually healed nicely, but it hampered him for two or three years. A letter he wrote to Josie headed "Kingman, Ariz. 2–9–34" gives glimpses of what life was like for all of them at that time:

> Your letter was rather an agreeable surprise as I'd given up ever hearing from anyone again. . . . Edith and I are geting along fairly well. She is boarding some men and I am working at a job where I don't have much to do. I haven't much use of my left arm and no strength in either of them but my neck is growing back in fairly good shape. The bones grew back almost straight and I think in time I'll be able to get around better. . . .
>
> Wish you would come down here. I think you would like this country. Down where Ann is its a desert, the worst part of the country, but back over in the part Edith and I are in there is plenty of water and it's a very good cow country. We have a good little place if I ever get able to put in some work on it. I didn't get much done before I got hurt. Got a good house built but no fencing or anything else done. What we need is some cattle but I don't see how we are going to get them now. . . . Cattle are sure cheap now if a fellow could just get some money. This would be a fine chance to buy some and they won't always stay down. *Good cows sold here last fall for a cent a pound.* . . .

The italics above are added to stress the dreadful situation in the 1930s throughout the cattle countries of the west. Those prices, as well as Ann's desert ground and Chick's broken neck, suggest the reasons why Chick and Edith eventually went back to Nevada and Frank and Ann sold out in 1937. Frank went to work for a time in Colorado for the Humphrey Gold Mining Company, and later for the Bureau of Mines as a sampler foreman. They moved from place to place in Wyoming and the neighboring states, spending time between jobs with Josie or over at the old Bassett ranch in Brown's Park.

Eb's loss of the Bassett land had been heartbreaking to Ann. All the family were proud of their pioneer heritage, but Ann's sense that she was a Bassett of

Brown's Park shored up her insecure inner personality. Since the home acres had not been included in the sale and were still in the public domain, Ann peppered the land office with requests to sell the land to her, stressing the cabin's historic value as well as its sentimental value to her as daughter of the original pioneers. Finally the land office agreed, and in 1944 she acquired legal title to approximately thirty-nine acres that included the cabin, the spring, the orchard, and that marvelous "cave" which had been her childhood playhouse.

When Ann acquired title, she and Frank built a cabin almost alongside the original Bassett cabin, which had gradually been going to ruin, occupied only by Eb's sweetheart. Mattie Edwards was still "squatting" there, clinging to her memories of the past. The situation irked Ann, and she asked Mattie again and again to make other arrangements, but Mattie procrastinated. One day Mattie returned from a trip to Craig to find the cabin had burned to the ground, although evidently the fire had been slow enough to allow someone to pile her possessions outside. Esther Campbell explained, "It was Ann's cabin—if she wanted to burn it she had a right to do so."

Mattie could not have immediately realized what a fortunate fire that would be for her. Forced to move, she settled in Maybell, found another husband, lived happily, and died at the age of one hundred and three.

Ann, her right to complete possession restored, loved her own ground with the same passion Josie had for her homestead on Cub Creek. For the rest of her life she spent her summers in that cabin. However, in the winters she and Frank went to Leeds, Utah. There was an abandoned silver mine, the Silver Reef, nearby with a "dump" of discarded, low-grade ore. The price of silver went high enough that it was worthwhile to "prospect" the dump. Frank had reached retirement age by this time; Ann and he, together with a couple remembered only as "the Majors," spent time out at the old mine going through the rockpile. Frank was not yet ready for the enforced idleness of old age.

Ann herself was busy with her own affairs, which had nothing to do with prospecting. In her older years she had found a new crusade, one just as important to her as the crusade of her youth against the Two-Bar. All her life she had kept diaries and written long, witty letters to her family and to her many friends. Now she used her writing in a crusade to defend Brown's Park against its new enemies—the writers of western pseudohistory.

Beginning in the 1930s, there had been a flood of stories in books, in magazines, and in Sunday supplements, of the "Old West" in Brown's Park. Ann, remembering the days when the people of the Park had been fighting the cattle barons, was enraged at some of the sensational, distorted accounts that had changed Brown's Park almost beyond recognition. It was shown *only* as a den of rustlers, thieves and murderers. Everyone in the Park was damned. The

Bassetts' reputation was badly soiled; even more importantly, the characters of Matt Rash and Isom Dart were dreadfully besmirched.

The basis of this new spate of sometimes libelous stories stemmed from a book, *Outskirt Episodes,* privately published in Iowa in 1927 under the authorship of W. G. "Billy" Tittsworth. The book was copyrighted by a Jean Tittsworth, probably his daughter or even granddaughter. The book is based on Billy's life in the wild, wild west back in the 1870s, supplemented by a garbled account of Brown's Park people and the Tom Horn story. By the time of these later happenings Billy had been long gone from the Park, and it is probable that he learned of these events from Charley Crouse, his brother-in-law; Billy's wife Jean was the sister of Charley's wife Mary.

It was at Billy's ranch, halfway between Rock Springs and Brown's Park, that Crouse and some other Brown's Park settlers had spent the winter of the Meeker Massacre. Not too long after that winter, when the Park people had fled from the Utes, Billy himself fled, not from Indian tomahawks but from the six-shooters of a dangerous outlaw named "Black Jack" Ketchum. With help from Charley Crouse, Billy bought the train tickets to take his family to Iowa, where he established a hog farm. The Park saw him no more, except perhaps for visits to his relatives.

According to J. S. Hoy, Billy had been in partnership with an "active, efficient and successful thief" named Powers. The two men eventually had a falling out and Tittsworth killed Powers. Billy maintained that he shot in self-defense, but since the fatal bullet had been found in Powers' *back*, he did not expect people to believe him. Black Jack Ketchum was a close friend of Powers. Billy fled to Iowa because he was afraid that, once Black Jack heard how his friend had died, Billy's own days would be numbered.

It is difficult to believe that Billy himself wrote *Outskirt Episodes.* It is not a straightforward account of remembered events; it is fiction, about two-thirds of it; in the other third the author draws either on Billy's stories of very early times or on the terrible tales of the Tom Horn days. The writing style is that of a bright high school girl whose inexperience caused her to use high melodrama and heavily contrived situations. It is therefore probable that Jean Tittsworth, the claimer of the copyright, was the actual author.

The book would have been harmless enough had the author not had such a vivid imagination in the fictional portion of the book, and if she had not used pseudonyms so transparent that the characters could be easily traced to actual Brown's Park inhabitants. Billy Tittsworth himself was the fine, honest, manly "Billy Buck"; Charley Crouse was generally identified as the genial "Clouse Caseberg"; and the evil "Nat Rasper" was unmistakably the murdered Matt Rash.

If there is one character around whom the story can be said to be built, it is the Negro "Ned Huddleston." The author's pseudonymic characters come and go, as do other characters who are identified by their real names. (Charley Sparks, Jim McKnight, Tom Horn, William Pigeon and "Judge" Bennett are all mentioned.) But Ned is always there, the typical shuffling, obsequious, cowardly, ignorant buffoon of so many stories in which a black man is used as comic relief. Ned is the butt of many jokes and always is referred to as a "nigger." (This was unforgivable even in 1927.)

Briefly, the story recounts the activities of the Tip Gault gang of the early 1870s, with whom Ned Huddleston is involved. It includes an unbelievably fortuitous coincidence when "Billy Buck" finds Ned, a friend he had not seen since their boyhood in Missouri, dying by the side of a trail on the Wyoming–Colorado border because of a shootout. The author describes Ned's subsequent romance with Tickup, an Indian squaw belonging to Pony-Beater who, when he comes to reclaim his woman, hacks off part of Ned's ear. Ned was more upset at the loss of Tickup's daughter Mincy than at the loss of part of his ear, for he had developed a protective and fatherly love for the little girl. The story continues through Ned's starting a farm in Oklahoma and educating Mincy, who has appeared in that area. He finally sees Mincy run away with Nat Rasper, a no-good yellow varmint from Texas with a fancy rig pulled by stolen horses and a leer in his eye for the pretty Indian maiden. They elope in a buggy, Mincy contracts smallpox, and Nat deserts her in the wilderness, to die alone among the sagebrush and the rattlesnakes. However, Mincy is rescued by Indians and eventually marries a white rancher. It is assumed that everyone lives happily ever after.

As if all this were not enough excitement for the poor, ignorant Ned to stir up, the author also declares that Ned was actually two other men: he had been "Tan Mex" south of the Mexican border, where he was a circus clown as well as a vicious killer; and he had also been "Quick Shot" who worked with a Chinaman in Rock Springs and was known for his toughness and his bad disposition. It seems that Ned's cowardice and laziness, heretofore his most dominant characteristics, had been a sham. Then, toward the middle of the book, this man, who has already been given three inexplicably different personalities, is positively and openly identified as Isom Dart of Brown's Park, the dignified and powerful black man.

The story is discredited by even the scanty statistics of the 1900 census. Isom was born in 1855 (and in Texas, not in Missouri as Tittsworth states). If he indeed traveled with the Tip Gault gang in the earlier 1870s, he would have had to be no more than twenty years old, with a career behind him that included two aliases and two completely different personalities—"Tan Mex" and "Quick Shot"—besides the shiftless and dishonest "Nigger Ned." While it is true that boys grew up early on the frontier, it is seldom that they turned into such sophisticated criminals at an early age. As for Matt Rash, the Nat Rasper of the story, he was eighteen years old, even a little less, when he came up the trail from Texas and went to work for Middlesex.

Then, in 1938, Charles Kelly wrote *The Outlaw Trail,* an entertaining, fast-moving story that must be classed as nonfiction even though Kelly used no footnotes and named no sources and wrote in a style more suited to the tabloids or pulp magazines. He seems to have started with the assumption that no honest men, except for the Hoy brothers, had ever lived in Brown's Park, and he saw the valley as one vast corral of stolen cattle waiting to be taken to Rock Springs and sold.

In addition to his use of the exploits of Tip Gault, Butch Cassidy, and Elza Lay, and of J. S. Hoy's descriptions of his neighbors, Kelly leaned on Tittsworth's book. The result was that, to a national audience—rather than the few people reached by Billy Tittsworth's privately published book—Matt Rash was branded as a villain from Texas who deserted a dying girl in the desert, and Isom Dart was identified as a former outlaw with the vicious Tip Gault gang. Matt and Isom became rustlers working together despite Isom's enmity because of Matt's dastardly desertion of Mincy in the desert.

Almost every settler in the valley suffered from Kelly's distortions. The Bassetts were described:

> Sam [sic] Bassett came in from Green River, Wyoming, and raised his family in the Hole. Bassett was an unassuming individual, but his Amazonian wife had the reputation of being able to outride, outrope, outshoot and outcuss any cowhand in that part of Wyoming. Her two daughters became expert in handling cattle. Ann, who earned her title as "Queen of the Rustlers," and Josie, who was quick on the trigger, were a pair of real desert queens.

Ann always used the following paragraph as an illustration of how little Kelly knew about either the Park or western life in general:

> Children grew into young men and women without benefit of education, except what little they may have had forced upon them in Charley Crouse's school house. Young men naturally became expert rustlers, but they were not to be outdone by the girls. "Queen Anne," according to stories told in the Hole, once stole a herd of five hundred cattle single-handed and drove them to the railroad where they were sold. Her exploit was conducted from the front seat of a covered wagon, the team being used as saddle horses as required.

Ann never forgave Kelly for this story, saying that no one would even try to herd five hundred cattle through the sagebrush from the seat of a wagon, and that she resented his making her appear ridiculous.

Two later books were published whose authors also drew on Tittsworth. Dick Dunham's *Flaming Gorge Country*, an engaging and unpretentious little collection of anecdotes from old-timers, told the story briefly. More surprisingly, John Rolfe Burroughs devoted many pages of *Where the Old West Stayed Young* to an elaborate exposition of Isom, Mincy, Tickup and Pony-Beater and Matt Rash's desertion of the dying Mincy. Both authors identified Isom and Matt by their real names. Neither presented any collaborative evidence. And neither one had the foolishness to repeat the final chapter of *Outskirt Episodes*, in which Mincy is so miraculously returned to life.

Thus did Tittsworth's tales become "official" history. It was this besmirching of the Bassetts, of the ranchers of Brown's Park as a whole, and of dearly remembered friends that started Ann on her own writing crusade.

Although Ann accused Kelly of exaggeration and misstatement of facts, in her zeal to portray Brown's Park in a favorable light, and to publicize the real reasons the ranchers were fighting the cattle barons, she also tampered with the truth in the interests of making a good story. For instance, in *Scars and Two Bars* she evidently thought that she could refute the Tittsworth picture of Isom Dart if she were to show him as less of a man than he really was. She therefore wrote, "Mother, whose parents had been slave owners, wanted a negro cook. She sent for Isom, and he, being anxious to serve someone who knew how to treat 'niggas', came and was taught cooking and became a handy man at the Bassett ranch." Such distortions as this disgusted Josie, who dotted the margins of her copies of Ann's writings with "B. S." In one marginal notation she wrote, "If bull shit were music, Ann would be a brass band." Ann's answer was that she gave people what they wanted—a good story.

Her first attempt at writing was "Anarchy Ann," a fictionalized story of her childhood in Brown's Park. This was started but never finished in her Arizona days, and only a copy of its opening chapters has survived. The theme is that of a little tomboy with a prim and proper older sister, and the writing is strained and self-conscious. A copy of a contract between Ann and another woman seems to indicate that she was using an editor, perhaps even a ghostwriter, as she wrote the book. (Ann must have regretted in her mature years her inattention while her teachers tried to drill her in spelling and punctuation.)

She most probably abandoned this project to start her crusade, in *Scars and Two Bars*, which she researched, she told Esther Campbell, in many libraries and newspaper files in Arizona, Colorado and Wyoming. Again, only part of the book has survived, those few installments published in the *Moffatt Mirror* in the 1940s. She subsequently withdrew publication rights because someone had tampered with her writing. The bulk of the manuscript was destroyed after her death.

By the time she wrote "Queen Ann of Brown's Park," which appeared in

The Colorado Magazine in 1952 and 1953, she had developed (perhaps with the help of a competent editor) an easy style, vivid and nicely colloquial, which is pleasant to read. The work appeared in four parts, and the last sections dealing with the struggle of the small ranchers to maintain their position against the large outfits are rational and accurate and agree with other accounts given by her contemporaries and by the newspapers of the times.

Josie had no quarrel with Ann's presentation of the history of the range, but she detested the fictionalized accounts of her childhood years. In an effort to show that the Brown's Park people were not ignorant, uncouth rustlers huddling in dirt-floored hovels, Ann describes her mother as riding through the sagebrush on a prancing thoroughbred, attired in a blue riding habit trimmed with brass buttons, with no mention of the buckskin or heavy denim skirts that Elizabeth most assuredly would have worn in her workaday world. Ann describes the original settlers as coming to Brown's Park in a caravan, traveling over grassy plains (one can almost hear the banjos playing) to an easy life unmarred by cold, heat or scanty rations, or the grinding work of establishing new ranches in a wilderness.

In all her writings Ann shows a bias toward women. She sees them always able to outshine and outsmart men. She also makes herself the heroine, the protagonist, the star. The whole world centers around Ann, and she makes her own role unbelievable. At one time or another, in her writings, Ann appealed in person to a governor of Wyoming to unmask Tom Horn; assisted the outlaw Elza Lay in a hair-raising elopement with his sweetheart; and saved a friend from an Indian uprising in the 1890s, later going to Washington, D. C. to give testimony about that uprising and protect her Indian friends from the injustice of the whites. Her stories are appealing; the one concerning the efforts of old "Slippery Jim" to reform her tomboy ways when she was a little girl is a delight. Josie, however, remarks in the margin of her copy, "Harmless but untrue. Slippery Jim was an old saloon character around Rock Springs whom my parents wouldn't have had on the place."

One of the most appealing of Ann's stories, to my knowledge unpublished, appears below. It has been only slightly condensed and edited:

THE GRAY WOLVES

During the year 1905, cattle, young and old, were being killed in great numbers by gray wolves, great, powerful beasts that prowled over the range, making a kill for each meal. Wolves do not eat "left-overs." They eat nothing but meat of their own kill and it must be fresh and tasty. The choosy beasts know how to pick the best, the fat and most often the young.

A large bounty was offered for the pelts but still they increased in overwhelming numbers. I grew impatient over the loss of so many cattle, and decided upon a personal campaign to get at least some of the meat eaters.

My first experience at wolf hunting was with a dog. A kindly disposed neighbor loaned me a trail-hound with a great reputation for trailing wolves.

I took the famous hunting dog on a leash to the fresh tracks of a couple of wolves that had killed a cow during the early morning hours at the Douglas Ranch. The trail was fresh and plain, too fresh for the dog. When I turned him loose on the sign he gave one mournful howl, tucked in his tail and fled for his kennel. This ended the dog hunting for me. So I hit the trail accompanied by a little six year old girl, Doris Morgan.

We came to a place where the wolf tracks circled the head of a rough gulch. When we found that circle of tracks, I knew the den was near. I also observed the fresh traces of two grown wolves. The paw marks were deep in the soft sand where they had jumped and run away only a few minutes before.

I rode fast in the direction taken by the wolves fleeing when they caught the human smell. After following the trail a short distance it became apparent they were out of sight and out of gun shot.

I went back to the gulch to a mound of earth that had been thrown out, and found the den. These tunnel-like openings are dug slope-wise in the soft sand or silt between ledges of rock and are a tight squeeze for the wolves to enter. I prepared to bring the pups out and kill them. Tying my horse to a tree, I broke off a long cedar limb to tangle in the pups' soft fur and drag them out.

I wrapped a handkerchief over my hair and stood my gun near the opening, as it could not be used in such close quarters. Then instructing Doris to stay on her horse, I crawled into the entrance of the filthy, dusty den. Holding a long stick with a tobacco sack of matches tied to it to supply light when I got near enough to reach the pups, I managed to slip my body through the tunnel by wiggling along like a snake.

When I was about ten feet from the entrance the light was completely shut out. I struck a match and could see several pairs of eyes in a large round dugout six or seven feet ahead of me. I had expected to find a very small pup at that time of the year, early in March.

Those big eyes and such strong growls indicated something much too active to be hauled out on a stick. I decided to get out of that den right then and started shoving myself backwards a few inches at a time. I had to hold my arms forward and slide. The going was not good and very soon I hit a tighter place.

The slope of the rock reefs were pointed and the jagged edges caught my corset stays. I could not get my hands back to loosen the hold and I was not strong enough in that position to break either the stays or the rocks. I was held fast in a trap, with the parent wolves lurking somewhere near on the outside, and the big pups glaring and snarling close ahead in the den.

I called to my little companion who sat her pony standing guard at the entrance of the den. When she heard me call, she dismounted and came to the mouth of the passage. I told her I wanted to stay in the hole—just then those words "wanted to stay" almost strangled me, for by that time I was numb with fright. I instructed Doris to ride back to the ranch, reckoned to be about eight miles. She should back track our shod horses, the tracks we made that morning in the soft earth. I cautioned her to be sure that the tracks she followed had shoe marks, that being very important.

I was fearful of betraying my trapped condition to the small child who was all I had between me and the jaws of a mother wolf. If Doris became frightened, or lost, we were both sunk. There were no other people near, no fences or roads to guide her over endless hills, but she was a child of the hills with natural instincts of direction and could be relied upon to do as she was told. With only shod horse tracks to direct her, the brave little crusader went cheerfully on her way, alone.

Lying there in a helpless position, stretched out like string in that unsavory den, was nothing to be enthusiastic over. With the eyes of the big pups glaring at me from the front and expecting the enraged mother to chew on me from the rear was not a pleasant situation.

Nothing could be done about it. I was forced to lie motionless and wait for one of two things. If help came all would be well, otherwise the wolves would make short work of me. The welfare of the little child was a cause for much anxiety. The child I had led into this uncanny circumstance in a head-on enthusiasm of wolf phobia. If the child became lost in her direction, it was reasonable to suppose that the old horse she was riding would eventually go to the ranch when he felt the urge to have the saddle removed. He would, of course, take his own time to do that and when night came on the tracks to the den could not be found.

After several hours, that seemed years, I heard my saddle horse call and he began to stomp and walk around in a nervous, uneasy manner. I knew instinctively that other horses were approaching.

I was filled with joy almost to the bursting point. After a short time all was quiet again. No sound of voices or footsteps came near the den. I slumped. The walking around of my horse was caused by range horses passing somewhere close and he had either seen or smelled them.

All hope was vanishing fast, utter despair was creeping over me. I was too weak to cuss, misery had completely engulfed me.

At last, I heard the ring of steel from a pick striking rock as it was thrown to the ground. And a voice said, "I'm here now, you can come out." I had worked myself into such a frenzy it was hard to believe my ears. However, I gained sufficient strength to shriek, "Come out, hell! I'm caught in here, fastened tight as a wedge!" After Jim had picked and shoveled for about an hour and I had received a few jabs from the pick and broken rocks, I crawled out looking like an animated clod covered over with cactus and wolf hair. I was blinking and wiping the dirt from my face, but never had daylight looked so inviting.

We proceeded to go after the pups in earnest and were bewildered to find two families in the den. Some of them were large and the others were very young. Contrary to all animal habits, two mothers had made this den their home. Living together and doing cooperative housekeeping to raise their young is something quite unbelievable in the animal world.

We killed the pups and carried them away to save the hides so we could collect the bounty. We set traps around the den and when we returned the following day one wolf was snared. The other had gotten out of the trap and escaped.

From that experience I found that corsets and trappers did not belong together and my first act after I was dug out of the wolf hole was to step behind a sheltering tree, to avoid further shock to my rescuer, a modest old bachelor. I then and there forever freed my carcass of that steel girder, so dear to feminine hearts.

With loud echoing words of profanity I cast the thing from me, to let it rust in peace in a quiet spot on the Douglas Mesa. In some future years that corset may be

> plowed up by an over-zealous dry farmer who will become worn by brain sag trying to classify an ancient race that clothed themselves in steel armor.
>
> And now, whenever I see a counter display of those slinky corset things, the gripping jaws of a hungry, angry mother wolf seem to be nipping on my hind quarters, urging my steps to quicken as I pass by the heap.

The story is one that the family delights in telling. The only detail they add, which makes the story even better, is that Ann had been wearing a handsome new riding skirt that day, and had spread it on a bush before she wriggled into that dirty wolf den. When she emerged, she was wearing *only* the offending corset! A sobering note is also added; when they returned to the den the next day to check their traps they found that the surviving wolf had attacked the bush bearing the scent of that skirt, tearing the foliage to shreds. Truly, it is lucky that Ann lived to wage her war with Two-Bar and tell her enchanting stories.

QUEEN ANN OF BROWN'S PARK

During their retirement years, only the winter snows drove Frank and Ann from their cabin on the site of the Bassett homestead. In the long summer months they often went to Craig, which was by this time the home of Josie's grandchild Betty Eaton. One day Betty was sitting in a dentist's office waiting for badly needed tooth extractions (which Josie paid for by giving her a heifer to sell) and becoming restive because the dentist was keeping her waiting for a long time. He came out to assure Betty that the delay was unavoidable.

"I have an old lady in there whose teeth have roots like a horse's, and I'm having to pull them with no novocaine. She's a tough old girl and insists that she does not believe in deadening drugs."

When the door finally opened, Betty was not surprised to find that the tough old lady was her Aunt Ann. Ann greeted Betty with aplomb, dismissing her extractions with a haughty wave of her hand.

In her old age, Ann was no different from the dictatorial aunt of Betty's childhood. Each time she came to Craig she would visit with Betty, upsetting her life just as competently as she had upset Josie's. For instance, Betty's little girl was allergic to bananas. Ann believed in allergies no more than she believed in novocaine, and was convinced that all children without exception needed this almost perfect food. Consequently she always brought bananas and fed them to little Judy, and even the normally assertive Betty found it easier to cope with Judy's rashes than attempting to cope with Aunt Ann.

In the summer of 1949 Duard Campbell, the teenager who had known Ann back in her South Fork days, reentered her life, bringing with him his wife Esther. Duard and Esther, after living all over western Colorado and eastern Utah, had bought a ranch up on Douglas Mountain at Teepee Springs, the site of Ann's Douglas ranch. They lived there in the summer and came down to Brown's Park in the winter so that Esther could teach in the Park's one-room school.

One day in late spring Esther answered a knock on the door of her school and opened it to a very straight-backed little woman with a high-held head who said, "I am sure you do not know who I am." Esther looked at her a moment, and then answered, "Well . . . I think . . . that you are Ann Bassett." Ann was delighted that Esther had remembered her from one short meeting many years before, and from this auspicious beginning arose a friendship that was to add sparkle to Ann's last years of life and give immense pleasure to Esther as well.

Esther had had an unquenchable interest in every facet of the cattle country since she first came there as a young schoolteacher. Because Duard had known the Ute Indians down on the Uinta Reservation, Esther came to know them too, had been present at their ceremonies, and had been given gifts that will be returned to the Ute tribe at her death because of their tribal significance. She also collected arrowheads, rocks and artifacts, but most of all she collected people and their stories of early times. After Duard and she retired and left Douglas Mountain, they bought the old John Jarvie place at the western end of the Park where the Green River breaks through into the valley. Jarvie's stone building still stood, sturdy and usable, its soft buff stones bearing the carved graffiti of more than seventy years. They turned the building into a museum for Esther's large and varied collection of relics and mementos. In the late 1970s when the widowed Esther sold it to the Nature Conservancy and moved to Vernal, she left behind many items of that collection, including a gorgeous pair of shocking-pink satin lounging pajamas once worn by Queen Ann herself.

Duard and Frank decided that it might be worthwhile to prospect together in the outreaches of Brown's Park, and eventually they filed a claim or two up on the flats beyond Irish Canyon, although unfortunately they were never to amount to anything. Ann had a heart condition and needed someone with her to slip nitroglycerine under her tongue in case she should have what she called "one of my tizzies." While the two men prospected, Esther moved into Ann's cabin and spent the summer listening to Ann's graphic stories about Brown's Park and its people.

Ann told Esther about "Scars and Two Bars" and about "Queen Ann of Brown's Park," which she was working on at the time. Esther herself decided to write a history of Brown's Park that would be more general than Ann's, and she plied Ann with questions. She would ask Ann, "Did you say that so and so happened?" and Ann would reply, "No, dammit, I said that it was such and such." She was a hard taskmaster. Even so, Esther enjoyed herself.

Somewhere around this time Duard went to Denver and happened to meet Sam Goldwyn, one of Hollywood's leading producers. Goldwyn expressed great delight in what Duard told him of Queen Ann and Brown's Park, and talked tentatively of producing a movie about Ann and her valley. The mutual interests of the two women in writing their stories and in developing the possible Goldwyn interest cemented their friendship. Through Ann, Esther met Josie and developed an acquaintance with her that was equally enriching to Josie and to Esther.

When Ann returned to Leeds in the autumn, she corresponded with Esther about the possible motion picture, the impending publication of Ann's writings, and Esther's ambitions for her own history. Esther herself was too outgoing and gregarious, too involved in community projects to submit to the self-discipline and solitude necessary to put what she knew on paper, but the correspondence provides insights into Brown's Park and into Ann herself that could have been preserved in no other way, as the following potpourri from Ann's letters reveals:

> I have thought for a long time that someone would make a picture of Brown's Park historical background. The one thing I have been afraid of was it might be taken from "Outlaw Trail" and that fact has worried me. The damned stuff Kelley put out was senseless and stupid and still people sucked it up. No doubt we could furnish more real more exciting and far more interesting historical facts if given a chance. . . . Josie puts all the little episodes of our daily lives in those early times down as too trivial and nonsensical for people to be interested in. She just shrugs it off and says "Of course Jack Rollas was killed so was Valentine Hoy. What of it—we buried them and that's the end of it. Why start that all over again." While I think all those things are important in a country's history. Josie says nuts to me. She knows its all true but thinks it's silly to write or tell it now after so many years. . . . Speaking plainly Josie won't be worth a tinkers damn to us on history. She will fit in as an old resident of the "Hole" and that is all. . . .

> I wrote not for publication but for the generations of Bassett clan who had read absurd publications lacking in even a shade of truth. I had Sam's boys and their children as well as more distant relations in mind. . . .

> I have lived in the Brown's Park and Douglas Mtn. country when and if you got a nice little outfit together just as you have by hard work and honestly, you would become a "cow thief." Rumor would be started floating around Denver, then spring up in Baggs and around Rawlins—seep to Vernal, etc. Then let the axe fall. The papers would slyly hint good riddence. Whisper "The Campbells were cow thieves did you know that?"—"Well I heard it"—"I did not believe it at first but—I guess it must be true, they got killed for it—I guess." Yes, I guess—it took guts and gumption to hold out and there was no guess work about that. Some of [us] were so mad and [foolhardy] we failed to see the danger. Injustice loomed above every thought of safety. . . . Hells bells I get strung out & cant quit, when Tom Horn is mentioned. I go off my trolly and see red. Shut her down Ann you bore me. So Long.

> Bill Titsworth could have written a true story of the country and made it good history if he had been inclined that way. . . . Mr. Hafen [editor of *The Colorado Magazine*] had read all that stuff. He also has J. S. Hoys manuscript. He told me that he could not publish it until he had worked it over and cut out the wicked

> personal venom that is so very obvious in Hoys writing. . . . I don't expect you to take up the subject of the *casteration [sic] of J. S. Hoy* in your history. However your club gals would be interested altho seeming to be very much shocked. . . . I could tell you a lot of such stuff. It would not be pretty. Some juicy scandel but I am not going to. I could implicate my self in some of the dirt. Some is funny. I am not going to do that either. . . .

The correspondence was interrupted in 1953 when Ann suffered a heart attack so serious that she was taken out of Brown's Park by helicopter to the hospital in Craig. When she found herself lying in bed, surrounded by people who all looked *down* at her—at her, Ann Bassett, who had always stood eye to eye with the world and dominated it with her five feet and three inches of height—she felt helpless, defeated, old and ready to die rather than submit to the indignities of illness.

When Betty was notified she hurried to the hospital, to be greeted with the phenomenon of her invincible aunt wearing black blinders over her eyes and refusing to acknowledge her presence. Uncle Frank was beside himself with sorrow and worry.

Frank informed Betty that Ann would not drink water, and Ann broke her silence to corroborate this statement, saying that she would not drink water from the Yampa River, no matter how many times it might be filtered, since it was contaminated by the sewage of up-stream Hayden. From behind her blinders she informed Betty that yes, she would drink the water from Betty's well. From then on, three times a day, Betty brought well water in a thermos, water so heavily sulphured that Betty herself could not drink it. Ann manfully downed the noisome water, then sank back on her pillows behind her mask, waiting—and willing herself—to die.

Betty called Crof, and he brought Josie to Craig. When Josie walked into the room where Frank and Betty sat helplessly, Ann did not know, behind her blinders, that Josie was there. For the first time in Betty's life she saw her grandmother cry. Josie stood there with tears running down her cheeks and dribbling off her chin. She was shaking all over, as if from bitter cold.

Finally she said, "Ann, you're the biggest horse's ass I've ever seen. You never could face facts or face the world. What are you doing, lying there with those whoopty-doopty blinders on your eyes!"

Ann said, "Well, Josie." Then they sat, holding hands and not saying much, the two sisters who had loved so deeply and fought so furiously all the days of their lives.

Ann made life miserable for all around her. A nurse came in to protest some noise actually made by an old person in the adjoining bed, and Ann threw a bedpan at her, shouting, "Don't you ever come in here again, you black bitch!"

Betty advised the nurse—who, incidentally, was not a Negro but a woman with black hair—that she would probably be better off if she really did not attempt to enter the room again.

Relatives were gathering—Josie, Crawford, brother Sam's son from Washington State, and "the Majors" from Leeds. They all descended on poor Frank and the unresponsive Ann, who continued to wear her blinders most of the time.

The worried Betty consulted the doctor, wondering if all these mourners were good for Aunt Ann and also upset by what Betty considered to be poor treatment and neglect by the nurses. The doctor told Betty that he knew he was dealing with a determined, obstinate woman who had decided to die, and that the only way he could help her was to instruct the staff to be so unsympathetic that Ann would decide to recover just to spite them.

The doctor was wise. In only a few days Ann asked Betty what kind of automobile she possessed. On hearing that it was a small one, Ann directed her to find a station wagon that could be fitted out with a mattress on which she could lie for the trip to their winter home in Leeds. As she informed Betty, "I *shall* not spend one more night in this filthy hole."

In April 1953 Ann wrote a letter from Leeds to the Campbells:

> The truth is, I am very much out of the running right now. About two months ago I was hit by a rather searious heart condition which has set me down a lot. If I do the slightest bit of arm exercise I go into a tail spin for sure. Then it's reach for the nitro-glycerine pill and slip it quickly under the tongue to get action. Dr. ordered me to quit work for a while—or else—ten minutes or less can wind up the tick in an old body. It does not bother me any, its very painful so I do the heavy sitting around and Frank does the work, not much to do. . . .
>
> I suppose you are fretting about the drop in cattle prices just as we did on that exact range many years ago. History of mankind goes around in circles but the old cow has sense enough to lie down under a tree when she fills her paunch and rests up until her cud is chewed. When cold and hunger overtake her she lies down and dies just as serenely as she chewed her cud with no fuss and bother about what work she left undone. I often wonder when we will learn as much as a cow knows without trying to learn. Prices go up and down and the change wont hurt the one who raises his cattle. He and she may have to tighten the belt a little but they come out of it. They always have. The one who trys heavy speculation on high prices has always been the loser. "Feed them and weep." Good steady stick to it and cattle will bring you out of it in the end. Old buzzards such as I will ramble on about a subject out of reach, knowing they would repeat their mistakes if given another chance to worry and groan.
>
> Its such a habit to hunt up something to grieve about. . . .

Ann knew she could not live much longer, and she proceeded to prepare her affairs. She wrote a will giving her husband Frank the use of the Bassett homestead for the rest of his life, but directing that the thirty-nine acres, with the cave where she had played as a child, were then to pass to Sam's son, Emerson Bassett, and from him to Frank MacKnight; from there it was to pass she knew not where, but it was never to be sold or mortgaged, and was always to remain under the ownership of descendants of those Bassetts who had come there in 1878.

But she lived on. It was not until May 8, 1956, three days before her seventy-ninth birthday, that she quickly and quietly died.

Even in death Ann Bassett Willis caused trouble. According to her obituary in the Craig *Empire-Courier*:

> Mrs. Willis requested cremation. Her ashes will be placed in the Bassett cemetery on the old home Bassett ranch in Brown's Park and be allowed to blow to the four winds.
>
> Her round-up days are over. Her heart has ever been in Brown's Park. She will be returned to its hills and valleys, of which she herself has said, "the only thing I ever selfishly loved."

As soon as her ashes were returned from the Salt Lake crematorium, Flossie gathered as many of Ann's nieces as were available and, with Crawford, went to Brown's Park to give moral support to Frank in his task of strewing Ann's ashes in the Bassett cemetery.

They found Frank in the cabin. He made no attempt to take them up the hillside for the strewing ceremony; in fact he put them off and seemed not to want to discuss the subject. They went home with nothing accomplished. Jane caused consternation later down at Jensen's store when someone asked her if she had helped bury Aunt Ann safely. Jane said airily, "Oh no, Frank's still carrying her around in the trunk of his car," and then was compelled to explain away the apparent gruesomeness of her remark.

Ann's ashes remained in the back of Frank's car. The family believed it was really Frank's business and not theirs, and put no pressure on him for a more fitting resting place. The mystery was finally explained when Frank visited Betty in Craig while Jane and Josie were also there. He had already gone to bed when the conversation came around to a discussion of what might possibly have happened to Ann's very beautiful diamond and platinum ring. Could it have been cremated with her body? Each woman looked at the others, and they mutually agreed that it would hurt nothing if they were to take a look inside the box in the trunk of Frank's car.

When they brought Ann's ashes in and spread them out on paper for the search, they realized Frank's problem. Even a "perfect" cremation does not create light and feathery ashes, and Ann's cremation had been far from perfect. As the women looked for Ann's ring, they found that Ann's remains were, in actuality, large, yellowish lumps. No wonder Frank kept Ann in his car! There was no way he could strew her ashes to be caught by a summer wind—he would have had to pitch those clinkers like so many pebbles.

Later Betty talked to the old man gently, trying to help him in his dilemma. Surely Ann's remains could be buried? Frank's voice quavered and his eyes filled with tears. "I can't!" said the man who had so willingly followed Ann's slightest wish for over thirty years. "Ann said that if I didn't strew them, she would rise right up and *haunt* me!"

Frank lived until the summer of 1963. For a while after Ann's death he continued to live in Leeds or in his Brown's Park cabin. When he finally needed care and could not live alone, Flossie and Crawford took him in. Before he left his cabin in Brown's Park he posted a notice on the wall:

> To my friends and neighbors everywhere.
> My wish is that when I die is to be buryed on the top of the hill N. W. of my cabin. I want a plain wooden coffin made by me or some of my friends. I do not want any undertaker to touch me or have anything to do with my body. Artificial work does not appeal to me.
> Frank Willis

As time passed, Frank became difficult. He wandered, he ran away, he became almost violent when Flossie's grandchildren irritated him; and he became so suspicious of friends as well as strangers that he kept a loaded rifle by the side of his rocking chair. Everyone had always loved Frank, but it was obvious that he would have to be moved. For a time he went back to stay with a family in Brown's Park, but eventually the day came when he had to be sent to a nursing home in Craig.

As he sat at the post office in Brown's Park waiting for the car to take him to the nursing home, he talked to the people there of his wife Ann.

"Did you know my wife Ann Bassett? What a hornet she was! One time I started to chew snuff, and Ann laid me out in the yard. She just"—he made a hand movement as though hitting someone over the head—"and that was that. Another time she laid for me by the door when I came home drunk. She knocked me out and left me till I came to."

The old man sat there, going over in his mind the things Ann had done to turn him into an acceptable husband, and he remembered them with more lovingness and received them more gratefully than he did the impersonal kindness that surrounded him in his last days.

When he died, the nursing home notified a family friend who arranged for a casket and made the funeral arrangements without knowing of Frank's requests. Edna Bassett Haworth and her husband Paul were living in Craig at that time, but Edna herself was in Arizona. The Haworths felt that this was the most appropriate time to dispose of Ann's ashes and that it would be quite suitable to bury them in Frank's grave. But when Josie heard of this, she insisted that Ann's ashes were not to be part of Frank's funeral. "He put up with her meanness all his life, and he is *not* going to be plagued with her in his grave."

It was a lovely funeral. Frank's wish to be buried under the big cedar tree could not be completely satisfied, for when his neighbors started to dig the grave they hit rock, and the gravesite had to be moved just a little. It was still in the general location he had selected, however, a little higher on the hillside than the cemetery in which the Bassetts were buried. A "lady minister" from Maybell read prayers at his graveside, and hymns were sung. It was a fitting service for a beloved and respected old man.

As the minister stood praying, her black gown fluttering in the wind on the high hillside, Betty happened to glance down toward the cabin and saw Paul Haworth walking up the hill to the open grave with the box of Ann's ashes in his hands.

Betty nudged Flossie. "Mama, stop him!" she whispered. "Mother will make a scene right here and now." Flossie left the graveside and went down to explain to Paul that he was carrying a bombshell; Paul prudently backtracked and returned the ashes to the cabin.

With that crisis behind them, the funeral went smoothly and afterward the mourners partook of lunch in Ann's cabin, as is customary at country funerals. When all but the family had departed, Flossie, Josie and the MacKnight children took Ann's ashes up to the cemetery and buried them in a spot that is unmarked, lest curiosity seekers disturb her. The provocative and troublesome Queen Ann was finally laid to rest.

OLD JOSE

Josie was seventy-one years old in 1945, and had been watching the cattlemen of the area consistently make money on cows ever since 1939. Although she had been defeated earlier by the see-saw of good and bad years and her family obligations, the times seemed ripe for another venture. She had lost her grazing rights through non-use, but with her own fields and the use of purchased hay, she was convinced that she could now make money in cattle.

She went to the bank and asked for a loan to stock her land with cows, but the bankers refused her, perhaps feeling that she was a visionary too optimistic about her chances, and positive that she was too old to be a good risk for a loan. After all, whether she realized it or not, she was an old lady.

Once she had worked out in her own mind what she believed to be a workable plan, Josie was not to be balked. She decided to deed her land to someone young enough to get the loan the bank had refused her. She had been "squatting" on her property since she had homesteaded it in 1913, at times too poor to pay the necessary two dollars or so for each acre, and always too poor to pay the taxes that would be assessed when she had once proved up. Now she proved up on her claim, signed her land over, and sat back to wait for the loan to be floated.

Six months later, surely more from misunderstandings and inexperience than from chicanery, her assignee sold her land to Harry Aumiller, who ran the Jensen store. The sale price was twenty-six hundred dollars; within the week Harry Aumiller mortgaged the property for six hundred dollars more than he had paid for it and stocked it with horses.

This old woman who did not feel like an old woman—who had lost what she had built with her own back-breaking labor, who had tried so hard to turn her ranch into more than just a subsistence living, who had always had such plans and such belief in its potential, who loved her land as dearly as she loved her children—was enraged almost to the point of insanity. She loaded her rifle with shells, got on her horse and headed for Vernal, determined to kill.

Her family rallied around her and, with the help of the sheriff, calmed Josie down. They themselves bore the brunt of her anguished threats, her profanity and her desire for vengeance. They grieved with her, even the sheriff, in her murderous despair. They got her home, and they still shared her grief, as they looked out her big window onto the pastures where she had hacked at the brush in her bib overalls and entangled her curly hair in the thickets. Nothing could be done about it, of course. She had done it to herself in her stubborn determination to achieve success after all the years of scrabbling. She finally had to accept her loss as fact, unchangeable fact.

Things could have been worse. Utah public lands are divided among the Bureau of Indian Affairs, the Bureau of Land Management and the National Park Service, and the lands owned by the state of Utah, which include "school lands." After Josie built her final cabin she discovered that it had been built on Utah school land, over the line from her homestead claim. When the parcel had eventually come up for sale, by great good fortune Crawford had bought the five acres on which the cabin stood and given them to Josie.

So Josie could still stay in her home and continue the life that was as necessary to her existence as the air she breathed. Even though she now looked down toward fields that were no longer hers, she still had her orchard and her garden, her chicken house and her corral, her spring and the pond where her geese and ducks swam quietly. She still had the box canyon behind her cabin where she could confine her horses and a cow or two. She could survive despite her loss.

The first years of putting up with Harry Aumiller as a neighbor were difficult. Harry did not live on the property during the winter, but he camped out there each summer in a tent-house, using a rustic shower contraption he had erected with water piped from one of "her" springs. Having him so near was almost as bad to Josie as living in town. She hated seeing Harry's horses in her old fields, and detested his intruding tent-house, which she could see if she walked too far to the east.

Even worse than Harry Aumiller was his pesky, nasty, vicious mule. The mule liked to nudge her horses when she hitched them to the wagon; worse yet, he had even killed Helen's new-born colt. When Josie saw that colt's mangled body, she hitched up her wagon and said to Jane, "Come on!" When Jane asked where they were going, Josie merely said, "You'll see."

As they drove the wagon down the trail, the mule followed them, pestering her team as usual. Josie made no attempt to drive him off but drove on down to a place where a deep gully ran alongside the road. Josie tied up the team and sat watching the mule as he wandered around looking for graze. When the mule had ambled over to exactly the right spot, Josie picked up her rifle, took careful aim and killed him with one shot. The mule tumbled neatly down to the bottom of the gully. Jane and Josie then turned around and went home.

Josie was more cheerful than usual that day—she had accomplished a good piece of work.

Josie was fair enough to know that she could not blame Harry Aumiller for buying something that was legally available. She finally said grudgingly, "I can't get rid of the damned old fool, so I'll just have to put up with him." Her family was actually glad that, at least during the summer months, the old lady who so stubbornly refused to move to town would have someone within call. After the mule-killing and after Josie's victory when Hugh Colton made Harry pay for the feeding of his horses, they settled down to being good friends and neighbors.

Josie became reconciled to what had happened, and as time went on she blamed herself more than anyone else for the disaster that had befallen her. From a practical standpoint it was not even that much of a disaster, for Josie became eligible for a monthly pension. With her land gone, in her defeat, Josie had finally found the "cash crop" that had eluded her for so long. It was not a huge check, but at least she had a source of steady income. She spent it with her usual open-handedness on things that were important to her: parcel post charges for the plucked, dressed geese and turkeys she sent to friends and family outside the area; a membership in the Audubon Society; daily milk delivery to a grandchild struggling to support her children after the breakup of her marriage; and essentials such as kerosene for her lamp, plants for her garden, and batteries for the radio that kept her in touch with the outside world.

In 1950 Dottie was thirteen years old and Jane was fifteen. Their years of staying with Granny Jose were almost behind them, for Dottie went young to Salt Lake City and Jane was almost ready for marriage. Most of the grandchildren had scattered: Amy was out on Willow Creek with her husband and children; Boon was married and making a good success of his ranch, although he had already developed the diabetes that was to blind and finally kill him; Frank was in the Army; Betty was in Craig; and Belle was up in the state of Washington.

Jane and her husband Bob Smuin stayed in the area, however, and as each year of the 1950s passed they became more important to Josie, and to Crawford and Flossie as well. Crawford loved the outdoors as much as Josie and had always taken his children on fishing trips and arrowhead hunts when he could find the time. Now he went with Jane and Bob on hunting and fishing trips in the mountains, and Bob became almost another son to him. Bob loved Josie and admired her, so Josie found herself another grandson. Even his eventual divorce from Jane did not break Bob's ties to her family; he still went hunting with Crof and continued to visit Josie and give her what help she needed. As the years passed, Josie relived her summers with her grandchildren when Gib, Jane's son, came out to the ranch to stay with her and plow her garden plot with one of the new-fangled little tractors.

Other people were always coming and going. Teenagers out riding in the country stopped to see her just because she was witty and sharp. The game wardens still dropped by for a meal of venison jerky gravy over hot biscuits. Duard and Esther Campbell came every so often, as did old friends from Brown's Park. The family was always ready for a big feast whenever one of the children came back home; then there would be huge picnic dinners with Flossie and Josie assembling mountains of food for the family and for anyone else who happened to come. They would sometimes have wine to celebrate, and Josie would give the toast that the proper Flossie hated so. Holding her glass by the stem and swirling the wine a little, Josie would look into its depths and say:

"Here's to the American Eagle
That flies from sea to sea,
And the wine glass
And the woman's ass
That made a horse's ass of me."

As she aged, Josie needed more help, and it became almost a tradition with the younger neighbors to come out for a visit and do her heavy work for her. Shirley and Berenice Ainge brought their children for a camping trip in many summers, and while he was there Shirley would patch the fences or move the outside toilet or do whatever else had to be done. A woman friend of Josie's brought her trailer out and spent the summer. Once Josie even brought home a couple of beaded and sandaled hippies who stayed with her until her lifestyle became a little too rugged for them.

Josie's longevity was building a bridge between the 1950s and the long-gone past, and she became a celebrity of sorts. Boy Scout leaders brought their troops out to see the woman whom they themselves remembered from hunting trips and summer days on Cub Creek with her grandsons. Joe Haslem's wife Ruth, a schoolteacher in Jensen, took her class out to the ranch, and Josie told them stories of the old days and took them over her ranch, a working exhibit of the old pioneer life. A women's program over in Maybell included a "short talk by Josie Bassett Morris," as one of Colorado's pioneers. Craig celebrated the centennial anniversary of its incorporation, and again Josie was an honored guest, the town forgetting her scandalous breakup with Charley Ranney and remembering her only as one of its first and leading citizens, who had planted plum trees and put up Craig's first windmill.

Ann was still alive when *Life* magazine learned that out in Utah an old woman still lived in the style of the pioneers, shooting her own deer and butchering her own beef. They approached Josie for an interview and hinted that the publicity could mean that possibly a movie would be made of her life. Josie was as distressed as Ann over the distorted stories of Brown's Park (so distorted that now one writer had told of her poisoning Jim McKnight at Sunday dinner!), but she was intrigued with the idea that she might make some money from the publicity.

Queen Ann and Frank were visiting her at the time of the interview and were there to drive Josie up to the Jensen store to meet the *Life* news team. Ann had come prepared to meet the press with clothes of the sort that had made her a legend around the country. Eleen Williams of Flaming Gorge tells of the time she saw a younger Queen Ann. A young schoolteacher bride, Eleen was sitting in the lobby of the hotel in Rock Springs, listening in a bored fashion to her husband and mother-in-law talk to other people from outlying areas who customarily congregated in the hotel lobby on their trips to town. She looked up as a plump, straight-standing little woman entered and stood surveying the chatting groups. The woman was dressed in a tailored leather coat and well-cut riding pants. She wore beautifully fashioned western boots and a western hat of soft leather rather than the usual Stetson felt. She removed her long leather gauntlets, which matched her hat and boots, and slapped them against her hip as she looked around. Two men accompanied her. After a moment or so, the small woman strode on to the hotel dining room and the two men followed her. When Eleen asked her husband about the woman who was dressed so beautifully and seemed in such command of herself and those about her, he told her, "That was Queen Ann."

Now Ann prepared herself as carefully as always when she was to meet the public. This meant that Josie arrived at the Jensen store two hours late. Josie herself wore a pair of overalls from which a torn back pocket had been neatly removed, her customary old sweater, a felt hat on her white hair, and the tennis shoes she almost always wore in her old age after she developed a troublesome bunion. *Life* had said she was to shoot and skin a deer? Then of course it would have been ridiculous to dress up. Since she was to work, she wore her working clothes.

By the time the full party had assembled there was quite a gathering of people. The family was represented by Josie in her overalls, Queen Ann in her riding clothes, Frank Willis of course, and Josie's granddaughter Jane, a slim teenager agog at all the important visitors. The most important local members of the party, however, were Joe Haslem and his wife Ruth, for by this time Josie had no cattle and they were to use Joe's herd for the necessary props.

There was also the problem of shooting a deer. Josie's shooting eye was not impaired by age, but her way of getting herself a deer was to slip up quietly and line herself up a good shot. There was no possibility of this, accompanied by a troop of people that included tenderfeet with cameras. *Life*'s photographers were fortunate that two teenagers were able to flush a deer out of the brush, and that their cameras caught a good shot of the two boys literally chasing the deer, in sharp silhouette against the sky.

The whole day was spent taking pictures. They concentrated on Josie in her old sweater, ignoring completely her sister, Queen Ann. (Josie was later very upset at one picture they used in the magazine because it showed her posed on a horse with a slack rope around the neck of a heifer—an unforgivable breach, which any of her ranching friends would notice in a minute.) Since the teenagers had been able to overtake the deer and shoot it, photos were taken of Josie skinning and dressing out the carcass.

Ruth Haslem became so bored that she left the scene for a while, but she revived when the photographers finally had enough of outside pictures and returned to Josie's cabin. There Josie made a meal for everybody of her hot biscuits and venison jerky. More pictures were taken of Josie serving dinner to her neighbors Joe and Ruth and to Frank Willis and Ann. Unfortunately, Ann's back was turned to the camera and the caption on the published picture identified her as "a friend."

For Ann, perhaps the worst moment of a disappointing day was at leave-taking when the *Life* reporter turned to Josie and asked, "Do you mind if we call you Queen of the Cattle Rustlers?" Josie gave him her beguiling smile and, perhaps with a sidelong glance at her sister, graciously responded, "Of course not!"

When the *Life* article was published on January 5, 1948, Crawford and Flossie and all the grandchildren were aghast. In Amy's words, "You could show the real Josie any way you wanted to, and never would she come up a 'Ma Kettle.' That *Life* article was awful!" Josie was indeed called the "Queen of the Cattle Rustlers" who had never bought a twenty-five cent hunting license. She was shown brandishing a rifle above her head as she stood triumphantly astride the fallen deer. The article was not unkind, but it was a caricature.

Josie defended herself to Crof and Flossie by saying that it was all for money—big money, if they used her life for a motion picture. They patiently explained to her that she had little hope of being paid anything at all since she had signed a complete release. Josie was crestfallen and apologetic for being such a fool.

Indeed a motion picture was made a few years later called *The Ballad of*

Josie, starring Doris Day, and still being shown in the 1980s on late-night television. However, even if Josie had not signed a release she could have expected no royalties; the only resemblance to her own life was the locale of Brown's Park. The movie was a hodge-podge of stories, including those told by Queen Ann about Elizabeth. A version of Josie's loss of Nig Wells was so highly fictionalized that it was completely unrelated to the old poisoning scandal; Doris Day innocently and antiseptically pushed a drunken husband down the stairs, conveniently breaking his neck. Amy and her husband happened to notice the title of the movie when it came to Vernal and they went to see it. Josie was still alive, but they mercifully spared her the ordeal.

The most heartwarming recognition given "old Jose" came about when Jay Searle, president of Vernal's roping club, decided to arouse interest in his amateur rodeo by promoting the theme of "the pioneers." There had been local rodeos in the old days; Ed Lewis and Joe Haslem, for instance, sponsored a Fourth of July rodeo in Jensen where the local youngsters showed their skills. As the country had grown more sophisticated, the small local events had grown into modern rodeos, with professional contestants competing for sizable purses. These rodeos had the normal opening parade featuring a pretty rodeo queen. Jay Searles wanted to reintroduce the small local rodeo with a strong local appeal, so he came to Josie and asked her to be his rodeo queen.

At first Josie refused. She had all sorts of objections, including her age, the fact that her mare Helen was too old to gallop around an arena, and that she herself could not afford to buy an outfit such as a rodeo queen should wear. Jay Searle overrode her objections by promising to finance a snappy Western outfit and a saddle in keeping with the occasion, and to lend her a suitable horse. Josie still smarted at the family's horror over the *Life* interview, so she talked to Crawford about Jay's proposition. When she was finally convinced that this particular undertaking would bring no shame and perhaps even local fame to the family, she agreed to go along with the idea.

There were two rodeos in Vernal that summer, the ordinary rodeo with a beautiful girl as queen, and the amateur rodeo featuring Josie Morris. It was a pre-election year, and Averell Harriman came to Vernal. Josie was introduced to him right along with the cute little blonde, and both rode in Harriman's car during a parade. Later she was taken to Salt Lake City to be interviewed for television. Josie kept up a pretense that she did not approve of television, but she must have been secretly delighted at the attention given her, especially since she was again outshining her sister, Queen Ann.

On the opening night of the rodeo, in the beautiful Western outfit provided by Jay Searle, Josie had to stand on a box to reach the stirrups of Jay's lively pinto. After all, she was seventy-nine years old and her legs were starting to give her a little trouble; her old thoroughbred Miss Helen always stood quietly when Josie tried to mount her. Esther Campbell was there, to give a final tweak to Josie's neckerchief and to reassure her that her boots looked all right. At the last minute, the boots from Salt Lake had not fit over her bunion and she was wearing Amy's old boots, polished to a high shine.

As the loudspeaker blared the announcement, "Old Jose" rose to the occasion. Her back straight, she stood up in her stirrups, her backside not touching the fancy saddle, and she put the pinto into a gallop as she rode around the arena, waving her hat at the cheering crowd. Seventeen-year-old Dottie listened to those cheers and for the first time she fully realized how out of the ordinary her Granny was. When Josie went on to run in a race and brought the pinto in for third place, Dottie could hardly see through her tears.

Later that same year the crumbling mortar in the chimney set fire to Josie's cabin, but since she was only seventy-nine years old she had no trouble in putting it out. She described the fire in a letter to Duard and Esther in January 1954:

> After a long time I am going to try and answer your nice and welcome letter. I have been full of business and not in the notion to write. I got my metal fireplace [Crawford and Neldon Eaton built a new brick heatilator fireplace for her] but have had some things to think about. I had a fire in my house and it left me a mess, it took the north end of the living room and bedroom, the paper burned and it looks bad, the fire was behind the paper. I took the bar and pulled down the paper, then the flame was on the floor. It got all my best clothes, some pillows, some rugs and so many things I can't mention. I got water from the spring and lost no time throwing it on. I took the wrecking bar and pulled down the burning logs and after hard work and some managing, stopped it. No one hurt bad. I blistered my arms but am all right. . . .

She later said about the fire, "If it had happened to anybody but me, they most assuredly would have cried."

Late in the 1950s Chick and Edith came to visit Josie for the first time in thirty-eight years. When they arrived in town they looked up Crof and then drove on out to Josie's place. When they got there the door to the storage cellar was slightly ajar, but nobody came out. They parked in front of the cabin, and Edith got out to question a little Indian boy sitting alone in the seat of a battered old truck. They strolled around for a few minutes, but still nobody appeared, and the little boy answered any questions with a frightened "I don't know!"

Finally the door of the storage cellar opened wide and Josie came out, wiping her hands on a towel and followed by an Indian woman. The obvious inference was they had been disturbed while cutting up some meat, possibly illegal venison. Josie looked blankly at the couple and politely asked what she could do for them. She did not recognize her son! When Chick introduced himself, her embarrassment was poignant.

Chick and Josie had written each other sporadically. Chick had suggested that it would be nice if Josie were to visit him, but he had never sent the money for a bus ticket. He might never have returned had it not been that Jane and Bob Smuin had stopped to see this legendary uncle when they had passed through Fallon, Nevada, where he was working with his first and last love, horses. Soon thereafter Chick came to visit Josie.

A week or so of family reunions followed. Then Chick went over to Craig to meet Betty and to look up his old music teacher. Subsequently he disappeared again and was to see his mother only one more time, when she was in the hospital in Salt Lake City. Family ties once broken are hard to reknit. Crawford and his children saw Chick as an amusing man with the ability to tell a good story; still, they were slightly repelled by a certain cynicism and sarcasm in his humor that reminded them uncomfortably of Aunt Ann. They were not unhappy to see him leave, nor did they miss him in his absence. Josie, who had been so embarrassed at not recognizing him, quickly forgot him too, because by his own choice he had become part of her past and nothing in her present.

As the 1950s waned, Josie suffered the inevitable losses of the very old. Ann's death left Josie's world a bit insipid, once Ann was not there to enliven it with her opinionated wit and nostalgic talk of the old days. George Bassett had died at Christmastime in 1951, quietly sitting in a chair while waiting for a neighbor to pick him up for a visit to Craig to see Ruby, lodged in Craig's nursing home. Josie was the last of her generation; but she was not one to dwell on the past, and even in her eighties she looked eagerly toward what was ahead of her.

Betty and Neldon went up to see Josie and to shoot a deer. The three of them had climbed up to the canyon's rim and were resting under a tree when Josie pointed out a path that some reconnoitering official had told her the electric power line would eventually follow. Josie eagerly spoke of how wonderful it would be to have electricity so she could stop using a battery radio. "He said it may be twenty years, but that it's bound to come sooner or later, and then I can have a line run right down to the cabin." Betty looked at her and thought, "My God, mother, don't you realize you're already over eighty?" Actually, Josie did not realize it.

In the winter of 1959 a teenager dropped in to see her, and Josie calmly told him that she was glad he had come because "I am afraid I should have some medical attention." She had been very weak and "off her feed" and finally a show of blood alerted her to the fact that something must be wrong. It was a bleeding ulcer; as if that were not enough, she fell out of the high hospital bed and broke her collarbone. Still she stubbornly went home and continued her own way of living.

Once she tried spending the cold months with Crof and Flossie, but she refused to change her ways enough to make such long absences feasible. When she went in that winter, Bob Smuin had to bring Miss Pig along in the back of his jeep, and all the time Josie was absent she fretted about Miss Helen who had been left to fend for herself. The snow was still on the ground when she insisted that she must go home where the familiar and beloved task of putting in her garden awaited her. Something was always wrong with her hand after the collarbone was broken and she could no longer piece her quilts. However, she could still do almost everything else, even split logs if she had to.

Occasionally one of the newspapers of the region would write a feature article about the old lady. Writers came too, and although she would talk at length about her homestead and her years in Jensen, when someone with a pencil in his hand asked about Brown's Park she always clammed up. She had seen too much twisting of facts to trust many people.

G. E. Untermann down at the Vernal museum was different, however. He was an old-timer, and he knew not only Josie but Ann and George as well. He had pleased Josie when he told her that he had met George up in Zenobia Basin when he had been sent there to try to stop an invasion of Mormon crickets that were eating everything in sight, and that George had been his idea of a true gentleman. Josie was willing to reminisce with Untermann and anyone he brought out, for he was a real gentleman himself and not another Charles Kelly, of whom she said, "When Kelly dies and goes to hell, the Devil will shun his company for lying about dead men."

With Untermann, and with Murl Messersmith of Dinosaur, Josie was more open than she had ever been, and talked almost freely of the old days in Brown's Park. They also asked her about her life on Cub Creek. When she was eighty-five years old she could nonchalantly tell them that on nice days she still rode Old Helen the ten miles to Jensen to pick up her mail, although of course Crof or Bob Smuin brought it out most of the time; that someone did her plowing for her, but that she still put in a big garden, still picked her berries, still made jerky, and canned most of her other foods; and that she had just reconstructed her storage cellar, doing most of the work herself. When they asked about her livestock, she said that she now kept only two horses and Miss Pig, a good dog and some cats, but had plenty of chickens and geese and turkeys. She did not bother to mention that her family was still receiving dressed fowl and garden produce, and that guests still always left with a present of some sort—a book, or some eggs, or a jar or two of her jam.

Murl Messersmith took her up to Brown's Park, and she pointed out the site of the Bassett homestead, of the first school down on Vermillion Creek, and where Uncle Sam's first cabin had stood. She showed them the cabin where she had lived with Jim McKnight, and identified old graves and other landmarks. There was nothing left in the Park for Josie; even her mother's apple orchard was gone. Most of the ground now belonged to the government or to the state of Utah, which had established fish hatcheries in the bottoms along the river. There were fewer farmers there now than there were vacationers who came to Brown's Park to launch their rafts for float trips down the Green. Josie told them, in a tone almost of wonderment, that at one time, when the dry farmers had started to arrive, sixty or seventy families had lived there. Only her innate courtesy and her refusal to brood over the past saved the day from being funereal.

Her mind was still sharp, although she had begun to talk to herself. When Frank McKnight teased her about it, she just smiled and said she could not believe it mattered, as long as she did not expect an answer. She had always loved to whistle, and now she walked slowly, pampering her tired old legs with short steps, hands clasped behind her back, whistling softly. Her granddaughters giggled affectionately as they followed her. They thought of her as indestructible, and seemingly she was. Bob Smuin drove her home from Crawford's, one bitterly cold night of wind and drifting snow when she insisted she must go home because the animals needed tending to. When Bob did not return on schedule, Crof and Jane became alarmed and went out to check for trouble.

They found Bob's empty jeep stalled two miles from Josie's cabin on a section of the road so narrow that Crof and Jane had to abandon their own car because they could not pass. The weather was so bitter that Jane became frightened that she herself would not endure the trip. They followed the tracks that Bob and Josie had made in the snow and came to a place where they had stopped to build a fire. Jane and Crof made a new fire for themselves and rested before Jane felt she could go on. Then again they followed those two sets of footprints, expecting at any moment to see only Bob's as he was finally forced to carry Josie through the snow. But the two sets of prints led straight to the cabin, and they arrived to find Bob and Josie drinking tea beside the fire. When Jane told Josie how frightened she had been, Josie made light of it, saying "Oh, I had no fear I wouldn't make it as long as I didn't walk too fast."

It could not go on forever, of course. In December 1963, Josie was expecting Crof to come soon to take her to spend Christmas with the family. It is easy to imagine her lying in her bed out on the porch, flexing her muscles and stretching a bit before leaving the warmth to go stoke up the fire in the kitchen range, put on her overalls and start a routine day.

She built a fire in the living room fireplace, using all but two logs. The stack had to be replenished, but first things first: her water bucket was empty too. She put on her sweater and started for the spring, enjoying the glitter of the pale winter sunshine on the icy ground. Old Helen was running loose; she was old like Josie and would never stray from home. The old horse was feeling frisky too on this nice sunny morning, and as Josie passed, the horse nudged her as if asking her to fill that bucket with some oats. Josie fell heavily to the icy ground and could not get up.

"Oh, pshaw! Look what you've done, Old Helen!" Josie scolded her horse. Something hurt dreadfully when she tried to move; she knew it was in her hip. She lay for a moment, her mind racing against the pain, planning what must be done if she were to survive. Then slowly, inch by inch, grimly refusing to think of how it tortured her, she pulled herself along the ground, through the log gate and across the yard.

There she rested a moment. She was going to need water. She reached out an arm and pulled the dog's dish over to her and piled it with snow. She dragged the dish along with her, up the step and onto the porch and through the door of the cabin. The door had to be closed, for she must conserve what warmth there was and must not run the risk of the dog coming in, or for that matter Miss Pig, who had once taken it into her head to see what was in the cabin and had ended up tipping over the flour barrel. As she inched past the daybed, she dragged down a featherbed lying on it. Only when she had reached the fireplace and covered herself with the featherbed did she allow herself to give in to the pain.

They never knew how long Josie lay there waiting. Her two logs did not last very long but she had the featherbed, and Old Cat would slip under it and help keep her warm. She lay in a chilly daze of pain, and finally in terrible thirst. Perhaps she lay there only one night, perhaps two. Josie lost track of time in her torpor, half sleeping and half dreaming.

Crof brought Wilda with him when he came to get Josie for Christmas, and as he came up over the ridge he saw that no smoke was coming from the chimney. He was braced for death as he opened her cabin door. But Josie woke and lifted her head and asked, "Is that you, Crof?"

He did the best he could for her. He built up the fire and heated some soup and gave her water to relieve her dreadful thirst. Then he left her—there was no other way, for he could not get her into his car without help—and brought back Bob Smuin and Jane and Boon. The four of them shifted her onto a blanket and lifted it, stretcherlike, into Boon's car. Then they went down the rough dirt road to Flossie, who cut Josie's clothes off and kept reassuring her, as she bathed her soiled body, that she certainly should not be so ashamed of wetting her pants. Only after Josie was made comfortable and warm and clean did Flossie allow her to be taken to the hospital in Vernal.

The doctors were not encouraging and talked gloomily of the danger of pneumonia. Josie had no intention of dying, however, and they were soon able to take her in to Salt Lake City to have a pin put in her broken hip. Then she came home to Flossie to recuperate. She used a walker, but the doctor told Flossie to keep her quiet because her legs would swell as she tried to move around. But there was no way they could keep Josie sitting in a chair; she was up constantly, moving as she chose. As spring came and the snow melted, she started talking of her garden and worrying because the ground needed turning early with a plow.

When they told her she could not possibly return to Cub Creek, her spirit started to weaken, and from then on it was downhill. In May she was retaining so much fluid that they took her again to Salt Lake City to live with her granddaughter Belle and be near her doctor. On one of the last days in May she wrote a note to Flossie, still begging to come home.

When death came, it took her unaware. She was making her slow, determined way down a hall when her heart stopped beating and she pitched heavily to the floor. From this last fall the indomitable Josie did not rise again.

REQUIEM

When they brought Josie back to Jensen, Flossie almost buried her in pants; a dress seemed inappropriate. That Josie had died seemed equally inappropriate, however, so Flossie yielded to convention.

Crawford arranged for a simple service in the mortuary. After all, Josie was so old and so many friends were already in the graveyard that the small chapel should be adequate.

But the bishop of the Jensen Ward of the Church of Latter Day Saints would not hear of it. Josie was to be buried from their church. The fact that she was not a Mormon made no difference to him. She had been a Jensen neighbor and that was enough. Amy was to play the organ, Dottie and her husband were to sing, and the bishop himself would conduct the service.

Strangers had caused grief and embarrassment to the MacKnights with their whispered stories of poison and shooting and rustling and bootlegging. Now strangers softened the family's grief with other stories. People they did not even know came up to them at the mortuary, telling why they had come to honor the old lady. She had given one a home for the winter; she had delivered the baby of another; she had given one family a dozen chicks when they could not afford to start a flock. The people of Jensen surely remembered her cattle trial, but it had paled to insignificance; now they talked of the haunches of venison and cuts of beef she had brought in her old wagon to the poor people. The list went on and on, as they recalled her kindnesses and her courtesies. When the family walked into the church for the funeral, its pews were full and overflowing.

They took her up to Brown's Park. When they arrived at the graveside there was another crowd of people from the Park and Rock Springs and Craig who had known her and who mixed near-love with their respect. When they buried her near the graves of Elizabeth and Ann, the last space within the iron fencing was filled. There would be no more burials on the hill overlooking the Bassett homestead.

APPENDIX

Confidentially Told

Thank heaven for librarians! Catherine T. Engel of the Colorado Historical Society unearthed for me "Confidentially Told" after I had despaired of running down this apocryphal piece that Ann mentioned in her correspondence with Esther Campbell as having been written by her husband Frank Willis.

The Historical Society obtained this manuscript from Mr. J. Monaghan, who had once edited the Civil Works Administration's historical reports for Colorado and who then went to Illinois to be State Historian for the Illinois State Historical Library. Mr. Monaghan sent the manuscript to Mr. LeRoy Hafen (editor of The Colorado Magazine *at the time Ann's biography was published in its pages) with the following covering letter:*

> *I am enclosing the article about which I spoke to you. It is entitled "Confidentially Told." There is really some very good northwest Colorado history in this manuscript. Unfortunately, the author whose name at present must be withheld, tried to make a story out of it and in so doing hurt the history. Frankly, I suspect that the author was Queen Ann, but I am not sure. In time it will come out. . . .*

Mr. Monaghan was mistaken when he attributed the manuscript to Ann, although she undoubtedly added her own touches and anecdotes here and there. However, from examination of this manuscript and Ann's own unedited writings, it is Frank's work, based primarily on his recollections of the times he worked with Hi on the Larry Curtin ranch in Brown's Park when Hi was running cattle there after his divorce from Ann. Frank is described by the MacKnight family as a prime storyteller with an almost photographic memory of long-past events.

As Mr. Monaghan pointed out, it is unfortunate that Frank made a story of his conversations with Hi Bernard. If it were possible to separate without question the things that Hi said and anything interpolated by Frank or even Ann that was obtained from other sources, this manuscript would be the definitive document on Tom Horn's employers in northwestern Colorado. Even so, the story is worth preserving because it points up so vividly the attitudes of the big cattlemen. The whole rationale of the range warfare in the Wyoming Basin is encompassed within its pages. And not unimportantly, it contains some very funny stories and a last intimate glimpse of our cast of Brown's Park people.

Frank's written style clouds his reputation as a storyteller. His spelling is often so bizarre that it is distracting to a reader. I have presented his manuscript with all its faulty sentence structure and punctuation intact, but the spelling has been corrected for fear Frank's excellent remembrance of what Hi Bernard said to him might be buried under a deluge of "sics."

I will repeat it as I heard it, from the low spoken words of Hi Bernard, the quiet reserved man of mystery. I spent the summer of 1917 with him on the old Curtin ranch in Brown's Park. We were out away from other human contact by the great barriers of mountains and stream. There wasn't much for us to do but ride over the meadows and foothills and watch the cattle and horses grow fat. The stock belonged to Joe Jones and Hi Bernard. I was representing the Jones interests. We were batching and I was kept on my toes when helping with the household chores, stepped up to exact precision of order and neatness, demanded by this punctilious aloof man, who could cook to perfection, and would sit down to the carefully arranged table to drink cup after cup of strong black coffee, and merely nibble at a few bites of the food so painstakingly prepared.

Bernard slept as sparingly as he ate. In some unaccountable way I could see a similarity between this man's life and Green River. The river silently slipping by the ranch, its deceptive surface broken occasionally by the backturn of the warring riptides, the undertow rebelliously rushing against the stream as if in protest to natural forces that were sweeping the churning quicksands into the thundering, gaping jaws of Ladore Canyon.

One day in midsummer, right out of the nowhere, came a visitor, the elderly, highly educated, James [Jesse] Shade Hoy. An eccentric recluse who lived ten miles to the north and on the opposite side of the river. His small log cabin was half hidden by giant cottonwoods, and set in the middle of his vast acreage of meadow lands. Hoy was one of the early settlers of Brown's Park. Upon his arrival, according to rules of Western hospitality, preparations for dinner was started, and to have a little extra special service for a guest, I went to the garden and picked a small pail of luscious ripe strawberries. Mr. Hoy offered to wash and hull the berries. He placed three dishes in front of him. Carefully sorted and counted each berry so there was a like number in each dish. There was one extra berry left, so he took a knife and cut it into three equal parts placing one part on each of the three dishes for greater equality. Bernard winked knowingly at me.

When we were seated at the dinner table, the conversation drifted around to Brown's Park, history, and to Hoys recital of how he had written articles to various newspapers, and to the governers of Colorado, Utah and Wyoming, suggesting ways and means to rid the country of migratory criminals. My protests were in vain he said until my brother Valentine Hoy was shot and killed by Harry Tracy while Valentine, with other settlers of the Park was trying to run down and capture the Utah and Wyoming murderers Tracy and Johnson. And that, remarked Hoy, was the beginning of the end of outlawry in Brown's Park. At that point Bernard took up the conversation and he added. Yes Hoy, you overstressed the desirability of Brown's Park as a perfect and secure retreat for thieves and outlaws. By your writings, many of them widely circulated, advertised the place that otherwise would never have been known to exist.

You put out the bait that attracted the flies. Some of your vicious writings gave all of the inhabitants of the park, yourself included, the reputation of being thieves and crooks of every description. A man that would write and have published such stuff about his own community, a place where he has lived for over forty years, and has valuable interests is a dam fool.

And because of your prenatal affliction, and the loss of a few mental marbles, which is no fault of your neighbors, you strike at them and write your vindictive brainstorms and sow your vengeance broadcast over the entire nation. Your publications are the foundation for a grave injustice to the people of this section. I will refer you to one article in particular. I have it here, and will read it to refresh your memory.

Quoting you. "Brown's Park is a den of unclean beasts, and a roost for unclean birds." In this writing that was published in a lengthy article, you make no exceptions, you classify your neighbors, your brothers and their families all in the one melting pot of criminality. You wind up with a special peck at Charley Crouse, by naming him as the bellwether of the whole bunch. You have been sending out such messages for twenty years or longer. What could you expect the result to be? Hoy gave a shocked reply. Bernard you are not a gentleman. And who are you to make such accusations? We the people of Brown's Park, have endured the slings of arrows, and suffered the hardships of pioneering life, but we were never disgraced, humiliated, and insulted, until you dragged your swinish carcass across our fair land.

The argument was gaining momentum by leaps. Bernard quickly picked Hoy up there, and opened fire on his past history. Hoy you are the first cattle thief to enter your "fair land" you stole a bunch of cattle belonging to the Interior Department and headed them for Brown's Park in 1870. Your outfit was picked up in Wyoming by Secret Service Agents and the stolen stock recovered. To keep out of Federal Prison, you sailed to Europe, and remained in France and Switzerland for several years. When your brother Valentine Hoy was killed, you were too cowardly to go with the Posse to bring in the body, you hid in your house until Mrs. Warren and Josie McKnight coaxed you out. By that time I was fidgeting in my chair. Again Hoy struck back, and hit the bulls eye. Bernard, you beetle browed scoundrel you hired Tom Horn to kill our respectable citizens to gain a footing in this country, when that failed, you married one of our most outstanding girls [Ann Bassett] to further your greedy cause. To emphasize that heavy blow below the belt, Hoy emotionally beat the table with his fist, and sent some of the food-laden dishes spinning to the floor with a loud crash, as he shouted. "How could she so disgrace Brown's Park? How could she?"

That question was to be answered by both men as they went stumbling for their guns.

I had anticipated just such a climax, and had been edging my chair a little closer to the gun rack in a corner of the room, and near where I sat. The old boys bore the reputation of being quick and accurate lead tossers. Seventy years, more or less on the rough, had slowed their movements down perceptibly which gave me a jump ahead of them on the gun grab. I stepped quickly into an adjoining room, and cached the deadly weapons in a closet and returned to the scene of action. The old codgers were throwing rights and lefts at each other with might and fury. It was an unscientific scrap, with more misses than hits. The intended haymakers that landed lacked punch, and ended with mere taps. They finally went into a clinch, then slipped to the floor, upsetting the table as they went down to become entangled in tablecloth, broken dishes and food. The fight then developed into a scratching, hair pulling contest, Bernard who was partially bald stole the show in the hair handicap, as Hoy had an abundance of hair.

When Bernard got a good hand hold and began to pull, I expected to see a toupee lifted from Hoys pate, but I was disappointed, the hair stuck. I had been told that he wore a wig, but his pulling incident was convincing evidence that I had been misinformed, for at each jerk, Hoy would let out a blasphemous yell of indignation. When the contestants were completely exhausted, and unable to do anything but lie on the floor and glare at each other, Bernard barked chokingly, Bill get that slimy old bastard off of this ranch. I took over, and helped Hoy to his feet, he regained his wind and made it to the corral on his own power. While I was saddling one of Jones's gentle horses for Hoy to ride home, he sat braced against a haystack dabbing a handkerchief at his scratches and bruises, and growled to himself. "Look at that, the blood of an aristocrat, my own blood, spilled by a lump of putrid clay."

Soon he spoke in a louder, more excited tone of voice, come here Billie, I may be severely injured. My head wounds are oozing clotted blood. I walked quickly to the injured man, and after a careful examination of his head, the greatest tragedy of the entire affair dawned upon me, and I said bluntly.

Man this is not clots of blood in your hair, its strawberries. And there they were, the juicy berries we had intended to eat for dinner, hopelessly mixed up in Hoys unsightly mass of hair. Until then I had watched the performance with impersonal amusement. The thoughts of a choice meal that I had been cheated out of, welled up, and changed my attitude surprisingly. My patience was exhausted. I spoke rather decisive[ly]. "Get on this horse Mr. Hoy I'm taking you to the boat landing, and will row you across the river, to your home."

The trip was made more uncomfortable by Hoys mutterings of vengeance against his adversary. I left him in his tree covered bower to restore his homeland to the *culture* he was so *boastful* about. When I returned to the Curtin ranch, the ravages of battle had been carefully cleared away, and a dinner of fresh cooked food placed on the table for me.

Bernard sat on the porch quietly smoking his pipe and watching the fluffs of smoke as they climbed up to join their kind, and float away into nothingness. After eating a hearty meal, I joined him, and lit a cigarette. As I did so, Bernard dusted the ashes from his pipe and placed it on an ashtray. He began to talk as if to himself. He did not mention the recent battle, and spoke as if he was hardly aware of his one man audience. He sat motionless, his cold blue eyes continued to gaze tranquilly over the tree tops, he talked of his boyhood. I was born in 1854 near Knoxville Tennessee. My father went away to become a soldier in the Rebel army, mother was left with my baby brother George and me, on a farm to make our living, with no help but an aged negro woman. In the beginning we had some stock and could raise vegetables and fruit to supply our needs. Then the Union Army came by our place on a raid and took most of our stock. Later they returned, gathered our crops for themselves, and took away our last cow. How we managed to live I do not know. Father came home wounded by a minnie ball. He traded the farm for a team of mules and an old covered wagon. Our household goods that could be hauled, were loaded on the wagon and we started west, on a long slow journey to Texas.

Some young boys might have enjoyed this trip as an adventure, but it will always remain a horror to me. I can remember my mother in a faded and patched calico dress, cooking our scant meals over a smoking campfire, and washing our ragged clothes by a creek. When we reached Texas father rented a small farm near Houston on shares. I came down sick with smallpox. I had to lie on a hard pallet in a desolate old adobe house, "alone most of the time," with nothing to do but count the bedbugs crawling up and down from one crack to another. Around us to the north and west was cow country. While the Civl War was going on cattle branding had been neglected, and the cattle had become as wild as deer. On moonlight nights they came out of the brush to graze in open country; anybody who could catch and brand them became the legal owner. Some of the most wealthy cattle men of Texas got their start in business by "moon shining" cattle.

Catching and branding wild cattle by the light of the moon. When I was twelve years old I was hired by *Chas Chisholm* to help with the moonlight roping and branding. With my first money earned I bought a secondhand Mexican saddle, chaps and spurs. On dark nights we worked in daytime, locating the best feeding grounds to be worked when the moon shone again. On one of these scouting trips, another boy and I were riding along a wagon through dense timber; suddenly, two armed and marked men stepped from the brush. They grabbed our horses bridle reins and demanded silence, then jerked our horses into concealment beside the road. The order for silence was wholly unnecessary, for we were so scared that neither one of us could have uttered a sound. There was dull stillness for a few minutes. Then we heard the brisk clap, clap of horses feet on the dry road, and a team and buckboard came into view. Two men sat in the front seat of the buckboard, and two men in the back seat. The masked holdups sprung in front of the team and covered the buckboard riders with shotguns, and ordered them to get out and line up.

The holdups tied the hands of the disarmed men behind their backs, and ordered two of them to get back into the buckboard. They tied a rope around the neck of each of these men, and threw the loose ends of the ropes over a limb that projected across the road. They tied the ropes securely, and untied the hands of the other two men, but did not give them their guns, and ordered them to get in to the buckboard and drive off. As the team started, one of the holdups jumped at the horses, and slapped at them with his hat. The team ran down the road at breakneck speed. When the buckboard was jerked from under the tied men they were left dangling by the neck from a high limb. The masked men turned to us and shouted. You kids get out of here and head for home. We did so and without any lost motion.

When we reached home, and very much excited, father told us that the County sheriff and his deputy had been held up and relieved of two prisoners, men that had killed a girl some distance to the east a few days before. I had seen my first lynching party in action and never went in that direction again. When I was fifteen years old, I started up the trail with cattle as a cowpuncher, with one of Mavricks [sic] herds bound for Wyoming. It was a herd of about eight thousand young steers, and we traveled right along, barring a few short delays, caused by mud, flood, and Indians. Milt the negro cook and mess wagon driver had made the trip up and down the trails several times, and he knew more about the trails, campgrounds, watering places, and fords, than most of the cowpunchers did. Milt bragged continually, "I knows every watah hole between Copus Christi Texas and de C-a-n-a-d-i-e line."

One feature of the trip Milt did not like too well, was the danger of encountering Indians. The Indian question sent chills of dread up his spine, and the cowboys were not making things easy for him. They knew Milts habit of keeping one ear to the ground when trail hazards were discussed, and of his special alertness when they went into a huddle and spoke low, to talk of Indians. The boys whispered among themselves, just loud enough for Milt to hear, that a negro's scalp was worth three or four times more to the Indians than a white mans. When the herd reached the Red River we were met by white men who warned us to look out for Red skins on the war path, saying several whites had been killed fifty miles west of us.

Milt listened attentively while this bit of news was going around, and when the time came for him to shove off ahead of the herd to pitch camp and cook supper, he hedged and made excuses.

He had forgotten his directions and was having dizzy spells, and might drop off of the wagon unless some of the boys went along with him. None of his lines worked, and finally Jack Hunter the trail boss used some persuasive words that started Milt on his way alone. He had been out of sight of the herd an hour or so, when more whites came and reported that quite a band [of] renegade Indians were on the prod, and were headed toward where the wagon was to camp. The boss became a little worried, and several of us lit out with him to overtake Milt, to protect his kinks, and save our grub.

We circled the chosen camp spot, and discovered the wagon top, but no smoke of a campfire.

We kept along the creek bank under cover of brush and trees, and cautiously approached to within a short distance of the wagon, what we saw was a whole flock of moccasins sticking out from under all sides and ends of the wagon.

Some distance away from the wagon stood Milt, backed against a clump of brush, with his head bowed respectfully, and his hands folded in an attitude of prayer, solemnly repeating over and over.

I sho wish yu ladies an gentimans would hurry up and git all yu wants outen dat ole wagon, and git it done as quick as yu kain, cause some cowboys will be long hea mighty soon now, and da is gwiner be awful mad at me ifin ah dont have sumpin cooked fo em to eat. They is mean hombres, sho as I live. "Iffen ah does live." We soon discovered that they were not hostile Indians, but just the usual grub hunters, mostly squaws and papooses.

Jack hunter fired a few shots into the air. We let out a war whoop and the Indians took to the timber as badly scared as Milt had been.

As we moved on Milt grew more nervous and watchful. When night came he would roost on top of the wagon. He would absentmindedly forget to salt the sourdough biscuits. Milt had something on his mind, and it wasn't feeding cowboys that were driving longhorn cattle, slowly winding their way north over a long dusty trail. When we got to Abilene Kansas where a company of Negro (Buffalo) soldiers were stationed, Milt walked up to the boss, half dragging a war sack, and said. Suh, I'se bin conversin with the ahma boys, and I's gwina jine up with um, and git mysef a wardrobe of blue, and a big long gun that shoots a mile, and no mo Injins is gwina git close to me any mo." The herd moved on north without Milt, and the U. S. army got another good buffalo soldier.

We delivered that herd of steers to buyers north of Cheyenne, Wyoming. Cheyenne, the town that never slept. The place where "Apple Annie" the bedraggled, haggish looking old woman peddled apples from door to door of every saloon in town, and saloons were thick. When the Wyoming cowboys met us to receive the steers, I went goggle eyed at the sight of their rich regalia. Clean Stetson hats, gauntlet gloves, and fancy hand stamped stock saddles, set on big proud looking cow horses. Most of these cowboys hailed from Texas and they had created a style of dress smooth and neat. The handmade boots and straight shanked spurs were as new to me as their tailored California riding pants. I never saw a pair of Levi overalls worn by Wyoming cowboys in those days. Levis were worn by ranch hands only. I made a firm resolution to join the parade, and take up cowboying in Wyoming, where wages and living conditions were better than they were in Texas. Courage failed me, for I was just a kid, lost and afraid, so I stuck with my outfit and went back to Texas. The following year I worked for the Goodnights. When I was seventeen years old I came up the Chisholm trail as a trail boss of one of the Goodnight herds. That was a big herd of slow moving cows and calves, strung out for miles. They had to spread out and graze often, with every toe pointed in the right direction. On this trip were two Negro cooks, Mose and Maston, burly black boys, each driving a mess wagon, hitched to a four mule team. Negroes and mules, both breeds, endowed by nature with an instinctive fear and dislike of Wokas [sic] eaters. Keeping a combination of that kind in line while traveling through Indian country in the early seventies was not cake. It required a lot of witchcraft to keep that bunch organized and pointed in a northerly direction. The blacks were good at preparing our regular fare of beef and sour dough biscuits, the devil winds added the sand and soil for seasoning. At each fresh butchering we were treated to a conglomerate of every part of a calf, except the hide and horns, the delicacy known to cowpunchers as a "son-of-a-bitch." Along the way we picked up a batch of green boys for horse wranglers.

They were ravenous kids, and took a fancy to this tasty dish. One of them asked Mose if he was going to have a "son-of-a-bitch" for dinner, Mose replied

"Ah spect us is, cause us had twenty-five fah breakfast." To keep his mules shoulders tough, Maston used blue vitamus, commonly called blue vitriol. In pictures and song the cowboys life would appear to be one of play. In reality range life was rather a hard and serious job. Most of the cowboy songs did not break forth from merriment, they were born of necessity, a rhythmic jumble of words made up by the negroes and adopted by the cowboys on night guard. The cowboys sang to soothe the herd, as they trotted their horses around the cattle in a wide circle, to keep them quietly resting on the bed ground. Our workdays began at four o'clock in the morning and ended by each cowboy doing his two hour turn at night herding between dark and daylight. On dark stormy nights, especially during electrical storms cattle are restless, and more inclined to run. Now and then a boy was killed in a stampede, but not many were lost in that way.

Our greatest trouble was buffalo, and we avoided the deep worn buffalo trails between their grazing grounds and their favorite watering places.

Buffalo came down those trails on the run, in a great moving mass that sent all living creatures scurrying to safety. We scouted, and listened for the rumbling of a buffalo run that could be heard for miles. We kept to high ground and moved the cattle rapidly when forced to cross such trails. Many herds of cattle of the same brand were being moved over the Texas trail to the north the same year, so every herd was branded with its own trail iron, in addition to the regular ownership brand. I split this herd of she stock we were trailing into two herds when we reached Ogalala, Nebraska, and we delivered the balance of them to buyers at the Canadian line. I did not make any more trail trips. I returned from Canada to Wyoming, and became range foreman for the Goose Egg Cattle Company. From then on I managed the range end of the cattle business for several other big cattle companies in Wyoming. The greater part of my life was spent that way, and I worked for their interests to the extent that no outfit under my management ever went broke. When small ranch seekers came to squat on our ranges, I was not in sympathy with them, and used every means in my power to move them on, using force if need be. Every poor family moving in a covered wagon, to settle on a lonesome claim with a family, to chuck into a little rough dugout, or a dirt covered log shack, brought back memories of bed bugs, my childhood and my little sad mother in poverty, drudging wearily along, and bravely enduring such an existence.

The thought of struggling individuals going the hard way, and bucking against odds they could not conquer, was hateful and turned me sour. I went to Rosebud Oregon and bought a home for my mother and father, so they could live comfortably. Oregon was becoming settled, and a better place for homesteaders.

Wyoming was strictly a cattle range country, and it suited me as it was, a big country to be lived in, in a big way. My employers never interfered with my range work, they lived in eastern cities and I did not see them for a year at a time. My job was to handle an investment that happened to be in cattle. The investment paid a big dividend to the investors. They were satisfied, they made millions on the open free ranges of the west, and they wanted to keep the ranges open and free as long as possible. I was paid a good salary with all my expenses added. The company furnished me with a checkbook, and gave me a free rein to draw on company funds in connection with any business transaction I thought best for their interests and they never questioned my judgment.

I put in a question. The land was open to homestead entry, and you were making money for the capitalists; why didn't you promote an outfit of your own? Bernards answer, I was independent, my work suited me, I understood cattle and liked to work with them, and wanted to remain free from financial worries. I lived well, kept good comfortable quarters at the ranches, and put up at the best hotels when I went to the cities. I spent my money as I saw fit, among all classes, some of the best and some of the worst, all of which I found were more or less alike in many respects, just human, with the same human instincts expressed in different ways.

There was no prospect of an immediate change taking place to upset range conditions. Naturally, towns were springing up almost overnight along the Union Pacific Railroad, and the coal mines were developing fast. All kinds of people were coming into the Territory, for progress was on the march. The towns and even our range headquarters were tuned up to a lively pitch, woman cooks, new furniture, and paint covering everything, including the cook's face. Life was moving right along, with plenty of work and money to spend, in a brand new West, where most people were too busy to be crooked. The towns had their share of tin horns and drifters, and a few "bad men" now and then, to kick up a row, and leave dead ones lying around in the way. With women, whiskey and movement, why should a young man want to change to something stale and grubby.

The most amusing and the most embarrassing situation I ever got myself into, happened at Lay, a mournful looking little alkali flat in Colorado. Business in connection with the Haley interests called me there shortly after Major Thornburg's troops had been moved away. Lay was the military base of operations during the Indian outbreak, when the Utes stuck a barrel stave down the Government agent Meeker's throat, and raised a lot of general hell all over that part of Colorado. Haley had a few ranches and a "one horse" cow setup on Lay Creek, but the only place to put up was at the Barracks, consisting of a post office, a telegraph office, and an eating house.

The old Army post was taken over and run by a sister of Dr. Higgins the founder of Lily Park. She was a widow about fifty years old, and she had the most silvery hair I have ever seen. The place was as shiny neat as the owner, the food was good, and served right on the dot, and the clean comfortable beds to sleep in made it a very inviting place to lodge. For a little diversion I saddled a horse and went to Hat Wards saloon, a shack on Bear River several miles from Lay. I got myself owlish drunk, returned to Lay in that condition, and rode my horse right into the middle of the widows clean kitchen. She serenely looked me over, stepped into the bedroom, and walked out with a shotgun in her hands. That gesture sobered me somewhat, enough at least, so I made a clean getaway while she was stuffing shells into the gun. It was getting dark so I quit my horse and dropped into the tall sagebrush. That was a lucky quick change for me, for the old girl filled my saddle full of buckshot as my horse ran away on a high lope. She hunted around for me a while, but she couldn't find me, I had left there in a hurry. I slipped through the brush on my hands and knees, keeping a watchful eye on the back trail as I hotfooted it to Hats filthy dump.

Something had to be done, and at once. I got in touch with Kelly the Haley foreman who was leisurely taking his ease at Lay, and chuckling at my unhappy predicament. He took his time, and meandered over to see me (for another good laugh). I gave him a signed check, and instructed him to buy the widow out at any price. It was evident that I could not go back while she was there. Kelly did what he was told, and I paid the lady three times the value of her holdings, only to find myself in another jack pot. The widow was Postmistress, and her Government obligations would keep here there indefinitely. However, the Postmistress did have a responsible deputy in the person of Al Wallihan the telegraph operator. He might be persuaded to take over her official duties, for a short time, and give the widow a vacation to visit her brother Dr. Higgins.

Lily Park is quite some distance from Lay, and decidedly out of shotgun range. So Kelly helped to promote her hasty departure.

When the cowboys gave the all clear signal, I crept out of the brush and made a leap for the table for a clean bite of food. Within a few days I was called back to Wyoming, and did not return to Lay for several years. In the intervening time the widow married Al Wallihan and they built a house a quarter of a mile down the creek below the old barracks, and they moved the Lay post-office there. Back at Lay and wanting to be on friendly terms with my neighbors, and incidentally to get my mail, I saddled a horse and rode toward the post office thinking as I went. Perhaps I did owe Mrs. Wallihan an apology for riding my horse into her clean kitchen, for after all that was an ungentlemanly thing to do. I walked into the post office, and before I got my bearings up popped that silvery head, and the Post-mistress pranced from the office cage lugging her old faithful shotgun. It didn't take much imagination to follow her intentions, and from past experience I knew exactly what she could do with a gun.

I ducked through the door like a frightened lizard and ran zig zag to cover. For the second time I had to desert my horse and take to the brush. It was getting to be a habit around Lay for the boys to gather up my horse while Mrs. Wallihan was gunning for me. I never did get over being intensely unnerved when I had to pass the house of that extraordinary Postmistress. The post office was located on the roadside smack between two Haley ranches. I was forced to go that way, and "big fraid" went with me every time I hurried by. Mrs. Wallihan has gone on to the happy hunting ground. From what I have heard, the two places are so much alike she won't be homesick for Lay. The double barreled shotgun has me worried yet, for I may be her thoroughly buffaloed neighbor again.

Eventually the granger class took up so many homesteads in Wyoming that the "longhorn" range game played out about 1893. Business and fortune turned to better grades of cattle. We began to get good grade white faced bulls from the midwest to breed, and build the herds up for more weight, and choice cuts of beef demanded by the markets. The change came about gradually, and increased the overhead. Railroad land had to be leased, and bull pastures fenced for selective breeding to produce summer calves of uniform age. This type of calves were weaned and fed heavily in the winter months. Whereas, in the old days the cows weaned their calves, and nature took care of them. The new way of handling cattle required hay. I came into Routt County Colorado, and bought several hay ranches for Haley. These ranches extended over a wide scope of the County, with both winter and summer ranges on all sides. Open public domain, all choice range and with few fences to hinder the movement of cattle for a distance of about one hundred miles in all directions. That constituted a pretty layout, and easy to handle.

It proved to be good. Haley made over a million dollars profit on his Routt county investment in less than ten years. And in that time he never saw the range end of the business but three times. He did not know a thing about it for he was not a range man.

Haley was a smart, and lucky financier. He came to Wyoming a bull-whacker, and started in the cow business at Laramie with three old dairy cows. He was smart enough to see opportunities and capitalize on them, lucky to find a sucker to handle a range cattle business better than he could, and he was wise enough to keep from meddling with the range end, where the payoff came from. That is a rare combination of human character.

I would like to ask a question if you care to answer it. Bernard thought for a long moment and replied. I believe I am thinking away ahead of you, and before I answer your question I must exact a promise from you. A promise that you will not repeat this story while I am living.

I readily jumped at his proposition, and said "fair enough," now tell me what you know about the Tom Horn affair? He went on talking calmly. I know a great deal about it, to begin with the people of Brown's Park brought most of that trouble upon themselves. First, by allowing J. S. Hoy to write and have published the explosive hot stuff he generated for his own amusement.

And second, they knew the Majors and Sainsbury ranches on little Snake River were for sale, and could be bought cheap. Those ranches were necessary to protect their eastern range boundaries and they failed to buy them.

That was poor judgment on their part. And another reason is, they were range hogs, for they were controlling a greater amount of range than they used, or could use. They pompously called this piece of selfishness "Protection of natural growth."

The Brown's Parkers did not realize the range was not going to be open forever, and they foolishly tried to hold it as a private reservation.

Bank robbers were permitted to pass over the country at will. The horses stolen by such renegades and ridden away, or the beef killed for meat by the robbers hiding out did not disturb the Brown's Park settlers. That was a minor loss anyway. In fact the reported presence of such characters helped to scare outside stockmen away from the gravy bowl. It was a no trespass sign, and it worked for a long time. But, if one of those bandits had come into the park with a herd of cattle, to graze off a spear of the "conserved" grass, or make tracks over the sacred ground, that unfortunate's doom would have been sealed, and he would have been kicked out pronto.

The bank and train robbers did not eat grass, therefore, the slogan was, let the banks and railroads take care of the bandits. A mere handful of people in Brown's Park set up a little kingdom—or queendom—of their own from the Utah and Wyoming lines to the little Snake River.

Except for their few ranches, all of it was open public land. A big area, covered with grass and forage, seeding itself and blowing away each year, and benefiting nobody. "It was that way in the beginning and must be kept that way." One of the Brown's Park "musts."

Well, time changes things, and it "must" be a hell of a shock to some of them to see the range grubbed to the ground as it is now.

The range used by the big cow outfits was not considered private, they were used by all stockmen. Our company ran a roundup and a mess wagon, and provided a simple, economical way for small cattle owners to handle their stock. We furnished everything, and did most of the work. All they had to do was get their stock after it was gathered, at no expense to them.

I went into Brown's Park to make similar arrangements and got cold-shouldered. My offer was rejected with ceremonial courtesy. On that mission to Brown's Park I did not meet Ann Bassett, but I received a letter from her soon afterwards, advising "That neither me, or the Haley outfit were desirable. And when, and if, it was necessary for me to visit Brown's Park, would I please confine myself to road travel, for the tracks of Two Bar horses, or cattle, were obnoxious."

That impertinent demand was not in the form of a joke. Not by any means, it was an open defiance straight from the shoulder.

That demand still rings in my ears, very pleasantly at times. I guess we all admire courage, and the sand to come out in the open, to stand pat for what we believe in, uncompromising as it may often seem. Getting back to my story. The following spring I was making a tour of range investigation on the remote Douglas Mesa section, and I met Ann Bassett riding alone. A smallish imp of a girl sitting straddle of a superb horse, and fitted as if she had grown there.

She was dressed in at least one gun, and reminded me of tales I had heard about the equally romantic, and lovable, Sitting Bull, mopping up at the Little Big Horn. My hands wanted to reach for something high overhead, I restrained them with difficulty and introduced myself, and spluttered about the number of lobos inhabiting the range country. I got a salty reply that gave me the idea that grey wolves were natives, and belonged. While I was nothing but a worm crawling out of bounds.

I had never been much of what might be called a "ladies man" but it seemed the women of Routt County like sidewinders were on my trail chasing me. That is right, they were chasing me—right out of the country. The women were not on a wolf hunt, this was a rabbit drive, and kept me on the hop from one brush heap to another. I could not let the news of my latest defeat get out among the cowboys in my outfit, for the boys would join the chase and laugh me out of the country. So, I kept mum on the subject, and the Two Bar outfit off of the Brown's Park range. In the meantime things were picking up speed elsewhere. Haley sent for me to meet him in Denver, I met him there and the question of range west of the divide near his Snake River ranches was discussed. Haley told me that Wiff Wilson and Charley Ayers were in Denver and they had given him a tip on Brown's Park conditions. Wilson and Ayers were prominent business, and cattle men, of Baggs Wyoming. They each had ranches on upper Snake River, and were old timers in the range country of Routt County. A meeting was scheduled for nine o'clock that evening at Haley's office. We went to dinner and returned to the office; an hour or so later,

Wiff Wilson, Charley Ayers, and John Cobel came in. Cobel was a man of affairs from Wyoming who had extensive range interests north of Cheyenne and he had been invited to attend the conference. The business at hand got under way immediately—with Wilson and Ayers bringing up the subject of range in Brown's Park. They condemned the place as an outlaw hangout, and a threat to the Haley interests. Both men stated what they knew about the reputation of the Park, and Wilson from personal experience, giving detailed information regarding his losses, he attributed to the thieves of Brown's Park and named Matt Rash and Jim McKnight as the individuals whom he knew were cattle rustlers.

Brown's Park's reputation as a hangout for outlaws was farflung. The sincerity and truthfulness of none of the speakers had ever been questioned, so far as I knew. Their repeated accusations were convincing. John Cobel had like grievances in his part of the country, and he offered a solution to the problem that would wipe out the range menace permenantly. He would contact a man whom he knew with the Pinkerton Detective Agency. A man that could be relied on to do the job, and no questions asked. A committee was appointed, Wilson, Ayers and I were to act for the joint interests in our range section.

Cobel would take care of his part of the country. Tom Horn was the man chosen by Cobel. Horn was not at the meeting, and Cobel acting for him, said that Horn was to be paid five hundred dollars for every known cattle thief he killed. Haley was to put up one half of the money, and Wilson and Ayers one half. Wilson and Ayers agreed to handle the financial transaction with Horn. Haley nodded consent to the agreement but he did not commit himself in words, he instructed me to furnish Horn with accommodations and saddle horses at the Two Bar ranches. After the meeting was over and Haley and I were by ourselves, he said to me, neither you, or I, can afford to lay ourselves open to this man Horn. I do not want him on my payroll to kick back, and collect money from me in a much more simple way than killing men for it.

Tom Horn was hired and given a free hand by the appointed Committee to make a thorough investigation of conditions in Brown's Park.

He was to produce the evidence, that cattle were being stolen, and find out who the thieves were. Horn went to Brown's Park. Soon after our Denver meeting a bunch of twenty-eight head of well bred heifers branded V D belonging to a man at Baggs Wyoming, on upper Snake River were missing. Horn reported that he had followed the tracks of a small bunch of cattle from Snake River, by way of Powder Wash to Limestone Mountain, east of Beaver Basin.

Wiff Wilson and I went back with Horn, and were shown parts of the cattle trail. It was an isolated country, the trail was old, but traces could be picked up in the clay soil. The cattle had been driven by two horsemen. They had camped and night-herded in a small canyon. Wilson and I did not go all the way to Beaver Basin. Horn's statements had been verified so far, and we instructed him to make an effort to locate the cattle. Horn reported back to the committee that he had found butchered hides bearing the V D brand. One of the hides was found at Jim McKnight's summer cow camp at Summit Springs, and one at Matt Rash's N S camp. Both places were at Beaver Basin. Rash and McKnight were using these summer places at the time, and had done so for several years. Horn brought the pieces of cow hide for Wilson, Ayers, and me to examine. We wet, and stretched, the pieces of hide and found the V D brand on each piece. That looked like the boldest, most outrageous, cattle rustling job I had ever seen, or heard of. Acting for the general welfare of all range users adjacent to Brown's Park, the appointed Committee gave Horn the go ahead signal, and cautioned him to be sure he got the guilty men only. Horn made a further investigation and killed Matt Rash and Isam Dart.

Horn did not go back to that part of the country after the killing of the negro Dart. I never saw Horn kill anybody, but his acknowledgment of the killing of Matt Rash went on record when Horn was arrested.

Horn expected to be acquitted of the charge against him, on the grounds of acting as a detective in the interests of law and order, and he thought he would be backed by the big cattle men and several hundred thousand dollars; his calculations misfired.

Wyoming officials took every precaution to see that he did not escape the law. He was tried, found guilty, and hanged. Horn was not the only one connected with that affair that should have been hanged. There was several of us that the country could have gotten along without. We acted too hasty, and for my part, I expect to pay the price in full. At the time I interviewed the Brown's Parkers on the range question, Sam Bassett, a very fine young man, was the only one of them willing to cooperate with me on the grazing problem. Sam was selling his cattle at the time and preparing to see Alaska, therefore he was overruled in the matter. McKnight and Rash were willing to use me as a buffer against sheep invasion, but they insisted on a strict deadline against the Two Bar Cattle. It looked like they could have something to cover up, and I could not make a personal investigation, it required a stranger to do that successfully. Wilson and Ayers claimed to know the facts concerning Brown's Park, and I accepted their word on face value. If the information, regarding Wilson's experience in Brown's Park had been passed on to me at the time, as it was four years later, the entire affair might have been quite the reverse of what it was.

Another angle of the case presented itself to me when Al McCarger of Baggs told me that several years before I came into Colorado, Wilson had bought a bunch of horses in southern Utah. The horses attempted to go back to their old range. They strayed into Brown's Park and were picked up late in the fall by Sam Bassett. The horses were in poor condition and Sam fed them all winter, and notified Wilson to come and get them in the spring. McCarger told me about making the trip to the Bassett ranch with Wilson, and he said, We found the horses in good shape, We spent the night at the Bassett ranch, took the horses and returned home, I heard Sam Bassett refuse payment for the care of the horses and also for our meals while we were there. This information was given to me by McCarger in the presence of Wiff Wilson who admitted it was true. I am not offering this tale to justify my actions in the Tom Horn case, but it does puzzle me, why Wiff Wilson, and Charley Ayers, were over anxious to move in on Brown's Park for the kill. Their ranches and range was about one hundred miles from the Park, and they never ranged any stock near the place.

It all sums up to the question of ground, the question that started when the first white man advanced westward. First, we killed the Indians to get it, now we kill each other for the same reason, and will continue to kill until the public land problem is permanently settled. I believe the western grazing lands should be taken over by the States and leased as school land is leased to stockmen, and the law should contain a clause, that no individual should lease more ground than is needed to graze five hundred head of cattle, or a like number of sheep.

If such laws were put into effect, and were under the supervision of men who understood range conditions, range wars and man killing for range would cease. But I am not a lawmaker, and this is just a lost idea.

I asked another question: Tom Horn took a shot at Ann Bassett, at the Bassett ranch, didn't he?

Bernard gave me a cold glance, he set his square jaw a little tighter, and firmly said; I do not believe that Tom Horn ever fired that shot. It is my opinion that someone from around Baggs got wise to Horn, they did the shooting, and left a plain trail on purpose, so the Brown's Park people could pick up a clue that would put them on Horn's trail. I have no idea who it was, the Wilson horse that was ridden to Baggs from the L 7 ranch was not ridden by Horn, as reported. The stable man at Baggs claims that he was asleep when the horse was left in the barn. The people in the Park think it was Horn, and proof to the contrary would have been useless. From what I have heard it did not seem to me that shot was intended to kill, and it could have been fired by any one of a number of men familiar with the country. It served its purpose, for it helped to quiet some of us down to keep thinking.

After the arrest of Tom Horn, a hush settled over the range country in northwestern Colorado, and along the southern border of Wyoming. The big cattle outfits were slowed down and satisfied to stay all in one package, if we could, for we were skating on thin ice until Horn was put out of commission. The Brown's Parkers were on the watch and wait, to be prepared if another raid was in the making. Ann Bassett grimly rode herd over her favorite hunting grounds, to be sure that Two Bar cattle did not eat the grass west of the divide. I was not in the mood to put my neck into another loop. Responsibilities kept me around Snake River, for one reason, there was a slight tinge of sentiment in the direction of Brown's Park, quite justifiable and excusable in view of certain facts. Sitting Bull did not have green eyes or reddish brown curls. You must remember, that we are men after all, and savage looking girls can be attractive, very attractive, especially so if they happen to be the first of the kind you ever saw, and the last of the kind too.

At that time I was thinking seriously of throwing my Colorado job overboard to try my luck in Oregon. Then I received a message, delivered by Tom Armstrong, an odd character, who was building fence for me west of Snake River. The message was a note from Ann Bassett, requesting me to meet her at the Douglas ranch. The message confused and pleased me at the same time. I didn't know what to expect, but I did know that little things like bullets were a minor consideration and would not stop me from trying to reach the Douglas ranch. I rounded up my courage and sloped out to keep the appointment.

When I arrived at Douglas Ann Bassett was there. Not the stern little gun toter I had seen patrolling the range on Douglas Mesa, but a girl wearing a pretty blue dress that went well with shiny hair. I was invited into a cozy cabin and frankly told why I was sent for. Ann was contemplating a partnership arrangement to stock the Douglas range with cattle, using the Bassett ranches as a winter base. She outlined the program in a very businesslike way and said, you are a cow man, and if you are interested just think the matter over and advise me of your decision at some future date. As simple as that. By that time cattle and range was the last thing on my mind. When we were called to dinner I had turned to ashes, and I did sure need a bracer of strong coffee to pick me up, for I had a counteroffer to make, and it needed a lot of backbone that I was unable to locate just then.

So far the most important part of the contract had been over-looked. I did not intend to let that slip away from me, it was not Brown's Park and a jumble of sand hills I was after. It was a wife. I braced myself and boldly said so. It seemed the most natural thing in the world for a man to fall in love with a striking young woman and want to marry her. She was not a kid but was well along toward her thirties. She was a capable woman with a mind of her own, she meant something more to me than a toehold on any country.

The woods were full of men and I was flattered to be chosen as her partner.

It was strictly cattle to Ann and she did not pretend otherwise. It was I, who became the unit in a business enterprise exactly the reverse of what you heard today. According to Hoys lights, it is a crime and a disgrace to Brown's Park, for a man to love a woman.

Mountains of hokum has been peddled far and wide about that marriage, made up by nose-ins who are setting up their own standards, and jumping at their own conclusions regarding a private affair that they were not consulted about.

Hoy and his tribe of gabbers did not dare to approach Ann on the subject. She hazed the rattle tongues to cover and dealt them a sizable cussing a time or two, for she understood the situation and was loyal about it. Loyalty is one of her admirable traits.

Together we built up a prosperous cattle business in Brown's Park, Ann rode the range with me, and that was not the hardest job I ever did. Ann can qualify as an expert in handling livestock of any kind, and she knows more about cattle than they know about themselves.

A few of the old pioneers were in Brown's Park when I came to live here in 1905, Charley Crouse was one of them. He was a regular westerner, enterprising and well liked by all his neighbors, except J. S. Hoy. Another was Uncle Sam Bassett, a grand old man, a bachelor who had made several fortunes in mining at various camps over the west. He mined at Virginia City Nevada, and he picked up gold nuggets at Sutters Mill in Californias boom days.

Sam Bassett junior became interested in mining in Alaska, he is married and lives there.

The most friendly one of the immediate Bassett family now living in Brown's Park is Eb Bassett. He lives generously, is kind to the human race, and has not dedicated himself entirely to animals.

Josie Bassett McKnight is a jolly good natured woman, she works like a steam shovel and then she hunts up some unworthy bums and gives away the proceeds of her labor. Her hobby is husbands, she has had five or six good men and discards them one after another without a backward glance.

George Bassett's chief concern is in being unconcerned, and he mosies about the business of life in his individual way. His little daughter Edna is six years old and she is sure a cute little trick. I think a lot of that little kid. Ann convinced me that all animal pets definitely take precedence over husbands.

The entire Bassett family is devoted to their father. I never could get acquainted with Mr. Bassett for he is a religious man and is away over my head. He peeps over his specs at me and seems to be smiling behind his long white beard as if he was amused at the antics of some strange insect he had come upon by accident.

The old Bassett ranch has some time or another housed most everyone in this part of the northwest. Charley Sparks made his home there, when he first came west as a boy, from North Carolina. Sparks is a wealthy man now and he has given over one of his ranches to be used as a home for all of the old broken down men that ever worked for him. He provides the best of food for them and gives them medical care when needed, and then he buys lots in the Rock Springs Cemetery and gives each of them a decent burial.*

We all practically come to the same drift fence in the end. Haley is paralyzed, and is being trundled around in a wheelchair. I go around knocking my hocks because of a weak heart that kicks up a fuss and fails to pump regularly. I was only a machine for Haley at any time, he oiled me up and I ran smoothly for too many years. When I began to backfire and wanted a new steering gear Haley junked me. He accused me of doublecrossing him, when I quit him to marry Ann Bassett. We had one hearty row and I haven't seen Haley since.

I wonder why I am telling you this long tiresome yarn, it must be a hangover, brought on by the fight with J. S. Hoy.

He is the direct cause of all of the tragedies that ever happened in Brown's Park, and the women feel sorry for him, they coddle and humor him, and the old steer shoots at the men whenever they go near his place.

The Brown's Parkers are a clannish lot. Ann would cook a big chicken dinner for Hoy, and stay in the house all day to entertain him, just because he was one of the old pioneers he had to be treated with great respect. Hoys heart wont bother him, for he hasn't any.

Eb Bassett said Ann is coming home to visit him this fall. I know the answers to that, Ann is not so much interested in seeing any human being as she is in rambling over the old Bassett ranch, and caressing every ugly, scraggy, cedar in Brown's Park. She is blended into the rugged mountains around here and belongs to them.

Of course, I'll be the happiest old fool in the world when I see her, and then cuss myself for it.

Ann and I were living on the Bassett ranch the winter of 1907.

There was a heavy snowfall and very cold weather in December, then came the January thaw, which often happens in the Park. The warm Chinook winds blew for several days and melted the snow, broke up the ice in the streams and turned them into raging torrents of muddy water carrying great floating slabs of ice.

---

* After his sojourn with Frank Willis at the Curtin ranch, Hi stayed for a while with Eb Bassett. As Hi grew older and finally became unable to care for himself, Charley Sparks took him to a hospital in Rock Springs and later buried him in the plot Sparks had bought and set aside for old cowboys. Hi Bernard died on February 3, 1924, at the age of 67. This information is found in Burroughs' *Where the Old West Stayed Young*.

Mr. Bassett had stretched a wire cable across the Vermillion for the purpose of getting mail to and from the *Star route Carrier.*

The mail carrier came once a week from the Maybell post office sixty miles to the east. Bedding and food for the mail carrier and feed for his horse was sent across the Vermillion by cable when the river was not fordable.

One afternoon during the high water period, we saw a man on horseback riding up and down the banks of the Vermillion directly opposite our house.

It was evident that someone wanted to communicate with us. I saddled a horse and rode to where the cable was anchored. I soon discovered the horseman to be Jack Chew, he was a recent settler who with his wife and several small children lived fifteen miles south and near the foot of Douglas mountain. They were without neighbors at that time of the year. The roaring water of Vermillion was deafening. We could not hear a word spoken. I beckoned Chew to the cable and by motions instructed him to wind the ropes when I fastened pencil and paper to the pulleys. Chews message came back that his wife had given birth to a baby the evening before. The baby had died. His wife was in a very bad condition and they needed immediate help.

I sent a note over to Chew advising him to return home, and we would be with them as soon as the night air checked the thaw from the incoming streams and lowered the wild Vermillion so we could cross.

I hurried back to the house and broke the news to Ann. We selected our most dependable grain fed saddle horses and got ready for an early start the next morning. It was necessary to take a pack horse to carry warm blankets, food and medicine, and grain for our horses.

The only crossing on the Vermillion with good landings was within fifty feet of a falls where the water dashed over a rock ledge to a lower level a hundred feet below.

We arranged to have several ropers—among them George and Eb Bassett—stationed on the bank where we were going to attempt a crossing. If a horse failed to swim, or became tangled in the debris and ice, it was possible for a horse and rider to be caught before going over the falls to sudden death.

When we were all set to take the plunge into the ice-jammed water, I stepped my horse in and he swam high and easy.

Then the cowboys shoved the packhorse into the water. By dodging ice and swimming strong he made the landing. Ann came last, her horse reared back and refused to take the plunge. He was a spirited animal, and when she raked him with her spurs he made a long jump and went under water and struggled frantically down stream. He gained balance and treaded ice and swam low to my horse on the right bank.

The horses were cold and scared and we lit out on a keen run and kept the pace for a mile. With cold air fanning our wet clothing we were soon covered with solid sheets of ice.

I roped the packhorse and built a fire in a cedar gulch to warm up a little. We removed our heavy coats and chaps from the pack, where we had them wrapped in a waterproof tarp.

We put our dry things on top of our wet clothing and rode on toward the mountains.

The shock of seeing Anns horse go under water so near the falls almost floored me. That was the first time I realized I had a bad heart. I dam near died and thought I could not hold out to reach the Chew dugout fourteen miles away. When we hit the dreary Lone Cedar flat the snow was deep and crusted, and going was slowed up. I believe the only thing that kept me alive that day, was Ann riding in the lead with her head thrown back in defiance of obstacles. On a mission of mercy bent and determined to reach a sick mother in time to help if possible.

We arrived at the Chew Camp about four o'clock in the afternoon and found Mrs. Chew very weak and having chills, as she tried feebly to feed her hungry brood. I immediately gathered wood and soon had a roaring fire. We heated rocks to warm the bed and gave her a stiff, hot whiskey toddy.

When Mrs. Chew was made comfortable, Ann pitched in and put the dugout in order, she prepared supper for the children and put them to bed, then she took the only blanket we had to roll up in, and put it over her saddle horse. We sat around an old caved-in fireplace, in a muddy dugout and watched over Mrs. Chew that night, and for several days and nights, until we knew she was out of danger.

I have never regretted that experience, Mrs. Chew is a noble woman, and a splendid pioneer mother who is worthy of any kindness that can be bestowed upon her.

Did you tell Ann about your heart ailment? I asked. No, he said, one does not tell Ann that kind of thing. Such an acknowledgement is a mark of weakness. According to her way of thinking a full grown man is not supposed to get sick. She takes life on the bounce and expects a man to do likewise.

I still carry in memory that scene of Anns unbeatable courage in swimming the river, and making that long, cold ride which she completely ignored at the time, and no doubt has long since forgotten.

I said, you and Ann Bassett are divorced, aren't you? Bernard said yes, Ann was a gay and exciting companion—too exciting, I guess—a man does not enjoy playing second fiddle to so many things, like cattle, and horses, and dozens of other animal pets. For instance, we had a whole family of tame chipmunks to live with us.

Ann spends very little time in a house. We had homes, several of them, orderly cheerful places, but a man wants to rate above a chipmunk in his wifes affections and I could not make the grade.

Have you seen the grave out yonder on the knoll? Bernard did not wait for a reply. That is where I buried Jerry. We were good friends and I miss him a lot now. He was small when he came to live with me nine years ago, but he grew to be a big fellow. Ann gave him to me when he was nothing but a little ball of fur, a tiny Maltese kitten. I must repaint the picket fence around him. It needs a new coat. Bernard pulled his wide stetson a little lower, he leaned wearily back against the cushions of his chair and sighed deeply—for Jerry.

NOTES ON SOURCES

General

The history of the Bassett family is based for the most part on the family's knowledge, the memoirs of Josie and Ann themselves, and information in courthouse and newspaper files. However, there are other sources to which I have turned consistently.

Where the Old West Stayed Young by John Rolfe Burroughs is the most complete story ever written of northwestern Colorado. A native of the country, Burroughs drew on his own knowledge of the area, and he wrote at a time when he could interview survivors of the pioneer era. In my research for this book I used Burroughs as a starting point. As I retraced his steps and went back to his sources as far as possible, I sometimes disagreed with his facts and interpretations, but this in no manner cancels the debt I owe him nor the admiration I have for his handling of a complex and controversial period in his home country's history.

Another rich source of information was the files of Glade Ross, the park ranger stationed in Brown's Park on the one small piece of land which falls within Dinosaur National Monument. He has collected a wealth of original material on Brown's Park (including the notes of both Esther Campbell and Marian McLeod) which not only gave me information about the Bassetts themselves but also clarified and deepened my understanding of the Park and its people as a whole.

I also benefited from an interview with Nick Meagher, Jr., a banker in Vernal, Utah, who gave me background on what living in Vernal was like during the years of the Great Depression.

Equal help was gained from others who will be credited in subsequent chapter notes. To all of these people, as well as to the authors I have never met and the unnamed personnel of libraries, courthouses, government offices and historical societies in three states, I give my sincere thanks.

Chapter 1. Arkansas Travelers

The county records and newspaper files of Hot Springs, Arkansas, have been decimated by fire. Even so, Inez E. Cline of the Garland County Historical Society in Hot Springs was able to unearth nuggets of information about the Arkansas Bassetts and to supply some names and dates of the Chamberlin and Miller families. Family traditions were corroborated by Herb Bassett's Army records obtained from the United States National Archives, a typed note evidently copied from a family Bible, and by a little red notebook with hand-written notations by Herb Bassett himself.

The nineteenth century theories about women's uterine focal point were outlined as early as 1849 by Frederick Hollick, M.D., in *The Diseases of Women: Their Cause and Cure Familiarly Explained.* They culminated in a "best-seller" printed in 1873 (Boston, James R. Osgood; reprint edition by Arno Press, Inc., 1972) by Dr. Edward H. Clarke, a Harvard professor, entitled *Sex in Education, or a Fair Chance for the Girls.* Both books are cited in *For Her Own Good* by Barbara Ehrenreich and Deirdre English (Anchor Press/Doubleday, Anchor Books edition, 1979). This latter book gives a comprehensive and often lurid overview of female physiology as seen by the scientific and medical communities in the 1800s.

Chapter 2. Brown's Hole

The difference between a "hole" and a "park" is not precise, which is understandable since each geographical location has its own peculiarities. In general, a "hole" is considered a flat place, surrounded by natural barriers, created by the action of a river. A "park" is normally larger, more a mountain highland than one carved out by water action. Brown's Hole/Park was created to a great extent by the Green River; however, it is open to the east, and is large enough that it can be classed as a park. It is interesting to note that although Elizabeth was prime mover in the use of the term "Brown's Park," her daughter Ann, in the 1950s, referred to "the Hole." Of course, Ann liked to be original, and by that time "hole" may have seemed more picturesque.

John Rolfe Burroughs described the Brown's Park settlers, as did Dick Dunham in *Flaming Gorge Country*. Their descriptions are supplemented by the memoirs of Josie and Ann, and by a taped interview with Joe Haslem (regarding Charley Crouse) found in the Public Library in Vernal, Utah.

The evaluation of the controversial Herrera brothers was based on the J. S.

Hoy manuscript, with its bias tempered by various other scraps of information, charity, and logic.

A. B. Conway is listed in Wyoming State's "Blue Book" of officials as Asbury B. *Conaway*. I have chosen to retain the spelling used by his Colorado contemporaries. Even official lists have been known to be in error.

The reaction of the Brown's Park people to the Ute uprising is described in Bourroughs's *Where the Old West Stayed Young*. The most comprehensive description of the Meeker Massacre and the events before and after it is contained in Marshall Sprague's engrossing book *Massacre*. Quotations from Dr. Meeker's reports to Washington were derived from the annual volumes of reports issued by the Commissioner of Indian Affairs.

Chapter 3. Cattle Fever

When Grass Was King (Frink *et al*) and *History of Wyoming* by T. A. Larson deal with the cattle craze that swept the west after the Civil War, its economic roots and its consequences. Dr. Larson graphically describes the lawlessness prevailing in the Wyoming Basin in the heyday of the cattle barons and quotes J. H. Hayford, editor of the *Laramie Sentinel*, who wrote on November 9, 1883: "As nearly as we are able to get at the objects of the meeting of the Association it was called for the purpose of devising ways and means by which the 'big thieves' could head off the 'small thieves.' " Larson also quotes the editor of the *Buffalo Bulletin*, Joe de Barthe, who wrote on December 24, 1891: "The big cattlemen . . . own thousands of acres of rich Wyoming land that they have deliberately stolen from the government. . . . They . . . gobbled up all the rich creek bottoms they could . . . and the rest of the state was their range . . . small stock men have been completely frozen out." John Rolfe Burroughs supplements Larson with his description of what was going on over the border of Colorado.

Chapter 4. Ranchers and Rustlers

The description of the Hoy brothers is derived from several sources: Ann and Josie Bassett, John Rolfe Burroughs, and J. S. Hoy's self-description in his manuscript.

Chapter 5. The Bassett Gang

The U. S. Census of 1900 lists Isom Dart as a head of household with no other household members. Isom did not furnish the month of his birth, but said that he was born in Texas in 1855. As for his mother and father, the notation is "information unknown." It is possible the census taker was negligent in filling out the form; it is also possible that Isom's parents were "sold away" in those years before the Emancipation. With such a possibly barren and deprived beginning, he is still listed as being able to "read, write and speak English," and as being the owner of an unmortgaged farm.

As for Jim McKnight, he came from the "aristocracy" of Utah, the closest to a theocracy the United States can offer since the Puritan colony. His father had first married Camillia Young, a niece of Brigham Young himself. When Camillia died after bearing two sons, he married a Harriet Painter. The number of children born to this second marriage is unknown, for Harriet "became upset over polygamy" and returned to the east, taking her children with her. McKnight's third wife was Mary Fielding, who came from a line of prominent and important Mormons related to the founder, Joseph Smith. He married Mary while Harriet was still with him, probably thus touching off her "upset" over polygamy. Mary blessed McKnight with nine children before he was cast out of the Church and left for Washington. This information comes from Arthur McKnight, Jim McKnight's son by a second marriage.

Brown's Park is today so isolated and sparsely populated that it has the only existing one-room schoolhouse in the state of Colorado. Although they are now unused, tiny cabins around the existing schoolhouse still point to the old custom of sending the children to live near the school during bad weather under the charge of a relative.

Chapter 6. The Harvest

The original postmaster in Brown's Park was the Dr. Parsons who attended at Ann Bassett's birth. He served from 1878 until his death in 1881. John Jarvie then took over the post office until 1887.

Chapter 7. The Survivors

"Ronickie" dun: Neither Webster's Unabridged Dictionary nor handbooks of western colloquialisms give any clue as to its meaning. English is indeed a living language, and sometimes a slang expression dies an early death.

Inquiry was made of Sister Miriam Ann of the Sisters of the Holy Cross, Saint Mary of the Wasatch Convent in Salt Lake, and of Sister M. Campion Kuhn, archivist at Saint Mary's, Notre Dame, Indiana, concerning the Bassett girls' enrollment at the old convent school in Salt Lake. The records are scanty and some of them are missing; however, although academic records are unavailable, the names of both Josie and Ann appear in their rosters.

Chapter 8. The Outlaws

Ann puts the date of the outlaws' Thanksgiving dinner at 1895. However, Butch Cassidy was in jail in Wyoming at Thanksgiving time in both 1894 and 1895. He was released in early 1896, and on August 13, 1896, Elza Lay and Butch robbed the bank in Montpelier, Idaho. If Butch and Elza did indeed participate in the Thanksgiving dinner, they must have returned to Brown's Park after the Montpelier robbery.

Esther Campbell's re-creation of the Thanksgiving dinner was put on for the entertainment of a gathering of women's clubs at Maybell, Colorado. The Maybell women dressed in period clothes and acted roles in a play that Esther wrote, based on Ann's account. Josie was a guest of honor, and she gave a short talk in which she said that she felt as if she were back in Brown's Park again, since the dinner and all the characterizations were so accurate. Since Josie disapproved of what she called "Ann's exaggerations," it can be assumed that her kind words about the play give Ann's descriptions authenticity, at least in their essentials. It is hard to believe that Ann would have remembered the "menue" in such detail after fifty years, but it is no surprise that she would remember the women's gowns. Ann was always clothes-conscious, and the dinner was a big occasion in Brown's Park.

Josie's version of how Eb Bassett brought in Judge Bennett to the Bassett ranch and how Bennett was arrested in the kitchen by Farnham does not conform to the story told by John Rolfe Burroughs. Burroughs, relying on a typed fragment of a manuscript attributed to J. S. Hoy, says that Bennett was arrested by three members of the posse before he and Eb entered the Bassett cabin. I have used Josie's version because Hoy was not present at Bennett's arrest and because Josie's small, homely details seem authentic.

Butch Cassidy's career is outlined by Dora Flack in *Butch Cassidy, My Brother*, and in Matt Warner's memoirs, *Last of the Bandit Riders*. John Rolfe Burroughs tells the story of the kangaroo court at which John Bennett acquired his nickname "Judge."

Chapter 10. Scars and Two Bars

T. A. Larson's *History of Wyoming* describes stock detectives such as Tom Horn; Burroughs tells of Horn's actions in Routt County. I owe the story of

Ann and Matt Rash's missing will to Burroughs, as well as the account of the Routt County sheep wars.

The description of Hi Bernard is based for the most part on "Confidentially Told," an unpublished manuscript by Frank Willis which is included here as an appendix.

In Ann's writings, she describes a terror-stricken night when she and her brothers crouched in the darkened Bassett cabin after an assassin's bullets had crashed through the window as they played cards. This could possibly be true, but it could also be an embellishment of the facts. Since the threatening note from Cheyenne passed through the uprightly honest Herb's post office, and since it was taken seriously by the people of the time, it is most probably authentic.

Chapter 11. Hi Bernard

When Avvon "Leath" Chew says she had already heard of "Queen Ann" when she was a little girl, she may have been leaning on hindsight. Ann's title did not come into general use until later in her career.

Chapter 13. The Drifting Years

The quotation from the Literary Society's newspaper, "The Budget," is posted in the museum that the Moffatt County Historical Society maintains in the courthouse in Craig, Colorado. The mainstay of that museum is Louise Miller, quoted elsewhere in the text. She has cheerfully helped me in many ways, not the least of which was sharing with me her own assessments of the country and its people, among them Queen Ann.

Minnie Crouse Rasmussen's insistence that Josie poisoned Nig Wells is supported by a taped interview with Minnie, found in the Vernal Public Library, and by Eleen Williams of Flaming Gorge, Utah, who knew Minnie intimately. (Eleen's home is located in "Minnie's Gap," the site of Minnie's original homestead.)

The only other on-the-spot testimony about the poisoning is Josie's. Once a grandchild asked her about it, and Josie repeated substantially what she said in her tapes. She turned the story into an opportunity to give her grandchild a lecture on the danger of saying things in anger which one does not mean.

George Bassett's wife Ruby McClure is not related to the author.

Chapter 17. An Uncommon Woman

By the time Josie shot two deer with one bullet and sent for Doug Chew, Doug had bought Ed Lewis's ranch. However, Ed was to remain in the general area until his death.

Chapter 18. Apricot Brandy and Chokecherry Wine

In speaking of Josie's brush with the revenue agents, Flossie MacKnight said, "Now that's one time that I was able to be of some help to mother! She still owed a store bill for sugar when Crawford made her stop, and I paid it for her."

Chapter 20. A New Crusade

Billy Tittsworth's story of Isom Dart/Ned Huddleston/Tan Mex/Quick Shot, taken as a whole piece of work, is unbelievable. However, somewhere in the stories that Billy told of his life in the west, and somewhere in the stories he may later have been told by Charley Crouse, there must have been raw material upon which Tittsworth elaborated. Isom Dart had a cropped ear. Tittsworth's story is that the ear was cut off by Pony Beater in a fight over Tickup, an Indian squaw, back in the days of the Tip Gault gang. At that time Isom would have been in his teens. It is very possible that he had made a trail drive from Texas before the one made with Matt Rash in 1883. One must sadly agree with Ann Bassett Willis, who said in one of her letters to Esther Campbell: "Bill Tittsworth could have written a true story of the country and made it good history if he had been inclined that way. He was a blow off and got a ghost writer to write what he told. Of course it was fiction. It need not have been damaging but he chose to make it so."

Perhaps Charles Kelly sought verification of what he read in Tittsworth's book. But in the years when he was writing, most of the eyewitnesses were either dead or scattered. Ann was returning to Utah only on visits at that time; Josie was in Utah (and was in any event known to be close-mouthed with reporters); the Hoys were no longer in Brown's Park. One of the few people left in the area was Minnie Crouse Rasmussen. Even Minnie would have had to depend on hearsay to answer many of Kelly's probable questions.

Minnie was also most easily available during the period when Dick Dunham and John Rolfe Burroughs were doing their research.

The Outlaw Trail, originally published in 1938, was reissued in 1959. The second edition contained an additional chapter based on Kelly's 1943 interview with Queen Ann in Leeds, Utah, and perhaps on material he later obtained from Ann's own autobiography in *The Colorado Magazine* in 1953 and 1954. The chapter gave a more sympathetic picture of the Bassetts. Moreover, many of the inaccuracies and distortions to which the old-timers in Brown's Park had taken such violent exception had been changed or softened. The book is still not good history, however.

"The Gray Wolves" was given me by Hilda Morgan of Vernal, Utah. Ms. Morgan is of the same family as the little Doris Morgan who accompanied Ann on the wolf hunt.

The beginnings of "Anarchy Ann" were discovered in a collection of papers belonging to Evelyn Semotan of Steamboat Springs, Colorado. After Ann's death, Ms. Semotan and Avvon Chew Hughel drove up to Brown's Park to visit with Frank Willis. When Ms. Semotan showed interest in Ann's writing, Frank gave her a random batch of papers from an old suitcase. Ms. Semotan's papers were seen by John Rolfe Burroughs when he was writing *Where the Old West Stayed Young*.

Chapter 21. Queen Ann of Brown's Park

Edna Bassett Haworth and young Sam Bassett's son Emerson later erected a very appropriate gravestone, outlining the family members buried there, and Emerson also placed a stone on Frank's grave. Moreover, Edna made the burial of Ann's ashes more secure than the MacKnights had been able to accomplish on the hurried afternoon of Frank's funeral.

The site of the Bassett homestead and the family graveyard is now privately owned and not open to the public.

BIBLIOGRAPHY

Concerning Brown's Park and Its Inhabitants

Betenson, Lula Parker, as told to Dora Flack. *Butch Cassidy, My Brother.* Provo, Utah: Brigham University Press, 1975.
Burroughs, John Rolfe. *Where the Old West Stayed Young.* New York: William Morrow & Company, 1962.
Dunham, Dick and Vivian. *Flaming Gorge Country.* 1947; Denver, Colorado: Eastwood Printing & Publishing Co., 1977.
Hoy, Jesse S. "The J. S. Hoy Manuscript." Unpublished manuscript, Colorado State University.
Hughel, Avvon Chew. *The Chew Bunch in Brown's Park.* San Francisco: Scrimshaw Press, 1970.
Kelly, Charles. *The Outlaw Trail.* New York: The Devin-Adin Co., 1938, 1959.
King, Murray E. *The Last of the Bandit Riders.* New York: Bonanza Books.
Monaghan, J., ed. *Civil Works Administration Reports, 1935.* Historical Society of Colorado, Denver.
Tennent, William Lawrence. *The John Jarvie Ranch: A Case Study in Historic Site Development and Interpretation.* Logan, Utah: Utah State University, 1980. (Now available through Bureau of Land Management, Vernal, Utah.)
Tittsworth, W. G. *Outskirt Episodes.* Des Moines: Success Composition and Printing Co., 1927.
United States Forest Service. *Routt National Forest, 1905–1972.* U. S. Government Printing Office, 1965, 1972.
Willis, Ann Bassett. "Queen Ann of Brown's Park," in *The Colorado Magazine*, 1952–1953. The Historical Society of Colorado, Denver.
Willis, Frank (attributed), "Confidentially Told." Unpublished manuscript, the Historical Society of Colorado, Denver.

General Background Material

Frink *et al. When Grass Was King.* Boulder: University of Colorado Press, 1956.
Larson, T. A. *History of Wyoming.* Lincoln: University of Nebraska, 1965.
Lyman, June, and Norma Deaver. "The Ute People, An Historical Study." Unpublished manuscript, University of Utah.
Nostrums and Quackery. Chicago: American Medical Association Press, 1912.

Pierce, Neal R. *The Mountain States of America.* New York: W. W. Norton & Co., 1972.

Redford, Robert. *The Outlaw Trail, A Journey Through Time.* New York: Grosset & Dunlap, 1976.

Report of N. C. Meeker, Indian Agent for the Year 1879. Annual Report of the Commissioner of Indian Affairs to the Secretary of the Interior for the year 1879. Washington: U. S. Government Printing Office, pp. 17–19.

Sprague, Marshall. *Massacre.* Boston: Little, Brown and Company, 1957.

Stegner, Wallace. *Mormon Country.* New York: Hawthorne Books, 1942.

Stoddart, L. A., *et al. Range Conditions in Uintah Basin, Utah.* Logan: Utah Agricultural College, 1938.

Vandenbusche, Duane, and Duane A. Smith. *A Land Alone: Colorado's Western Slope.* Boulder: Pruett Publishing Co., 1981.

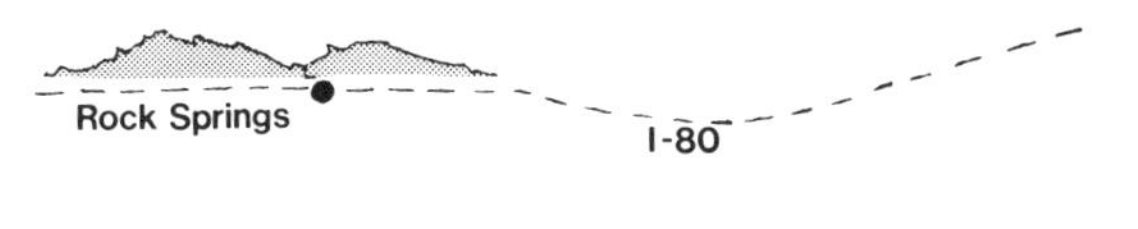

Locator

Browns Park area
not to scale

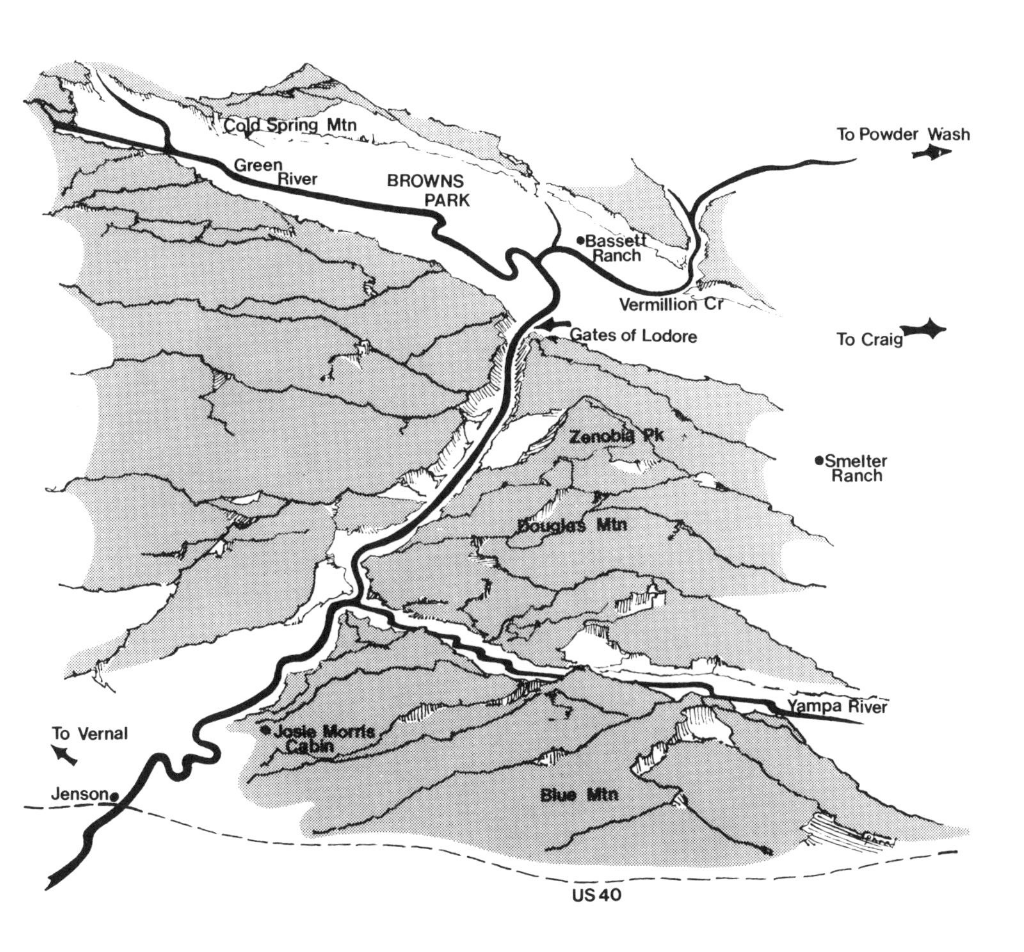